Fates of the
Performative

Thinking Theory

Grant Farred, Series Editor

Fates of the Performative

From the Linguistic Turn to the New Materialism

Jeffrey T. Nealon

Thinking Theory

UNIVERSITY OF MINNESOTA PRESS
MINNEAPOLIS • LONDON

The University of Minnesota Press gratefully acknowledges financial support for the publication of this series from Cornell University.

Lines from *I Don't Have Any Paper So Shut Up; or, Social Romanticism* are reprinted with permission of the author, Bruce Andrews. Lines from Jack Spicer's "The Redwheelbarrow" are from *My Vocabulary Did This to Me: The Collected Poetry of Jack Spicer,* copyright 2008 by the Estate of Jack Spicer; published by Wesleyan University Press and reprinted with permission.

Published by the University of Minnesota Press
111 Third Avenue South, Suite 290
Minneapolis, MN 55401-2520
http://www.upress.umn.edu

ISBN 978-1-5179-1085-3 (hc)
ISBN 978-1-5179-1086-0 (pb)
Library of Congress record available at https://lccn.loc.gov/2020048344.

Printed in the United States of America on acid-free paper

The University of Minnesota is an equal-opportunity educator and employer.

28 27 26 25 24 23 22 21   10 9 8 7 6 5 4 3 2 1

Contents

Acknowledgments

Previous versions of some chapters have been published, in quite different forms, in *Cultural Critique* (chapter 1) and *Critical Inquiry* (chapter 6). Material from the Conclusion is reworked from my contribution to the collection *Neoliberalism and Contemporary Literary Culture*, edited by Mitchum Huehls and Rachel Greenwald (published by Johns Hopkins University Press), and material later in chapter 1 is repurposed from my essay in *What's Wrong with Anti-Theory?* edited by Jeffrey DiLeo (published by Bloomsbury Academic). Thanks to those editors and readers for their invaluable input along the way.

I've also received helpful feedback when delivering preliminary versions of these chapters in several sessions over the years at the MLA convention (thanks to Jeffrey DiLeo and Jane Gallop, as well as Jean-Michel Rabaté, Cary Wolfe, and Ewa Ziarek from the Philosophy and Literature Forum) and the Society for Phenomenology and Existential Philosophy (thanks to Alan Schrift). I also benefited greatly from invitations to speak and interact with colleagues at State University of New York at Albany (thanks to Vesna Kuiken), Wayne State University (thanks to Steve Shaviro and Jeff Pruchnic), the New Materialism Network in Amsterdam (thanks to Iris van der Tuin), CalArts West Hollywood Lecture series in Los Angeles (thanks to Arne De Boever and Peggy Kamuf), DePaul University (thanks to Russell Ford and Michael Naas), the University of Utah (thanks to Kevin Deluca), and Loyola University Chicago (thanks to Paul Jay and Pamela Caughie).

Rich Doyle has done his usual yeoman's work over years of weekly lunches and happy hours, vetting every thought offered here—though he will strongly disagree with the Thoreau material, methinks. Gregg Lambert has likewise been there every step of the way, helping me separate the bull from the shit.

Thanks to the Penn State graduate students who helped immensely in working through this material, and for showing me where it could go, with help from my colleague and neighbor Claire Colebrook. And special thanks to Stacy Alaimo, who graciously agreed to visit my graduate class when this was all in a nascent form.

At the University of Minnesota Press, thanks to Grant Farred for encouraging me to write this book for his series, as well as his friendship and sharp commentary at every stage, and to Doug Armato for his good humor and great advice in marshaling it into print. Thanks are also due to John McGowan and Branka Arsić, whose readers' reports offered incisive and immensely productive suggestions for revision. Finally, thanks to Mike Stoffel for doing a great job copyediting the book, though of course all remaining mistakes, gaffes, or outlandish claims herein remain solely my responsibility.

In the end, none of this adds up to anything if not for Leisha, Bram, and Dash: the performativity of the everyday is the baseline of this little thing called life.

Preface

Why the Performative?

I am no longer sure what counts as performative.

—JUDITH BUTLER, *New York Times*, July 10, 2019

As a quite singular example of what Edward Said called "travelling theory," the performative has enjoyed a wild ride since its birth in J. L. Austin's ordinary language philosophy of the 1950s. From those quite staid origins in the British analytic philosophical tradition, the performative has migrated across numerous national, linguistic, and disciplinary borders to become a key concept in several other fields that are quite far afield from the lecture halls of Oxford. So, for example, the performative became a linchpin for deconstruction (both for Derrida's philosophy and for American deconstructive literary theorists like J. Hillis Miller, Shoshana Felman, and Paul de Man); in an even more unlikely transformation of Oxford ordinary-language thinking, performativity became a central practice for thinking about resistant identities in the feminism and queer theory of the 1980s and '90s (most intensely in the work of Judith Butler and Eve Kosofsky Sedgwick), branching out from there to become an important concept in ethnic studies and its overlaps with performance studies (for example, in the interventions of José Estaban Muñoz, Fred Moten, and Diana Taylor), all the way to Marianne Constable's work on performatives and legal speech. If we fast-forward through the early 2000s to today, we see an even more unlikely spread and triumph of performativity as the key to understanding the workings not merely of subjects and identities, but of objects (say, in Bruno Latour's actor-network theory or Jane Bennett's concept of vibrant matter, with their insistence on the lively performativity of what were previously thought to be inert, passive things).

Finally, in what is surely the most sweeping wholesale transformation of Austin's original concept, Karen Barad has argued that the very status of matter itself—the most basic quantum "stuff" of the entire universe—is best understood as performative. As Barad writes in *Meeting the Universe Halfway*, "*Mattering is a dynamic articulation/configuration of the world . . . All bodies, not merely 'human' bodies, come to matter through the world's iterative intra-activity—its performativity.*"[1] In short, Barad summarizes for us the current consensus shared by various strands of "new materialism": matter *is* nothing other than what it *does*, and thereby the basic processes of the universe itself are performative. Which, if nothing else, constitutes quite a roller coaster ride for the performative—from its humble birth in the cloistered drawing room of an Oxford language philosopher of the 1950s, through various resistant identitarian political movements of the 1980s and '90s, all the way to infinity and beyond in the twenty-first century (hereafter, C21).

Which is maybe only to say that the performative is a rich vein to mine in the genealogical recent history of literary theory: as a generative and evolving blend of theory and practice, the performative is second to none when it comes to its influence on recent humanities theory in North America. Its only serious contender for unlikely and wide-ranging theoretical spread from its original context would probably be Saussure's thinking about the workings of the signifier, specifically his insistence that the signifier–signified relation is a conventional one. In short, Saussure shows us that meaning in language is *constructed* through a network of systematic effects, not *found* within a list of Adamic names whose meanings are guaranteed by an essential link between the word and the existence its referent in the world. Famously, for Saussure that relation between the signifier and the signified (between a word and what it means) is arbitrary and social, not necessary and essential: as Saussure puts it, "in language there are only differences[,] without positive terms."[2] This insight about the workings of language became the cornerstone of almost all structuralism and poststructuralism, movements Richard Rorty dubbed "the linguistic-turn," which entailed far-reaching revolutions in thinking about everything from the nature of kinship systems (Lévi-Strauss) and historical events (Hayden White) to the workings of political power (Althusser), all the way to the understanding of the unconscious (Lacan's famous dictum that the unconscious is structured like a language is scaffolded on Saussure's relation between the signifier and the signified). The truism that "there are no positive terms, only differences" got translated far beyond Saussure's insight into the workings of human language, and in the end this linguistic insight found itself exploded into the near-universal claim that there is no meaning in itself or in the world (against the "essentialist" position that takes meaning to inhere in an essence within persons and things); rather, on the Saussurean reasoning of the linguistic turn, there exists only a series of differential, social (re)productions of meaning—a social (re)production machine that pretends to be based on natural or self-evident truths but is in reality laden with ideological power plays and hidden political interests that require constant critical demystification. Saussure's thinking about language in his 1906 lectures lay dormant for many years, until it exploded more than a half decade later and launched a thousand successful tenure cases, most of which demonstrated in one way or another the axiomatic linguistic-turn conclusion that "x or y is socially constructed."

However, precisely because of this linguistic social-construction paradigm and its saturation within structuralism and poststructuralism, Saussure's work has not been well placed to survive the backlash against the linguistic turn that happens in the C21—the various critiques of the linguistic turn's primary "anti-essentialist" modus operandi, whereby any given *realist* or *essentialist* claim is shown to be *constructed* in and through the human conventions and language of social power. The era of the linguistic turn was, then, simultaneously the era of social constructionism, and its axiomatic sense that any claim to transhistorical truth (any claim to a final "signified" of guaranteed meaning) was in fact a contextual linguistic power play (a series of socially constructed signifiers) dressing itself up in the language of unassailable objectivism.

While Austin's work on the performative was also born in an insight into the workings of language, Austin's performative has shown itself to be better placed to live on after the linguistic turn of (post)structuralism, insofar as the Austinian performative was not primarily concerned with demonstrating the social construction of meaning (though its insistence on social convention would avail itself to that use, if need be); rather, the upshot of Austin's work on the performative primarily concerns the irreducibility of a kind of immaterial force that is not created by language but is characterized by the traversing, "greater"—one might even call it "living"—illocutionary force that courses through questions of language, meaning, or normative disciplinary convention. It is this emphasis on performativity as immaterial force that lives on most decisively in the C21, or so this book will argue.

This book constitutes a long-delayed sequel to my 1998 *Alterity Politics: Ethics and Performative Subjectivity*, where I was arguing for a fate of the performative beyond the linguistic turn of demonstrating meaning's (or identity's or anything else's) impossibility. That book's sustained critique of understanding performativity as the work of lack, negativity, or undermining was, it now seems in retrospect, part of retooling the work of performativity away from a narrowly humanist linguistic concept (undermining truth or certainty) and more onto other terrains of ontological or ethical inquiry. But of course a series of other, unforeseen performative forces has also decisively intervened in those twenty-plus years—changes within the discourses of theory, indeed the discourses of the humanities themselves, and those decisive changes are also woven into the fabric of this book.

Most starkly, almost no one within a humanities discipline was talking about the end of the humanities in the mid-1990s; whereas today, it's just about all anyone talks about at department and professional society meetings. And it was likewise taken as axiomatic in the heyday of theory that the linguistic or social construction of meaning was a—if not the—decisive pivot for understanding the world more generally, and the flow of students into the English major was taken as decisive proof of that generalization. Now, I think we have (yet) to come to terms with the fact that literary hermeneutics (the performative making of meaning in language) is no longer seen as a widely decisive factor in people's everyday lives; the ins and outs of interpretation begins to look, to many students and the general public, like either an expensive hobby or an antiquarian curiosity. If the performative remains an insight into the narrow workings of language, and not an insight that helps us to understand the larger fabric of the social, scientific, and cultural world, then I think it's probably lost its usefulness. But I'm going to argue here, alongside a series of kindred spirits, that even after the death of the linguistic turn, several versions of the performative are alive and well, while other concepts associated with performativity have passed their prime, become ineffective in thinking against the day in our present moment.

Chapters 1 through 3 chart the rise of the performative in North American theory circles, from its birth in the linguistic turn, through deconstruction and the performative identity years, all the way to the new materialist version of the entire universe's performativity. Chapter 3 ends with the general conclusion that, if everything is in some sense "alive" (active, self-overcoming, attentively enmeshed with other entities) in the world of new materialism, then performativity has today become biopolitics, and vice versa. Chapter 3 also ends with some wonderments about the new materialism's abandonment of critique, and chapters 4 through 6 attempt to reimagine what it might look like to deploy a performative discourse dedicated to a critique of neoliberal biopolitics, but a critique that doesn't depend on the linguistic-turn model of unmasking, paranoid social constructionism. All in all, taking the diagnostic measure of the performative in the present—what's living and what's dead?—will be the project that informs the following pages.

Finally, a few words about the title *Fates of the Performative*: especially in need of comment is the word *fates,* given the fact that fate is hardly a hot theoretical category these days. Most simply stated, this book charts the mutation of performativity as an academic concept: from its initial emergence as a linguistic phenomenon at work in speech acts, through the deconstruction and performative-identity years, all the way to its current deployment as an instantiation of new materialist ontology (and back again, returning to the question of performative force in language). So I'd originally considered calling it "Genealogy of the Performative: From the Linguistic Turn to the New Materialism." While that title is in many ways descriptive of my project (trying to locate—in Foucauldian parlance—how performativity today is different from yesterday), I decided against it because I fear that genealogy has become a worn-out concept. These days a "genealogy of x" is most often a "history of x" with a bad conscience; and besides, here I'm not primarily engaged in writing an exhaustive retrospective account of performativity.

If I am doing a genealogical history in some ways, I'm very specifically concerned with tracing the role of force-as-performativity in academic discourses about language, deconstruction, identity, and/or matter. Given that project, I particularly like the (admittedly odd) terminology of fate because it carries with it a sense of compulsion, futurity, and uncertainty, as opposed to the rather imperial idea conjured by calling something a "history." Given the centrality of force in my rendering of performativity, it seems important to insist that performativity can fruitfully be explored as a series of fates, transformative events that befall—and thereby define—it; and these fateful performative outcomes emerge, as most everyone including Austin insists, despite the original intentions of any individual or group. Fate implies an endgame, of course, but it also suggests that such a terminus is unknown to us in the present. It's in this sense that I limn out performativity as a series of fates, rather than a linear history.

PART I

Genealogy of the Performative

The Truth Is a Joke?

Performatives in Austin and Derrida

There are disadvantages in being excessively solemn.
—J. L. AUSTIN, "Performative Utterances"

Through comedy then.
—JACQUES DERRIDA, *Glas*

The genealogy of this opening meditation on jokes and performativity comes not so much out of a happy, laughter-filled context, but in the context of a death, most specifically Jacques Derrida's death. I was asked in 2014 to write something about Derrida's legacy on the tenth anniversary of his death, and the initial impetus on such an occasion is to follow out a trajectory that one learns from Derrida himself: when asked to mourn someone in print, immediately double down on the question by looking at how the topic of mourning is treated in his or her texts. And that could indeed present a rich itinerary: few people have engaged the work of mourning as centrally as Derrida.[1]

But I have to say, thinking back on Derrida's work, on what I found most admirable and useful within his texts (and given the few dozen times I had interacted with him over the years, what I took away from his personality), it was not mourning that I wanted to recall—not the Derrida of lack and loss, prayers and tears[2]—but the Derrida of a certain kind of malicious performative joy. The Derrida of *Glas*, for example, who gleefully links G. W. F. Hegel, that great thinker of normativity and dialectical progress, with the saint of queer transgression, Jean Genet. Whatever else it is, a text like *Glas* is a tour-de-force comedy routine (and the genre is literally comic, a circle—the beginning is the end, *Finnegans Wake* style).[3] And the joke is aimed squarely at that most serious and tragic of philosophical projects, Hegel's. Indeed, to what two specific episodes does Derrida very economically reduce Hegel's entire corpus in the opening pages of *Glas*? (1) Hegel's discussion of the phallic columns of India; and (2) the status of flower-religion.[4] These two seemingly frivolous throwaways in Hegel, like so many other bits of marginalia (recall what Derrida does with Nietzsche's "I have forgotten my umbrella"),[5] go on to be shown to be the heart and soul of a very serious project, and Derrida will perform this analysis in a magisterial and singular way . . . with numerous lowbrow jokes thrown in as well, musings, for example, on the chiasmic crossings between Derrida and derrière. In any case, to close this opening parenthesis, it's the joyful way Derrida does his work—its *performative* aspects, the illocutionary force of his work—that has really stayed with me over the years.

And of course 1974's *Glas* is just the warm-up for Derrida's real comic tour de force— "Limited Inc," his late-'70s back-and-forth with John Searle over Derrida's essay on J. L. Austin and performative utterances. I'll get to all that soon enough, but I can't help but note right off the bat that Searle, if he had taken time to look twice at Derrida's work, should have seen it coming: the great comics really know how to take down hecklers.

In any case, it's this underappreciated, comic, performative Derrida that I want to think about in this chapter, and while this Derrida certainly doesn't get as much methodological play as the "prayers and tears" Derrida, I'm going to try to make some larger claims about the joke being crucial to Derrida's itinerary, especially surrounding his attraction to the performative. (I'll likewise suggest that even as Austin tries to keep the joke under control, its logic remains central to his work as well.) To anticipate some things I'll repeat and expand upon later, the joke allows us to think in a very economical way about the performative deployment of force and provocation; about the necessity and nonsaturability of context; the signature style of delivery, the idiomatics of timing; and about the success or failure of a speech act being largely delinked from intentions (everyone *intends* jokes to be funny, but that intention is irrelevant when it comes to getting laughs: in the end, the only marker for the successful execution of the joke remains its uptake and countersignature by the other). Indeed, even the backdoor work of mourning must be considered in a discourse dedicated to laughter: there's always a chance the routine will fail, and as they say, you'll die out there. In a sideways nod to the irreducibility of the joke, Austin famously renames unsuccessful speech acts as "unhappy performatives"; but as you know if you've ever watched a routine go bad at Uncle Chuckle's Comedy Hut, the phrase "unhappy performative" doesn't begin to describe the anguish of jokes that don't work.

I'll have to admit right up front that the actual jokes in Derrida are hit and miss—there's for example a real bomb in the *States of Theory* collection, when he tries to milk a laugh out of the fact that "California is the state of theory!"[6] (at a conference in Irvine, no less). Then there are Derrida jokes that kill, like the Wizard of Oz routine: when asked, in a hostile way, whether deconstruction was in the end just like Oz (a tyrannical fantasy land run by a petty white-haired little man, who's finally exposed behind the curtain by the little dog Toto), Derrida responded something like: "Yes, deconstruction is like that . . . if you mean the dog."[7] Here, however, I'm going to be less interested in focusing on particular jokes—as in Slavoj Žižek's collected *Žižek's Jokes*, or as Sigmund Freud does with his categorizations of various brands of humor in *Jokes and Their Relation to the Unconscious*. (Nor am I necessarily interested in producing an overarching theory of the comic—as for example in Simon Critchley's *On Humour*, Terry Eagleton's *Humour*, or Jerry Palmer's *Taking Humour Seriously*.) I'm less interested in this or that Derridean joke than I am in a more pervasive kind of "comedy" sufficing Derrida's work: his obsessive interest in the idiom; in a certain kind of sarcasm; in timing; in dwelling obsessively on the philosophically "inappropriate" detail; and his extensive deployment of the comic unit of the routine (which may, better than the genre of the essay, describe Derrida's mature writing and speaking practice—

like a comic, he follows out thematic bits or clusters, putting together
a full performance of routines, rather than grinding toward an inevitable argumentative conclusion). You see this nowhere more clearly
than in "Limited Inc abc . . . ," which begins not at the beginning (section A) but with the false start of the letter D, and runs through twenty-
three routines, up to Z. In a bit of insult-comic bravado, he both uses
and mentions all the letters of the alphabet, which make up all the
words of Searle's essay, almost all of which he likewise repeats by citing them in a different idiom. Of course, all this is done in the name
of the performative, and succinctly demonstrates the grammatologi-
cal delinking of words from their supposed original intentions and
contexts—the triumph of comic reinscription over the serious "original" locution.

    Still in the introductory mode, it's probably also worth remember-
ing the role of "Limited Inc" in Derrida's American reception—the role
of the performative and the joke in laying the groundwork for what
people of my generation came to know as "Derrida" in the United
States. "Limited Inc" was first published in *Glyph* 2 (1977), after Searle
had published his critique of "Signature Event Context" in *Glyph* 1
(both Sam Weber's translation of Derrida's text on Austin and Searle's
response had been published in *Glyph* 1, earlier in 1977). *Glyph* was
among the first of the "theory" journals dedicated to translating European thought into English (those first two issues contain essays by
Paul de Man, Louis Marin, Rodolphe Gasché, Jean-Luc Nancy, Phillipe
Lacoue-Labarthe, and Sam Weber, among others—looking back, Searle
is a puzzling outlier in this group). It's also worth remembering that a
shortened version of "Limited Inc" was (according to J. Hillis Miller) the
first public lecture that Derrida gave in English at Yale[8]—and recall also
that "Limited Inc" was republished in English more than a decade later
in 1988, with a very long afterword-interview conducted by Gerald Graff.
I say this partially to remind us of the historical context surrounding
this signature event, but also to mark the fact that, consciously or not,
"Limited Inc" and its surrounding texts laid some substantial groundwork for Derrida's reception in America. In short, it may not be odd that
I initially took Derrida for a certain kind of combative, funny thinker,

as he didn't arrive on these academic shores sporting a prayer shawl and toting a box of Kleenex to dry his tears. Derrida came ashore swinging and telling jokes.

Just to rehearse the details surrounding Derrida–Austin–Searle debate concerning the performative: Derrida's "Signature Event Context" is published alongside Searle's critique of it in an essay called "Reiterating the Differences: A Reply to Derrida." Derrida's blistering comic response, "Limited Inc," is published several months later. I suppose the first thing we note about Searle's essay, which will take up the task of correcting Derrida's reading of Austin, is that the title—"Reiterating the Differences"—contains a kind of humorous gaffe, at least it's funny if you're a Derridean. *Re*-iterating is of course redundant, as iterate means repeat, so to "re-iterate" something is to "re-repeat" it—which of course Derrida is arguing happens always already when it comes to the performative nature of language. To say something, even the first time, is a kind of repetition (for reasons that Austin himself insists upon—all speech acts are dependent on conventions, social contexts, and one has to repeat coded formulas in order to be understood, or even misunderstood). So one is of course always repeating (in fact, always re-repeating), and in the process confronting the irreducibility of differences. So, though Searle says he doesn't understand Derrida, he's got it all right there in the title, "Reiterating the Differences." We might also note that the malapropism "reiterate" comes into English usage through a phenomenon that linguists call "hypercorrection"; which is to say, everyday users add a redundant performative mistake to an existing word or formula to make it *seem* correct. So you say "please RSVP" or they offer you a coupon for a "complimentary free game" at the bowling alley. Such hypercorrection—adding mistakes in a desperate attempt to make something seem more correct—is the ironic essence of Searle's project in "Reiterating the Differences," but you don't need to read past the first word of the title to get there.

Searle infamously argues that the "confrontation" between Austin and Derrida "never quite took place" (a phrase that Derrida lingers gleefully over, more of his territory), but to loop back to my opening performative promise to try and limn out the satirically funny Derrida in relation to jokes and the performative, I would point out first and foremost that the tone of his exchange with Searle (and Austin), like the tone of so much of Derrida's writing, comes from texts under consideration; one responds in and to the idiom of the other. (Why there are so few jokes in the work on Heidegger, for instance.) In short, the mean-spirited tone of "Limited Inc" comes from Searle, while the jokes and sarcasm come from Derrida's careful reading and consideration of Austin. And the stake of "Limited Inc," recall, is the all-too-pious place reserved for "seriousness" in philosophical discourse. I'll allot most of this opening chapter to talking about performative force and the joke in Austin, then very briefly discuss how Searle missed the joke (or perhaps he's just the straight man in all this), before closing with a return to Derrida and the question of legacy and the performative— Austin's legacy for Derrida, Derrida's legacy for us.

Austin

I suppose the first thing to recall concerning Austin, for our purposes, is that *How to Do Things with Words* (a lecture series given at Harvard in 1955) is actually funny, rife with a kind of Monty Python-esque English humor. There's a lot of comic material here—everything from schoolyard stuff, such as "In saying 'iced ink,' I was uttering the noises 'I stink,'"[9] to Austin's bestiary of absurdly comic examples—his routines about marrying monkeys or baptizing penguins (24)—all the way to dark comedy like "there are more ways of killing a cat than drowning it in butter" (48). In fact, I await the inevitable animal studies essay denouncing Austin's exemplary cruelty to animals.

But most of the humor in Austin is self-deprecating and directed at the dullness and pretention of academic work. Recall in this vein the end of "Performative Utterances," where he quips, "it's not things, it's philosophers that are simple." He goes on, with impeccable comic timing: "You will have heard it said, I expect, that over-simplification is the occupational disease of philosophers, and in a way one might agree with that. But for a sneaking suspicion that it's their occupation"—full stop, end of speech. Thank you and good night, I'm off the stage before you realize that I've just called you all simpletons.[10]

I don't want to bore the reader with a lengthy rehearsal of Austin's work on performatives (which are of course speech acts that bring something into being—like marrying, promising, insulting) versus constative speech acts, which may be said to be true or false. I'm assuming that's all familiar and will just recall that there are two primary targets of Austin's work on the performative: first, most famously, he questions the logical positivist sense that the only sentences worth worrying about are those that can be categorized as either true or false, "constative" phrases. On first naïve glance, it looks like performatives are parasitic on the "normal" constative usage of language to tell the truth about things; in other words, it seems common sense that doing is logically dependent on a prior understanding of being. However, Austin patiently reverses that polarity throughout *How to Do Things with Words*. As he sums up what he's doing in the lecture course, "thus we are assimilating the supposed constative utterance to the performative" (52). We are, in other words, in the business of showing that true/false statements are also performative statements, sentences that make something happen.

It is, as Derrida recognizes immediately, Austin's gambit to show how the supposed abnormal case of the performative contains the logic of the whole, rather than the usual philosophical procedure, which subordinates all other kinds of statements under the constative primacy of the true. And Austin's methodology is also something of an outlier— his is an experimental and materialist method: *what about this? what about that? not sure, have to make it up as we go along.* As he sums things up about halfway through his lecture series, to a no-doubt bewildered audience at Harvard, "I must explain again that we are floundering here. To feel the firm ground of prejudice slip away is exhilarating, but brings its revenges" (61). Seven lectures into his twelve-lecture series, he in fact utters the speech act "we failed" when it comes to distinguishing rigorously between constative and performative utterances, and hence "it is time then to make a fresh start on the problem" (91). In the end, to his own opening question, "can saying make it so?" the answer astonishingly turns out to be "yes." As Austin puts it, "'to say a few certain words is to marry' . . . or 'simply to say a certain something is to bet'" (8). To say a few words is to speak the truth. No joke.

At the abandonment of the constative/performative binary opposition, Austin pivots to perform an experimental topology of myriad kinds of performative forces (rather than philosophical meanings). As for the general thrust of his project, Austin sums it up like this: to "distinguish [between] force and meaning" (100) and finally to suggest, quite simply, that constative "meaning" is always beholden to performative (illocutionary) force, rather than vice versa. As Austin sums up in "Performative Utterances," "besides the question that has been much studied in the past as to what a certain utterance *means*, there is a further question distinct from this as to what was the *force*, as we may call it, of the utterance . . . What we need besides the old doctrine about meanings is a new doctrine about all the possible forces of utterances."[11] And Austin goes a long way in this direction, taking seriously a whole vast array of speech acts that most philosophers of language want nothing to do with: bets, vows, promises, insults, penguin baptisms . . . all kinds of things, but not, alas, jokes. An exclusion to which we will return.

The second (and related) target in the lecture series, this one a bit more wobbly, is Austin's questioning of intentionality, and it follows along immediately from his isolation of the performative as the kind of language use that *does* something, brings something into being (a marriage, a bet, but somehow not a laugh?). So in Austin's most famous example, if you say certain words in a certain approved context, you're married: whatever your intentions are (good or ill, loving or mercenary), you're married. Likewise, whether you intended to pay the bookie or not, if you made a bet, it was accepted, and the Bears don't cover the spread, you'll have to come up with the money . . . or learn to walk with a cane. Here, Austin is trying to impeach intentionality and its various meaning-guaranteeing avatars—"perhaps it should be 'mind' or 'spirit'" or maybe even "'heart,' but at any rate some kind of backstage artiste," he says, quite derisively.[12]

When discussing the near irrelevance of interior states in treating speech acts, Austin introduces a refutation coming from his fictional foil, a pious religious man: "One who says, *'Promising is not merely a matter of uttering of words! It is an inward and spiritual act!'* is apt to

appear as a solid moralist standing out against a generation of superficial theorizers."[13] However, this solid moralist, Austin suggests, is at
another level merely an excuse-generation machine—introducing into
discourse what will become the weasel politician's home playing field,
the highly plastic space between "what I said" and "what I meant." The
utterance, Austin argues over and over again, is not "(merely) the outward and visible sign . . . of an inward and spiritual act" (9); and for
Austin this is primarily an ethico-politico insistence, because reliance
on the "fictitious inward act" (10) consistently provides "the bigamist
with an excuse for his 'I do,' and the welsher a defense for his 'I bet.'
Accuracy and morality alike are on the side of the plain saying that *our
word is our bond*" (10, emphasis in original).

Austin, in short, is attempting to drive out the ghosts from the
machines of linguistic analysis, by treating language not primarily in
terms of meaning or truth (which is usually to say, some preexisting
intentional content represented by the words themselves) but as a performative doing (which can never be guaranteed, but can be brought
about only through a deployment of force and discharged by the performance of another, future set of actions). Austin reorients what we
look at when we look at a sentence, when he asks us to look away from
what's before or behind the words (the facts, the truth, the inward spiritual act of intentionality), toward the force of utterances and what the
words oblige us to do in the future.

So when Austin jokes at the opening of his "Performative Utterances" that the audience should come away thinking, "it could be that
he simply means what he says" (233), or when in the opening lines
of *How to Do Things with Words* he promises that what he has to say
will be "true, at least in parts" (1), those speech acts function both as a
kind of comic set-up and more importantly as a deadpan performative
statement of his core critique of linguistic meaning: any work that
these words might do, including being true or not, has to be done
by the words themselves, delivered with a certain illocutionary force
within a particular pragmatic context, rather than seeing their meaning as guaranteed by some intention that may or may not lurk behind
them. As he expands on his famous "marriage ceremony" example,

Austin insists: "Here we should say that in saying these words we are doing something—namely, marrying—rather than reporting something, namely that we are marrying. And the act of marrying, like, say, the act of betting, is at least preferably (though still not accurately) to be described as saying certain words, rather than performing a different, inward and spiritual, action of which these words are merely the outward and audible sign. That this is so can perhaps hardly be proved, but it is, I should claim, a fact" (13). In short, for Austin, the event and its context should trump the supposed signature of inward intentionality. The only constative ("I should claim, a fact") is the irreducibility of the performative ("saying certain words").

Now of course Austin waffles on this, and his waffling is what the better part of Derrida's reading lingers over—suggesting that Austin is of course onto something, but he doesn't push it far enough, especially around the question of phonocentrism (speech acts versus written acts) and the related question of "literature" and its supposed lack of "seriousness." As Austin infamously states his methodological caveats for treating speech acts, "Surely the words must be spoken 'seriously' and so as to be taken 'seriously'? This is, though vague, true enough in general—and it is an important commonplace in discussing the purport of any utterance whatsoever. *I must not be joking, for example, nor writing a poem*" (9, my emphasis). This sentence functions a little like fetish porn in the deconstructive literature surrounding Austin and the performative—people return to this line, and its preemptive exclusion of literature from serious philosophical discussion, again and again. And this question of literature (and whether it's taken "seriously," carefully scare-quoted twice by Austin and/or his editors) takes up a fair amount of space in Searle's response to Derrida's original essay. Austin has to exclude literature, Searle argues, because logically you have to deal with the "normal" cases before you can move on to the abnormal, "parasitic" ones (constative before performative); so it's not surprising that Derrida returns to the question of literature, and returns to it hard, in "Limited Inc."

Here, however, I'm less interested in literature's status in all this than I am in the joke—because Derrida (and the flood of work on literature and speech acts that came in his wake) definitively shows how Austin's whole logic is dependent on something like the logic of literature, rather than being somehow pristinely uncontaminated by literary language.[14] So I don't want to go over that ground again. I will just point out in passing, though, that the reason Austin wants to set poetry aside for the short term isn't a traditional concern about seriousness—that's clearly why he wants to exclude jokes, but it's not why Austin excludes literature (though it is why Searle does so—because literature is a set of "pretend" speech acts). Austin wants to set aside literature not because it lacks gravitas—Shakespeare is hardly frivolous—but because literature is not "ordinary" discourse: you can read "The Waste Land" all day long, but no one will actually "show you fear in a handful of dust," nor will you see any "lilacs breeding out of the dead ground." When Ahab yells "lower the boats" in *Moby-Dick,* you're under no serious obligation to do so; nor can you intervene by taking Ophelia aside at the theater to explain that Hamlet is only pretending to be crazy—even though you might be ethically compelled to do so in so-called real life. As Austin puts it, "If the poet says 'Go and catch a falling star' or whatever it may be, he doesn't seriously issue an order."[15] So you can perhaps forgive Austin for trying to put literature in a separate category, because he doesn't see it as ordinary language, and he's an ordinary language philosopher.

Oddly, this special or "nonordinary" status of literature is what Austin most obviously has in common with his later deconstructive interlocutors. Surely for de Man or Hillis Miller, and unambiguously for Derrida, literature is not just one kind of language usage among others. Contra the caricature of deconstruction that suggests that Derrida saw literature everywhere or reduced everything to literature, he states quite straightforwardly in "The Double Session" that "there is no—or hardly any, ever so little—literature."[16]

If you're an ordinary language philosopher, you can be forgiven for setting aside the extraordinary question of literature. But how can you set aside jokes? Jokes are a part of even the most mundane ordinary experiences: not only are they to be found abundantly in dry Oxford philosophers' talks, as Austin shows, but any trip to the dentist's office or any idle banter with strangers while you're waiting for the bus tends to be peppered with jokes; while poetic diction, one would have to say, tends not to come up in most everyday discourse. We've all seen people spouting something that sounds like poetry on the subway, but in those situations we tend to move away from, rather than magnetically toward, the bard in question. Which drives an initial wedge between Austin's dual exclusions of "joking, or writing a poem," as far as ordinary language philosophy is concerned—or at least it suggests the problems that they present are inverse: literature is serious but not ordinary language usage, while jokes are ordinary but not serious usage.

The joke is excluded by Austin possibly because it's the most dangerous form of everyday discourse to link with the logic of performativity, and more potentially infectious precisely because of its ordinariness. Philosophers over the years have shown a need to protect the "seriousness" of their discourse at virtually all costs; and as such, Austin's excluding the joke is a recognizable first order of business. But while symptomatic, Austin's exclusion remains puzzling because he consistently shows—*performs* or *demonstrates* rather than *states*—that jokes function as performative discourses par excellence. As with the bet or the promise, the joke is ordinary discourse that is neither true nor false, but happy or unhappy, felicitous or infelicitous. It brings something into being, rather than stating something constative that could be verified. No one ever interrupts a joke to ask, "Wait a second: How'd the gorilla get into the bar in the first place?"

And in fact jokes have one monumental advantage over promises, bets, or wedding ceremonies as examples of everyday performativity: unlike bets or promises, which can always summon the "backstage artiste" of intentionality (I meant it or didn't mean it), jokes are wholly dependent on the context and pragmatics of the situation—not on the teller's intention to be funny, which is almost completely irrelevant to the happiness or unhappiness engendered by the joke as speech act. It's all in the performative delivery. Often, in fact, the more desperately someone intends to be funny, the lamer the joke becomes. At the end of the linguistic day, your joke is your bond—either the joke does things with words (gets a laugh) or it doesn't, regardless of how much you meant it to be funny (or not). But as many jokes as Austin performs, he can't bring himself to set up the joke as a privileged paradigm for the performative, so he has to try and banish it from the content of his discourse (his constative "theory"), even though comedy comes back again and again with a performative vengeance.

Another possible line of defense against taking the joke seriously in Austin might be to recall that, given the itinerary—breaking down the constative/performative binary and constructing instead a typology of illocutionary forces—one could object that jokes are not examples of illocutionary force at all, but that laughter is (merely) a perlocutionary effect. Recall that Austin introduces a tripartite scheme in the ruins of the constative/performative binary: there are locutionary acts (saying something), illocutionary acts (force itself), and perlocutionary acts (an effect you can bring about by saying something). So for example there's the statement "Let me persuade you" that X is the case (a "locution" or statement with a "meaning"); then there's something like persuasion "itself" (illocution—the action of persuading), and all Austin's illocutionary examples are gerunds: "informing, warning, undertaking, etc., i.e., utterances which have a certain conventional force" (109); and finally there's the perlocutionary effect or outcome (you are or aren't persuaded). If the project is to study illocutionary force, you could say that the joke needs to be excluded insofar as joking is primarily characterized or recognized by a perlocutionary effect (laughter or amusement), not an illocutionary force of its own—and thereby may be interesting but is not what we're studying here, as Austin constructs his typology of illocutionary forces.

Maybe, but if you look at Austin's definition of illocutionary acts, the water gets muddier: in short, you can recognize them insofar as "illocutionary acts invite by convention a response or sequel" (117). Austin goes on to suggest that there are "three ways . . . in which illocutionary acts are bound up with effects" (118): "[1] securing uptake, [2] taking effect, [and 3] inviting response"; "and," Austin insists, "these are all distinct from the producing of effects which is characteristic of the perlocutionary act" (118). In short, Austin insists that illocutionary force can't be reduced to (or wholly sublated within) the perlocutionary effect. There has to be uptake, effect, and response for there to be an illocutionary act, but what one might call the virtuality of the illocutionary force is not reducible to the actuality of the perlocutionary effect. (Here we could signal not only Derrida's reading of Austin, but Deleuze and Guattari's reading of him, around the question of the order-word, in the "Postulates of Linguistics" section of *A Thousand Plateaus*).[17]

And if this is indeed the logic of illocution, it's even harder to see how the joke can be kept at bay. The joke depends solely on illocution—uptake (someone has to "get" the joke); taking effect (the force has to transfer somehow—a largely involuntary smile or chuckle); and inviting response (laughter or groan). Indeed, one might say that the illocutionary force of funniness isn't funny any more than the force of insultingness is insulting—it's just force, measurable only through outcome but not reducible to that outcome. And of course it's not simply the words themselves that deploy the force either: two people can tell the same joke, word for word, and one may bomb while the other gets a big laugh—due to a whole series of contextual and virtual intangibles that Austin calls "illocutionary force." Likewise, Austin is perfectly willing to talk about somewhat shady language usage like betting or insulting as illocutionary force; as he observes, you can't bring about the perlocutionary effect of someone being insulted merely by uttering the locution, "I insult you" (30). But neither can you induce laughter simply by saying "I am being funny right now," suggesting that jokes are at least on an illocutionary par with insults. In fact, as I've been insisting throughout, jokes have a diagnostic performative edge on most illocutionary actions—including insulting someone—because they allow no convincing recourse to intentions. You can't mop up after the failed joke by explaining that you meant to be funny. It either works or it doesn't. With the insult, however, one can always walk it back: "Oh, sorry, were you insulted? What I really meant was . . ."[18]

So, how to explain Austin's lack of interest in investigating jokes, given his consistent usage of jokes throughout his lectures, and given the tight theoretical and even tighter performative fit between his comic discourse and his philosophical commitments—to ordinary language and to the exploration of illocutionary force? In Lecture 10, Austin returns to jokes one last time, only to dismiss them again out of hand, this time with a slightly different rationale. "Finally, we have said there is another whole range of questions about 'how we are using language' or 'what we are doing when we are saying something' which we have said may be, and intuitively seem to be, entirely different—further matters which we are not trenching upon. For example, there are insinuating (and other non-literal uses of language), joking (and other non-serious uses of language), and swearing and showing off (which are perhaps expressive uses of language)" (122).

So, why this second list of excluded kinds of speech acts—insinuating, joking, expressing? We can dispense quickly with expressing, which Austin parenthetically dubs an "odious word" (75) in an earlier lecture. Men of a certain generation, especially Oxford philosophers of a certain generation, were demonstrably not interested in what we now call "sharing," so expressive language (the evolution of the earlier exclusion of poetic language?) can as quickly be dispensed as "swearing and showing off." It would I think be quite difficult to bracket expressive swearing and showing off if one wanted to study ordinary discourse today (as my father liked to say, *fuck* is now America's favorite word), but I can see where it'd be less fruitful territory in 1955. In any case, expression, as countless poststructuralist theorists have shown in the wake of Austin, is not where it's at with language usage (mostly because expression depends so heavily on "fictious inward spiritual acts"—an interior truth that is "expressed" outwardly). Similarly, insinuating, while interesting as a kind of language usage, does seem hard to study as a performative, as it also depends on a preexisting or two-tiered discourse of "meaning" (what I "actually" mean versus what I'm "insinuating") and opens perhaps onto an entire psychoanalytic discourse concerning depths and levels of signification that might be very interesting to Freud, but not to Austin.

So no insinuating or expressing yourself, as both summon yet again the "backstage artiste." But that still leaves us with joking—an almost pure illocutionary force, dependent on nothing but the categories of uptake, effect, and response. Again, the question keeps coming back, to take its revenge: why dig a trench around jokes—or, to follow Austin's metaphor a bit more literally, why refuse to "trench upon" joking? Possibly because it would indeed comprise a kind of prolonged trench warfare—you may never make much progress in the war to eradicate jokes from your theory of performativity, and you'll likely lose a lot of personnel along the way.

It's hard to say definitively why Austin refuses to take jokes seriously, but I think it's safe to say his commitment to capital-p Philosophy might explain Austin's uncomfortableness theorizing about comedy or including jokes within his "serious" discourse on ordinary speech. The endgame of his analysis, remember, is to suggest that constatives are performatives. As he reminds us in the final lecture, "to state [something that is true or false] is every bit as much to perform an illocutionary act as, say, to warn or to pronounce . . . 'Stating' [the truth] seems to meet all the criteria we had for distinguishing the illocutionary act" (134). In the end, "We see then that stating something is performing an act just as much as is giving an order or giving a warning."[19]

This being the punchline (truth is force, not reference), it may be that Austin has to understate or downplay jokes as the privileged paradigm for illocutionary acts, because if you don't, you're left with a syllogistic problem on your hands. The syllogism might look something like this:

> All statements of truth are illocutionary or performative.
> The illocutionary or performative is best understood or displayed in jokes.
> Ipso facto, all statements of truth are best understood or displayed in jokes.

As funny and self-deprecating as his lectures are, Austin can't I think bring himself to wonder outright whether "the truth is a joke." It's one thing for Austin to say, "with the performative utterance, we attend as much as possible to the illocutionary force of the utterance, and abstract it from the dimension of correspondence with facts" (146). It's another thing altogether to suggest that facts themselves are a kind of joke—and while he will never trench upon truth directly, he certainly does undermine any naïve correspondence theory of the true throughout his lectures. There's for example a funny routine about the statement "France is hexagonal" (143). How do we confirm this, Austin asks? We confront it with the facts—as he says, "in this case, I suppose, with France" (143). In short, correspondence is a joke: how can you confront a massive geopolitical entity with a three-word English sentence and say they correspond in some way? And true for whom? As Austin suggests, channeling Phil Silvers's Sergeant Bilko, France as hexagon "is good enough for a top-ranking general, perhaps, but not for a geographer" (143).

So what's the upshot of all this, for us? In the main, deconstructive work on Austin and the performative has tended to collapse the question of "joking" entirely into the logic of "writing a poem," and while there are obvious similarities, I've tried to isolate them a bit, and consider jokes on their own terms, rather than collapsing them under the larger (and, frankly, more philosophically reputable) logic of literature. In the end, this of course only strengthens and supplements Derrida's work in "Signature Event Context" and "Limited Inc," but I think there's a certain something about the joke—its sense of provocation, even inappropriateness—that makes it worth thinking about on its own terms. Or just consider it this way: philosophers, especially continental philosophers in the wake of Heidegger, are quite used to saying that the truth is a poem, or that truth is literary in some essential ways (narrative, open-ended, elliptical, idiomatic, world-forming, and so on). But even that continental tradition, or at least that portion of it still huddled in the shadow of Heidegger, still remains hesitant to say that the truth is a joke, or is comic in some essential ways. Though Derrida, of course, does.

Searle, Very Briefly

Searle's "Reiterating the Differences" is a flat-footed routine if there ever was one, almost a performative parody of seriousness. In any case, one can say with confidence that, despite his insistence that he is Austin's true heir, Searle's essay is absolutely foreign both in tone and style to Austin, who importantly reminds us that "there are disadvantages in being excessively solemn."[20] However, Searle—somewhat puzzlingly—wants to insist on both seriousness and intentionality as key components in Austin's work.[21]

I've spent so much time discussing Austin's project at least partially so I can more easily make it clear how patently absurd Searle's reading of Austin really is. Given all we've just seen in Austin, especially his summary dismissal of "backstage artistes" and "inward acts," how is it that Searle can, with a straight face, pretend to correct Derrida by arguing that for Austin, "in serious literal speech the sentences are precisely the realizations of the intentions. . . . understanding the utterance consists in recognizing the illocutionary intentions of the author, and these intentions may be more or less perfectly realized by the words uttered."[22] First, what do these locutions mean—"serious literal speech," "more or less perfectly"? Is perfection the kind of thing that exists "more or less"? If it is, then wouldn't that "more or less" be catching, and maybe even infect "serious literal speech," making it always already "more or less serious literal speech"? But in any case, Austin is engaged in a straightforward critique of this intentionalist position. To quote from Austin's "Performative Utterances" essay: "if we slip into thinking that . . . utterances are reports, true or false, of the performance of inward and spiritual acts, we open a loophole to perjurers and welchers and bigamists and so on" (236). So unless Searle intends to add "philosopher" to Austin's list of scoundrels, it's not at all clear where in Austin Searle got the idea that "understanding the utterance consists in recognizing the illocutionary intentions of the author," or how he's able to say something like "hearers are able to understand [an] infinite number of possible communications simply by recognizing the intentions of the speakers in the performances of the speech acts."[23] In any case, to even the most casual reader of Austin, Searle the defender or advocate must seem more like Searle the welcher or perjurer of Austin's legacy.

In the end, Searle takes the full force of Derrida's sarcastic ire not primarily because of the nasty ad hominem things he says about Derrida—though Searle is nothing if not nasty. He insists that Derrida's arguments aren't clear, and then says there aren't any arguments at all. But even though there are nothing but unclear nonarguments in "Signature Event Context," Searle is assured in saying that Derrida has "misunderstood Austin" and makes "major mistakes"—or in the essay's best howler, "Derrida has a distressing penchant for saying things that are obviously false" (203) about Austin. These are surely unkind things to say, and most of them are in fact "wrong"—Derrida will take particular delight in quoting and "refuting" virtually every word of Searle's essay. But I don't think in the end it's the personal attacks that draw this level of Derridean fire. I think it's more the way in which Searle has set himself as the sole legitimate protector, interpreter, and inheritor of Austin, a thinker to whom Derrida owes some debts, and for whom Derrida has great admiration (as well as some substantial disagreements). This I think is what really angers Derrida, that Searle is involved less in a scholarly debate than in a police action: trying to cordon off the legitimate and serious legacy of Austin (to which Searle somehow has privileged access) from what Searle has decided are illegitimate and frivolous performative uses. What a joke.

The Punchline?

As Austin jests in his final *How To Do Things With Words* lecture, "I have as usual failed to leave enough time in which to say why what I have said is interesting" (153)—and I in turn haven't nearly devoted enough time to discussing the text that got me thinking about this topic in the first place, Derrida's "Limited Inc abc . . ." Suffice it to say that in "Limited Inc abc . . . ," Derrida employs the joking, sarcastic performative discourse of Austin in his onslaught against Searle, at least partially to defend the multiplicity of Austin's lineages against the kind of "serious" stupidity that would suggest that Searle really knew what Austin's intentions were. The very last performative of "Limited Inc abc . . ." perhaps says it all: the essay (even in the original French) ends simply with the English word "Quite." Here Derrida gives Austin the last word in the debate, citing his terribly English idiom for bemused dismissal: "John Searle knows my intentions? Quite."[24]

This, it now becomes clear, is what really attracted me to Derrida all along: the upshot of Derrida's work on the performative, like the upshot of all his work, is also and necessarily political and institutional. As he reminds us in Z, the final section of "Limited Inc abc . . . ," "there is always a police and a tribunal ready to intervene each time that a rule is invoked in a case involving signatures, events, or contexts. . . . If the police is always waiting in the wings, it is because conventions are by essence . . . precarious, in themselves and by the fictionality that constitutes them."[25] Just as surely as academic spats, political power today configures itself through performative means. Now more than ever, we've come to realize that the power of saying and repeating something trumps any politics run by mere fact checkers.[26] Stephen Colbert's "truthiness"—the pervasive cultural sense that it feels true because I've heard it so many times before—is maybe the dark side of the triumph of performativity, and those of us who live in the United States certainly saw that kind of bad-affect politics on display with the rise of Donald Trump.

Which of course makes the truth dangerous political terrain, but it also importantly reminds us that the arsenal of ideology critique (take down the false with the power of the true) is no longer the effective toolkit that it once was. Most of my leftist friends lament what they consider the loss of "reality-based" politics in recent years, and they rehearse the untruths that have ruled over U.S. foreign and domestic policy in the C21: there were no WMDs to justify the Iraq War, and besides Saddam Hussein had nothing to do with 9/11; tax cuts don't pay for themselves, not to mention the fact that taxes were double their present rates during the "golden age of capitalism" from the 1950s through the '70s; God doesn't decide when a woman gets pregnant; climate change is real and human made; President Obama wasn't born in Kenya but in Hawai'i; and everything that has ever come out of Donald Trump's mouth was a lie. Likewise, people who twenty years ago roundly denounced Darwinism (and often "science" as a whole) as misogynist and totalizing (the same people who reveled in pointing out science's dependence on literary devices) now festoon their Subarus with bumper stickers touting the empirical facts of evolution against dangerous creationist fictions. Real politics, it seems, means siding with the constative.

But on Austin's or Derrida's account, political truth functions not on the logic of the fact but on the logic of the joke (uptake, effects, and response, largely outside the guarantee of original intention—which remains in play, as Derrida insists, but can no longer rule the chain). That being the case, you can't outflank performative truth solely by serious appeals to the really true. You need only late-night fare—everything from comedy monologues on the talk shows through *The Daily Show* and its successors like the Samantha Bee and John Oliver shows—to show you that, in fact, the joke is the most effective means of calling bullshit in the current political climate. Serious people in tweed coats or lab coats, arguing in scholarly journals or on news programs, won't get the whole job done. So if theory really does want to engage the world, it had better learn to tell some good jokes. Taking a hand in the game of power requires performative engagement, not solely insistence on the unforced force of the constative "truth." This, I think finally, is why Austin, Derrida, and the performative remain crucial topics for us today.

But that's not, oddly, the way things are trending in continental political theory. In fact, much of that political theory today harkens back to an analysis of dominant power not as dependent on precariously performative illocutionary force but as essentially fascist, brooking little to no resistance (I'm thinking here mostly of Bernard Stiegler and Giorgio Agamben, but there's a pervasively tragic strain in most continental political thinking—Foucault and Deleuze being the obvious exceptions, reminding us that you don't have to be sad to be militant). So, for example, in correcting Hannah Arendt's notion of power along the path of tidying up Michel Foucault's mistakes on the same topic, Agamben writes in *Homo Sacer* that "the radical transformation of politics into the realm of bare life (that is, into the [concentration] camp) legitimated and necessitated total domination": "the camp—as the pure, absolute, and impassible biopolitical space (insofar as it is founded solely on the state of exception)—will appear as the hidden paradigm of the political space of modernity."[27] For Agamben, the machine that animates all the others today is not a disciplinary panopticon, a sexual identity, or a biopolitical stock exchange, but a Nazi concentration camp—a "pure, absolute and impassible biopolitical space" dedicated to "total domination." (Right now, update your Facebook status to "Totally Dominated"!) And much explicitly political work on the performative remains tied to this tragic tone—in Judith Butler's texts, for example. Even Žižek, surely the contemporary political theorist who tells the most jokes, tends to understand them as compact figures for some traumatic core of Hegelian negation (why his jokes revolve around what he calls "a little piece of reality . . . related to 'dirty' topics"—often death, violence, humiliation, degrading sex acts, racism or sexism, and the like: "the whole enjoyment of a joke is that there must be someone who is hurt, humiliated" Žižek concludes).[28] It may be that Paolo Virno's work on jokes and innovation is the sole island of performative optimism (though even Virno spends far too many pages on Carl Schmitt, who's soooo not funny, even in the legendarily unfunny company of other Nazis).[29]

In any case, the hegemony of the performative, and of the joke, should offer us a productive swerve around political theory's tragic pathos: resistance is not scarce or nearly impossible, but far rather it's everywhere—ordinary, as ubiquitous as the joke. Politically, I can't see how it's a helpful or accurate diagnosis of contemporary power—how it works and what it does—to say as Agamben does that we in the wealthy countries live in a kind of concentration camp. (I guess both the Luftwaffe and DirectTV can overwhelm us from the air, but c'mon now. . . .) If anything, political power today seems more like an endless amateur nite at the comedy club—it is often funny, despite itself, even though the blundering consequences of political (in)action are too often unambiguously tragic. In short, it gives away far too much for political theory to agree that contemporary power is what it says it is, a top-down, sovereign form of power much like the parodic SARL corporation that Derrida (de)constructs in "Limited Inc abc . . .": a powerful conglomerate that's in command, in control, knowing both its own intentions and ours.

In the closing lines of "Limited Inc abc . . . ," Derrida takes stock of the politics and ethics of the whole comic affair with Searle and company.

He wonders, could the upshot be that "I do not take their seriousness very seriously?" (107). In the end, such comic performativity remains a sharp provocation for the political future of thinking. In short, it's in and through the comic emphasis on performative, illocutionary force, rather than the tragic emphasis on failed constative meaning, that produces the logic of the joking truth. It's not that truth is farcical or irrelevant, "fake news"—quite the opposite. But political, environmental, scientific, and social truth is beholden to emergent and transforming fields of force, rather than tragic failures of constative totalization. Fake news, as much as bad jokes, continues to produce effects, regardless of constative content. And an emphasis on the performativity of force keeps us trained on those emergences and transformations.

Derrida, Searle, Communication:
Turning Away from the Linguistic Turn

Prior to the obviously joke-laden postscript with Searle, perhaps the first thing you notice about Derrida's initial encounter with Austin's performative theory in "Signature Event Context" is that the entire essay is scaffolded by a broadly comic set of appeals or evasions, or at least mirthful provocations. Imagine you're Derrida, and you're invited to give a keynote speech on the theme of "communication" at a conference dedicated to same, peopled by scholars who work in a field likewise named "Communication." The conference takes place in Montreal, and everyone knows that the Canadian French have a bit of a chip on their shoulder when it comes to the Parisian French. So, what's the first thing that Derrida does in that address dedicated to various senses of "communication"? He suggests that the concept of communication is both naïve and impossible—take that, Canadian Communication Careerists. Or at least Derrida insists that communication is not primary when it comes to language's usage and function. Common sense on the topic, which Searle nicely sums up as "the idea of communication as the communication of intended meanings,"[30] suggests that meaning necessarily comes *first* in any language usage: anything else that might follow after a speech act (understanding, subjective agency, response, or conversely the absence of these outcomes) depends on the prior drama of communicating some content. Everything that might follow from any given linguistic act seems like it logically depends on whether a receiver can "get" what the speaker is trying to communicate (or not, as in the case of the unhappy or misfired speech act). As his primary example of this logical priority, Searle argues that "one could not have the concept of fiction without the concept of serious discourse"[31] precisely because, on his commonsense account, the "serious" notion of intentional communication is necessary to the understanding of any concept whatsoever—philosophical or fictional, serious or frivolous.

Not so fast, Derrida warns in "Signature Event Context," where he wonders in the very first line: "Is it certain that to the word *communication* corresponds a concept that is unique, univocal, rigorously controllable, and transmittable: in a word, communicable?" (1). Rather than get right to the point, to start communicating with his audience right off the bat, Derrida argues that "one must first of all ask oneself whether or not the word or signifier 'communication' communicates a determinate content, an identifiable meaning, or a describable value" (1). The Derridean answer to those questions is of course "no" (the concept "communication" far outstrips any univocal "content," "meaning," or "value"), but it's important to understand why that is the case— especially if one is concerned about Derrida's work and its relations to language and the linguistic turn. There are two primary Derridean reasons one can't simply boil communication down to a univocal concept or transmittable meaning: the first and most recognizably "Derridean" reason is constituted by his insistence that communication is carried along not by intentional subjective intentions but by asignifying performative forces: communication "designates non-semantic movements as well. . . . a shock, a displacement of force" that "does not involve phenomena of meaning or signification" (1). In short, what makes communication possible and effective is not (primarily or originarily) a representable meaning or content, but a force. Communicating is first and foremost responding to the force of the speech act (as Austin would have it, the illocutionary), rather than understanding the semantic content of the utterance. Linguistic "meaning" or "intention," then, is made possible by structurally more powerful forces, ones that do not in themselves "mean" anything at all at the level of the communicated concept or content. It is precisely this insistence on an always already immaterial (illocutionary) force, rather than on its byproduct semantic meaning, that from the beginning situates both Austin's and Derrida's "language" philosophy far beyond the kind of hermetic prison house that came to be associated with the linguistic turn. Derrida's prey in his work on the performative is the question of (asignifying) force and its role in communication, not the issue of linguistic meaning's impossibility (demonstrating the lack of a determinate signified for any given signifier) nor meaning's overdetermined social construction (demonstrating the inevitable excess of meanings for any given language usage).

Derrida's second or parallel point to be made in all this, then, is not simply that some kind of overflowing, undecidable, or natural force comes first because of an inherent or essential polysemic vitality within a word or concept—wherein the force of language's rich, originary meaningfulness constitutes an overflowing, excessive force like lava from an active volcano. Such an appeal to an originary, essentialist polysemia would be to recast the drama of communication into the problem of whittling down language's rich, overflowing content—akin to the overfull intentionality of the human subject—into a decipherable message. In contrast to this kind of romantic linguistic realism (the problem of communication as the problem of containing or paring down an originary excess), for Derrida it is a question of demonstrating that something like the determination of a meaning will always be secondary, inscribed, supplementary—always outside the words themselves and/or the intentions of the speaker.

In short, any communication that might unfold "in" language is always already beholden to the field of forces that make up the performative event, chief among them the "event" of delivery (written, spoken, or otherwise) and the sibling problem of delimiting a "context": words don't "contain" overflowing intentional meaning, impossible to contextualize, but the determination of said ranges of meaning is the performative event of building a context. For example, "ordinary language" is only locatable in a kind of contextual frame, insofar as an ordinary language philosopher would require some external criteria for separating out two events, ordinary and nonordinary speech acts: the marshaling of the criteria does the locating work, not the content or meaning of the speech acts. This is the contextual framing problem that haunts all the other kinds of speech events that Austin tries (and fails) to separate out from one another—behavitives, imperatives, descriptives, and the like. Words are only meaningful inside a context, but such contexts are always iterable or reconfigurable (always beholden to prior and future performative events); hence, this entire drama of meaning finds itself marshaled and orchestrated by deployments of nonlinguistic performative forces. It's not the overflowing intentional force of the words themselves that is the home turf of the performative; rather, the configuration of a communicative context parses out the event sending and receiving the "message," and that configuring has more to do with force than with meaning.

Language 2.0? Rethinking Derrida on Language

In fact, the driving apparatus of the linguistic turn—the hermeneutics of suspicion and its bedrock faith that any claim can be endlessly recontextualized—becomes the linchpin of Bruno Latour's critique of deconstruction, taken up by Rita Felski in *The Limits of Critique*: they share the sense that "context stinks" as a way to think about social determinations of meaning, because sooner or later you simply have to give up on that endless contextualization, precisely because it's otherwise an interminable process (akin to the Hegelian "bad infinite").[32] If, as Derrida concisely puts it, "no meaning can be determined out[side] of context, but no context permits saturation,"[33] then maybe the larger grid of intelligibility offered by linguistic context has to go, at least in part because that skeptical procedure of endless recontextualization has in the C21 mutated from a tool used primarily by leftist hermeneuts of suspicion, to become the preferred tactic of right-wing climate-change deniers and political purveyors of "alternative facts." Much more on this as the book progresses, but suffice it to say here, the new materialist critique of contextual meaning is that the formerly prized moment of factual conclusion or consensus—scientific, literary, or otherwise—is downgraded by deconstruction to the moment of the process's arbitrary exhaustion (you have to stop somewhere), arrived at not by satisfactorily completing the contextual deliberative process but by simply running out of time, throwing up your hands or shrugging your shoulders.

From Derrida's point of view, however, that giving up on endless contextualization is thematized not as a moment of frustrated surrender but as the generative, performative moment of decision—the event where one engages an outcome that's never guaranteed by the process (in the moment of deliberation, you can't know if it's the "right" decision) and (luckily) always open to recontextualization. As Derrida writes in the Afterword to *Limited Inc*, "A decision can only come into being in a space that exceeds the calculable program that would destroy all responsibility by transforming it into a programmable effect of determinate causes. There can be no moral or political responsibility without this trial and this passage by way of the undecidable. Even if a decision seems to take only a second and not to be preceded by any deliberation, it is structured by this *experience and experiment of the undecidable [expérience de l'indécidable]*" (116; emphasis in original). While there is no theoretical limit to the performative events of iterability and recontextualization (such an iterability of the mark, a gesture's repetition that nevertheless introduces difference, is the compulsory "real" in Derrida), there certainly is a practical limit to endless recontextualization—the performative necessity of action and decision without which there would be no ethics or politics. But that ethical decision or political action is based not on the sureties of intentional states and guaranteed outcomes, but on the undecidable calculations of contextual possibilities. Derrida will elsewhere call this iterable contextuality "justice" (the necessity that everything is so calculated that calculation does not have the last word over everything)—so named because any given ethico-political decision is inexorably open to revision in the future (for better or worse): to speak phenomenologically, the "event" that is today is part of a mesh with the retention of yesterday, and the protention of tomorrow. This explains why for Derrida justice is "undeconstructable": because justice is deconstruction itself.

And thereby any narrow linguistically based example of this deconstructive larger process, like the contextual emergence of meaning or the process of subjective decision making, is necessarily carried along by a structurally more powerful set of disseminating forces that go by many iterable and recontexualized names in Derrida's work—the aforementioned justice, for example, or performativity, iteration, the structure of the remnant, pharmakon, supplement, shibboleth, trace, *différance*, hospitality, chora, and so on. The most famous general moniker he gives to those disseminating forces is "writing," but of course that immediately leads us back to the (still-dominant) thematization of Derrida as a hopelessly "linguistic turn" figure, who suggests that human language—in the form of textuality—is finally what makes the world go round: there is nothing outside the text. On this line of reasoning, deconstruction shows us the embarrassing fact that we used to think the really real was to be found in the intentional metaphysics of presence that animates human speech; but Derrida (especially in his debate with Searle) may seem to teach us the opposite—that the real is (un)grounded in a metaphysics of difference and deferral modeled on human writing practices.

Such a narrowly linguistic understanding of Derrida, however, seriously underestimates the stakes of his notion of writing, which he insists should be taken not as synonymous with human inscription but in a more general (let's call it universal, just to be provocative) sense as "the iterability of the *mark beyond all human speech acts*. Barring any inconsistency, ineptness, or insufficiently rigorous formulation on my part, *my statements on this subject should be valid beyond the marks and society called 'human'"* (134; emphasis added). So the performative trace structure of the iterable mark is open to recontextualization precisely because any given mark or singularity—me, you, the bird, the worm, the orchid, the wasp, the napkin dispenser, the North American power grid, the earth—is not identical to itself. And that structure of universal nonidentity certainly isn't *caused* (or really in any significant way impacted) by humans and their language. Rather, this structure of the mark, the remnant, or iteration is the performative condition of (im)possibility for the event of being itself—human, animal, plant, planetary.

Which is to say in more prosaic terms that withering and passing away is the condition of possibility for something to come into existence in the first place; so the event that is any given entity—the performative emergence of everything that's come into being—necessitates that being is never fully present to itself. Which is why for Derrida the emergence or life of a being or object is not opposed to its death or disappearance, because finitude is integral to being itself: the ability to pass from the scene inevitably and inexorably marks anything that emerges. And that law applies even to large-scale entities such as the formation of the Earth or the emergence of the human species itself—both of which will pass away eventually, taking the highly circumscribed entity of human logos with them. And such finitude is not merely an avoidable accident that befalls some existents: passing out of existence eventually happens (or at least structurally can happen) to them all; in effect, the eventuality of disappearing is the signature event that *marks* and prefigures all contextual emergence and presence. In Derrida, that necessity of finitude (the performative coming into being and passing away of all things, alive or otherwise) constitutes a philosophical "real"— that which far exceeds the human species, much less the arcane intricacies of human linguistic activity.

But if deconstruction is not primarily a linguistic-turn discourse, if the performative structure of the mark is finally about a much larger field of forces than human language, how did Derrida's work get understood in the heyday of theory (and subsequently dismissed in the new materialist era) as the stern warden guarding the prison house of language, the linguistic-turn discourse par excellence? Well, deconstruction caught a lot of heat from its enemies, from the very beginning, around the question of meaning's endless recontextualization and its (supposed) political upshot in a kind of shoulder-shrugging nihilism. Terry Eagleton's hugely influential 1983 primer *Literary Theory: An Introduction* summed up deconstruction like this: it "frees you at a stroke from having to assume a position on important issues, since what you say of such things will be no more than a passing product of the signifier and in no sense to be taken as 'true' or 'serious'. . . . Since it commits you to affirming nothing, it is as injurious as blank ammunition."[34]

As I argued over a quarter century ago, and will not belabor again here, this picture of deconstruction (as a linguistic game of showing how language strives after and inevitably fails to attain the status of univocal meaning) may in fact have been the project of American (literary critical) deconstruction associated with the Yale School, though it shouldn't be confused with Derrida's (much different) horizons of engagement; but you don't have to take my word for it, as even Eagleton admits that the upshot of Derrida's work is more complicated than this project of revealing that all language usage is "literary" insofar as it's undecidable. As Eagleton writes, "Deconstruction in the Anglo-American world has tended on the whole to take this path" of rather monotonously "demonstrating that literary language constantly undermines its own meaning" (125). In short, deconstruction got as much help from its friends as it did from its enemies in being painted as a discourse that's wholly caught up in language—in showing the impossibility of meaning in the world as it is in the text. In the heyday of theory, both its proponents and its detractors seemed to agree that deconstruction was primarily in the business of understanding the workings of the world in terms of an understanding of language and the linguistic turn (a rendering of world-as-text that is simultaneously triumphalist in its reduction of the natural world to the human and somehow at the same time completely impotent to change that world). As we've seen in subsequent years—and could have seen at the time had we been paying a different kind of attention—Derrida's philosophical prey lies far, far beyond these literary critical arguments about human language, reading, literature, and meaning (or lack thereof).

Decades later, it may strike us with limpid mirth that differing paradigms for thinking about philosophy, literature, culture, and ontology were ever thought to have had any rough and ready widespread political implications. But let's face constative facts: performing even the most faithfully Maoist reading of *Two Gentlemen of Verona* seems very unlikely to change much politically, in the past or present. But that sense of instant theory translation—from *PMLA* to the streets!—continues to live on, mostly these days in a negative way, in the endless parade of articles suggesting that poststructuralist theory (and even more specifically deconstruction) can be held responsible the "posttruth" world dominating our current political landscape. The argument, in short, is that the new global authoritarian regimes, and their endlessly recontextualized "alternative facts," are the obvious heirs to deconstruction's corrosive skepticism concerning meaning. I really don't want to engage that discourse here, with back and forths defending poststructuralism and deconstruction from those who accuse it of being responsible for nurturing neofascist liars and their spin doctors worldwide. If I were to engage that discourse, however, I might point out first of all that Donald Trump probably skipped the contemporary continental philosophy course in college, though Hungarian strongman Viktor Orban did study at Oxford with the eminent Hegelian Zbigniew Pełczyński, and I don't see anyone suggesting that Hegel or communitarian political theories of mutual recognition are responsible for Orban's brand of self-serving doubletalk.

Second, I'd simply note that political propaganda enjoyed a long, illustrious career before deconstruction became the rage in literature departments in the 1970s and '80s, and such propaganda in the internet era seems unfortunately well positioned to have far outlived the era of deconstruction as well. Third, it simply is the case that truth constitutes, as Foucault put it, a political question—what does the sequoia, the mosquito, or the washing machine care for "truth"? That's our problem, not theirs. Wishing it were not so, or newly fashionable theoretical appeals to a "really real," can hardly guarantee positive political results. Or one might note that realist metaphysics, all the rage the first few thousand years of human thinking in the West (until Hume or Kant, as the story goes), hardly stopped brutal massacres, colonialism, and slavery; nor did philosophical realism bend the first few millennia of Western political regimes toward democracy, and the new realism doesn't necessarily seem likely to do so in the present or future. Like humanism, it may be that liberal democracy is a recent invention, and one nearing its end, due to structural reasons far more powerful than the reach of academic theories.

But in any case, no matter what the backs and forths on the issue of the linguistic turn and its legacy (critiques that could continue ad infinitum), for now I will cut the string here and agree with critics of the linguistic turn on at least one point: if Derrida's primary theoretical-political insight was in fact into the performative workings of language, a series of linguistic mechanisms that then could explain everything else (the endless, "undecidable" making and unmaking of human linguistic meaning as the fulcrum for thinking about the world, or even the universe), then there's not much "new" remaining for deconstruction to discover or shed light upon in the C21—especially around the question of exposing essentialism as social constructionism, which seems like double-down on human linguistic exceptionalism, any way you slice it. It seems not only wrong but the height of humanist hubris to say that gravity, for example, needs to be demystified as a human construct: (a) because gravity is not a social construction, and (b) because such demystification of the "natural" world tends to reinforce human exceptionalism—the sense that the universe is, at its core, what we've made it.

In short, the broad outlines of the critique of the linguistic turn strike me as being correct—the general sense that human language and its workings cannot effectively serve as the linchpin for understanding the workings of everything else. So if deconstruction is or was a discourse completely subtended by the linguistic turn and the question of meaning, then I think interest in deconstruction going forward will remain largely historical. But my opening gambit in this book is to suggest that, while he did indeed write hundreds and hundreds of pages on the question of language, Derrida's core insights—about performativity as much as anything else—were never primarily *linguistic*.[35] Derrida's rewriting of the performative opens onto the comic question of force in and beyond language (comic because it's a circle; you always have to return to the question of force relations), rather than remaining territorialized on the straight-line, tragic question of (meaning's) failure within language.

What Is Performative Force?

If you're emphasizing the importance of illocutionary, performative force over the seemingly more empirically locatable perlocutionary

outcomes (such as success or failure in transmitting "meaning"), critics are rightfully going to ask after a definition, or at least a more concrete sense, of that performative force. I would begin answering that
question by returning to Austin, and his sense that you need to find
a new way to proceed in the wake of the collapse of logical positivism's
rigid dichotomy between constative truth and falsity (a philosophical
approach dominated by the question, "what does this speech act *mean?*");
instead you ask the performative question, "what does it *do?*" Recall
that Austin's entire project is to shift philosophical thinking about
language away from dependence on a master binary opposition (true/
false) toward deploying an experimental topology of forces, uses, and
linguistic effects—warnings, promises, vows, questions, insults, and
the like. To toggle from constative to performative also then slides the
philosophical procedures at play, from the human subject from making a decision or categorization ("this statement is true or false") to
a diagnosis ("what relations are at play in this field or statement?").
Ironically, the latter performative question concerning the play of illocutionary forces is superior to the former constative statement concerning truth or falsity largely because the performative way of proceeding
proves itself to be more realist or empiricist: it looks squarely at things
that happen in real time. In responding to the situation at hand, the
performative procedure is not dominated by a mystical "backstage
artiste" of successful or unsuccessful intentions or meanings. Indeed,
if you look at all the mentions of the word "force" in *How to Do Things
with Words* (72, 75, 100, 109, 150), you'll see that they all involve
illocution—speech acts *doing* something rather than *being* true or false
or *having* a meaning.

However, force "itself" (answering the straightforward question,
"what is force?") remains elusive in Austin, precisely because his notion
of force remains characterized almost wholly by the illocutionary—
which is the closest thing to a kind of metaphysics in Austin. As we've
seen, the illocutionary force of an utterance can't merely be explained
away by its perlocutionary outcome—as for example you could say it
works in Habermas when he speaks of the unforced force of the better
argument (i.e., you can infer the force of reason or unreason from the

reasonable or unreasonable outcome of the deliberation). Insofar as force in Austin—and also in the subsequent genealogy of the performative—is immaterial, it necessarily requires always an analysis or diagnosis to limn out its fault lines. This force of the performative doesn't guarantee anything in particular other than that the field under consideration (a text or a practice or a living being or even matter itself) is in flux, and is likely to remain so; therefore, the emphasis falls not on the (constative) terms but on their (performative) relations: this is the methodological first commandment of performativity, whether it be in the (very different) voices of Austin or Derrida, Butler or Barad— whether the formations under consideration are linguistic, bodily, or take up the question of matter itself.

So force is less a "thing" that can be defined than it is a methodological imperative, a mode of doing critical analysis somewhat akin to the work that Theodor Adorno says he wants to perform in his lectures on Kant's *Critique of Pure Reason*: "what I would like to do is retranslate this philosophy from a codified, ossified system back into the kind of picture that results from a sustained X-ray examination. That is to say, I should like to urge you to conceive of this philosophy as a force field, as something in which the abstract concepts . . . come into conflict with one another and constantly modify one another."[36] And maybe this is a Kantian aside, but I think dedication to this performative modus operandi is why Austin (no less than someone like Adorno) turns away from the dogmatic question of reference or constative truth and toward a mode of critique that works through diagnostic topologies of force. This retreat from the constative is in a way a very traditional Kantian move beyond analytical judgments: such statements are "true" but largely if not completely at the cost of tautology. The most famous example of a Kantian analytic judgment, "All bachelors are unmarried" is of course a true statement, but it hardly constitutes or leads to a synthetic principle or force that could transform anything at all. Such analytic truths have no bearing on a life nor really on a field of knowledge. Truth, at that level of the logical-positivist constative utterance, is largely worthless because it's force-less: what's "done" with or by a constative truth such as "all bachelors are unmarried" is severely limited;

it's true, but it's also more or less a joke. Methodologically, the turn to performativity as force is not a question of resolving issues and tidying things up around what they really mean, but of working with and through the dynamism of any given situation. In the end, this methodological turn from categorization (is it true or false?) to emergence (what does or can this thing do?) is the primary fate and triumph of the performative, in whatever form it takes: any given entity is a field of force rather than a truth hidden or distorted.

In short, performative force keeps an analysis focused on relations rather than terms (or the methodological caveat that any term or phenomenon is a series of relations); hence, far from a safe harbor for the paranoid social-construction thesis (lurking inside any truth is a social construction) that some have taken away from performativity, I would argue that emphasizing a topology of forces (rather than an undermining of truths) pushes the philosophical procedure of performativity no longer in the service of "exposing" anything at all, or certainly not about exposing the constructed nature of the supposedly natural. As we'll see throughout, that dog won't hunt in a world of ubiquitous performativity. In short, in throwing my lot in with performativity as force, my major claim here is that performative critique is not inherently a paranoid, unmasking, or tragic mode dedicated to showing the performative failure of any constative truth—though performative critique certainly has taken that road in its social-constructionist, linguistic-turn modality (much more about this in chapter 2). Emphasizing forces rather than meanings tilts performative procedures away from showing a kind of falsity buried beneath any seemingly decided truth, but instead to diagnose what I'm broadly calling the "comic" (again, because it's a circle not a line) entanglement of forces that inheres in any seemingly settled state or being.

To give the simplest yet most ubiquitous example, take what Samantha Frost recalls for us concerning atoms—the building blocks of matter—not as "things" but as a series of force fields: "To think of matter as energy that feels substantial because its movements or shifts are curbed or circumscribed [by countervailing forces] is not to say that the solidity of matter is 'not real,' as if up until this point we have been mistaken or deluded. Rather, it is to say that the solidity or substantiality of the matter we encounter daily is an effect of the constrained flow and interrelation of energy."[37] As the upshot of this performativity of force at the atomic level of matter itself, Frost suggests that we should "conceive of living bodies in terms of energy-in-transition rather than in terms of stuff-built-or-composed" (104). In short, whether you're talking about language or atoms, the performative emphasis falls on a diagnosis of forces, and critique takes off from what Frost calls "the conceptual primacy of processes and activities" (121). Understood as such, the performative constitutes then a diagnostic discourse to be sure, but not a symptomatic one—which reduces all diagnoses to a root "cause" that is somehow obscured by the symptoms. After the linguistic turn, the performative analysis doesn't *end* with the demonstration of such a conceptual primacy of flux (the tragic undermining of a seemingly solid object or truth); rather, it *starts* with such a flux as a methodological basis point, and from there goes to map relations—some of which may be social or political, or human influenced, some not.

In following out the comic circle of performativity, you come back again and again to the shifting terrain of emergence, rather than following a hubristic, tragic, unmasking, or ungrounding line. This may in fact limit performativity's social usefulness as a straightforward unmasking critique—at this point, "things are more complicated and fluid than they seem" is just that, a truism that's as available for use by all kinds of political actors, from the most enlightened to the most sinister. The force of the paranoid relation of critical unmasking—to demonstrate the social construction of this or that by human discourse—has morphed from being the consequential truth of performativity to become an inevitable or predictable punchline: "Why did the chicken cross the road? Because it was socially constructed." So if performativity is going to live on as a vibrant critical tool after the linguistic turn, it will be as a broadly comic mode of attention to forceful emergence, rather than a tragic discourse dedicated to demonstrating meaning's inevitable or tragic failure.

Two Paths You Can Go By

Judith Butler and Eve Kosofsky Sedgwick

> Bodies that matter is not an idle pun, for to be material
> means to materialize, where the principle of that
> materialization is precisely what "matters" about that body,
> its very intelligibility. In this sense, to know the
> significance of something is to know how and why it
> matters, where "to matter" means at once "to materialize"
> and "to mean."
>
> —JUDITH BUTLER, *Bodies That Matter*

> Repeatedly to ask how certain categorizations work, what
> enactments they are performing and what relations they
> are creating, rather than what they essentially mean, has
> been my principle strategy.
>
> —EVE KOSOFSKY SEDGWICK, *Epistemology of the Closet*

For those who weren't hanging around the theory watercooler in a North American humanities department in the 1990s, it's very hard indeed to *under*estimate the reach and scope of academic discourse on the performative in those years. Hot on the heels of deconstruction, a theory about which everyone was expected to have an opinion in the 1970s and '80s, the questions congealing under the heading "performative identity" were central to humanities debates in the 1990s. In retrospect, it's easy to see how the twin discourses of deconstruction and performativity were linked in that second generation: performativity's major theorists of the 2.0 era, Judith Butler and Eve Kosofsky Sedgwick, both took their PhDs at Yale during the apex of the deconstructive moment (Sedgwick near the origin of the Yale School with a 1975 literature dissertation directed by J. Hillis Miller, Butler toward the twilight with a 1984 philosophy dissertation on Hegel's reception in C20 French thought). And it may well be that deconstruction and/ as performativity was the last "key" theoretical movement in literary and cultural theory—by which I mean that deconstruction and performative identity were maybe the last ideas about which everyone in a literature department was obliged to be somewhat familiar and to have something to say, positive or (more likely) negative.

As John McGowan points out in *Democracy's Children: Intellectuals and the Rise of Cultural Politics,* for better or worse the discourse of theory got fragmented in the C21. As he writes from the vantage point of 2002, "we seem to be in a phase of assimilating, sifting through, and putting into practice the various new concepts and approaches theory suggests. There has been no 'big' theoretical book that 'everyone' must read since Judith Butler's *Gender Trouble* and Eve Sedgwick's *Epistemology of the Closet,* both of which are now more than ten years old."[1] And today, two decades after McGowan's insight, I think we still remain in that "phase of assimilating, sifting through, and putting into practice" the insights of the high theory era, performativity foremost among them. Or at least that's one of the arguments forwarded by this book.

But of course, that isn't to say that nothing has happened in and around theory in the C21, far from it. We've seen the emergence and consolidation of vibrant fields like postcolonial studies, globalization, critical race studies, critical animal studies, even plant studies or object-oriented thinking; relatedly, we've seen the emergence of robust discourses on trans identities, Afro-futurism and Afro-pessimism, Latinx studies, and an enhanced attention to the global south, all the way to a growing archive of humanities work on extinction and climate change. Much of this emergent work in the C21 can be categorized under the rubric of "new materialism," a loose catch-all phrase for discourses that emphasize the situated stickiness of the lively human body and its necessary imbrication with other forces and actants (nature, animals, plants, objects, bacteria, the environment) that were long (mis)understood to be inert slates awaiting the inscription of human linguistic recognition before they could "matter" to us. Various new materialist discourses have insisted on the return of "realist" facts and scientific principles as crucial drivers of humanities work, especially surrounding climate change, and a related theoretical distancing from the linguistic turn's axiomatic hermeneutics of suspicion (which dedicated itself to showing the impossibility of such constative or essentialist truths).

In any case, my point is not that any of these new movements is insufficiently new (though later on, I will wonder whether this commitment to the "new" isn't the most traditional thing about new materialism); nor do I argue that theory then or theory now was always already reducible to some insight about performativity. Rather, my point is that most of the emergent scholarly work in the humanities today grows out of a challenge posed by the second round of thinking about performativity (represented by Sedgwick and Butler) in the 1980s and '90s—to wit: whether *language* was the primary grid of intelligibility for humanities inquiry or whether an emphasis on identities and some kind of extralinguistic *force* was where the theoretical action was located. And, concomitantly, these C21 theory discourses (and many more— just think of the various new twists on the question of reading, be it postcritical, distant, surface, descriptive, and the like) are almost all scaffolded on a rejection of at least some tenets of the linguistic turn's "social construction" thesis.

In short, there's been nothing more universally worried over in recent humanities scholarship than the axiomatic sense that "everything is socially constructed" in and through the grid of intelligibility offered by the social mediations of language. This axiomatic social constructionism constituted the terrain of the linguistic turn, as I outline above, but I think it's uncontroversial to say that the linguistic is no longer a humanities terra firma that we theorists live solidly upon. So that narrowly linguistic sense of the performative—the sense that language is the skeleton key to everything else—is no longer quite where the emphasis falls. But of course there's another—or as we cleverly wrote back in the day, *an other*—deconstructive performativity that, as we have seen in chapter 1, has always already been at work beside or traversing the linguistic: performativity as (illocutionary) force—performativity as a force field that's much larger and more powerful than the social constructs of human linguistic activity.

Following recent work in new materialism, we might call this more robust, force-field concept a "performativity of all things." Take the sense, for example, in which Bruno Latour limns out the anti-Copernican revolution of recent thinking about life on Earth being constituted more by a mesh of co-constituting actants than by a competition among preexisting organisms—sometimes known as the Gaia hypothesis, which lines up with Latour's actor–network theory in arguing that all things in the world are forceful agents, lively if not in some sense biopolitically "alive":

> Before Gaia, the inhabitants of modern industrial societies saw nature as a domain of necessity, and when they looked toward their own society they saw it as the domain of freedom, as philosophers might say. But after Gaia these two distinct domains literally don't exist anymore. There is no living or animated thing that obeys an order superior to itself, and that dominates it, or that it just has to adapt itself to, and this is true for bacteria as much as lions or human societies. This doesn't mean that all living things are free in the rather simple sense of being individuals, since they are interlinked, folded, and entangled in each other. This means that the issue of freedom and dependence is equally valid for humans as it is for the partners of the above natural world. Galileo invented a world of *objects* placed beside each other, without affecting each other, and entirely obeying the laws of physics. Lovelock and Margulis sketched a world of *agents* constantly interacting with each other.[2]

The linguistic turn of axiomatic social constructionism lived and moved in what Latour here dubs the "pre-Gaian" world, where any given being's "nature" is seen as a constraint upon its freedom, constituting an essentialist "domain of necessity"; and therefore any argumentative appeal to nature (as in "this is human nature" or "this is the nature of gender roles") deploys, for social constructionist thinkers, necessarily an appeal to a kind of unearned, lock-step determinism, where the way things "are" in nature is prescriptive vis-à-vis the (human) cultural realm. On the other side of that same essentialist coin, it is only in a social world where we can demonstrate (in short, uncover through critique) the linguistic construction of those natural prescriptions that we have any chance of freeing ourselves from these otherwise determinist dictates (with critique re-igniting the Enlightenment torch whereby humans, as Latour puts it above, "looked toward their own society" and "saw it as the domain of freedom"). In short, in the era of the linguistic turn, only in a domain where we recognize thoroughgoing social construction can we perform freedom, and unlock the ability to intervene in the world and exercise the agency necessary to change our circumstances. The linguistic turn of social constructionism was, to put it bluntly, an attempt to wrest performative, human political or social agency (however limited or constrained) from an otherwise determinist realm of "natural" essentialist or constative necessity.

Take, as a representative example of this axiomatic linguistic-turn social constructionism, Judith Butler's critique of Deleuze and Guattari in her 1987 book on Hegel (a revision of her Yale dissertation), *Subjects of Desire*. Butler reads Deleuze and Guattari's hard critique of linguistic social constructionism—what they call the endlessly lacking "interpretosis" that infects any discourse dedicated to the signifier and its inability to reach the signified—as a naïve, essentialist, and politically dangerous "appeal to a precultural eros [that] ignores the Lacanian insight that *all desire is linguistically and culturally constructed*." She continues, "the postulation of a *natural* multiplicity appears, then, as the insupportable metaphysical speculation on the part of Deleuze. . . . The Deleuzean critique of the prohibitive law and the subsequent reification of desire as that which is always already repressed, requires a political strategy that explicitly takes account of *the cultural construction of desire, that is, a political strategy that resists the appeal to a 'natural' desire as a normative ideal."*[3] Here, Butler is defending as axiomatic—simply as settled law—"the Lacanian insight that all desire is linguistically and culturally constructed," and arguing along a parallel track that any attempt to critique or swerve around that law of social construction must necessarily appeal to a kind of unrestrained (implied here as fascist) notion of free, sovereign, natural desire.

This is relatively familiar turf, as Butler is performing a classic American-style deconstruction of the nature/culture binary, showing the privileged term "nature" to be always already beholden to some forms of cultural mediation; but what I want to highlight in particular here is the equally axiomatic relation implied between ontology and politics (in a slightly different parlance, facts and values): for Butler, because the realm of essences is socially constructed by various linguistic apparatuses (scientific, cultural, political, religious, and so on), the configuration of any supposed "essence" (of gender categories, for example) is always already soaking in political power. Which is, on her reading, simultaneously to insist that any such positing of a nonconstructed nature is always already an appeal to the way things "should" be, politically speaking (because all supposedly disinterested research on something like gender roles is necessarily interested all the way down, which is to say such research is always infected or inflected by the power relations of its social context).

This rhetorical appeal to nature—"the way things really are"—comprises the political danger of metaphysical essentialism for Butler, appealing always to the social values lurking within supposedly neutral objective facts. But I would mark again that this axiomatic fact-value relation (the sense that any appeal to the "fact" of nature is a bogus maneuver deployed to earn "value"-laden argumentative high ground in a political disagreement) is itself an insight that is inexorably linked to the social-construction hypothesis and its grounding opposition between a relatively inert sense of nature and the human social realm of meaning or knowledge; but I don't think that brand of critique—unmasking any claim to the real as a humanist social construction—can swim effectively outside the waters of the linguistic turn. In fact, with new materialism's rejection of social construction-ism's demystifying critique (the constant unmasking of the real as a linguistic construction) also gets jettisoned, it seems to me, the very fact-value distinction upon which so much of that critique was based, insofar as the fact-value distinction wholly depends on a sharp separa-tion of the human from the natural world. Back in the day, if you could show that gender, for example, was not mandated or guaranteed by an essential nature, but merely a social construction, it was assumed that some kind of liberatory social outcome would (or at least should or could) arise from that revelation—that, in short, a change in facts (their disruption or confirmation) will inexorably lead to a change in human values. I don't know if that was ever the case—at the time, Sedgwick famously suggested it wasn't: "I remember the buoyant enthusiasm with which feminist scholars used to greet the finding that one or another brutal form of cultural oppression was not biological but 'only' cultural! I have often wondered what the basis was for our optimism about the malleability of culture by any one group or program."[4] So there were good reasons to be skeptical about the iron link between facts and values, even in the linguistic-turn era; for that matter, we might do well to recall that Saussure (the grandfather of the linguistic turn) famously suggested that the social or arbitrary nature of the sign actu-ally made it highly resistant to social change: as he writes, because there is no natural or scientific "reason to prefer soeur to sister, Ochs to boeuf, . . . the arbitrary nature of the sign is really what protects lan-guage from any attempt to modify it."[5] The social conventions of lan-guage are functionally highly conservative in Saussure's rendering; so whatever else you might think about it, deploying a Saussurean understanding of the signification as your primary grid of intelligibil-ity is unlikely to lead to revolutionary social change.

But in any case, once we take our leave from the linguistic turn and drink the new materialist Kool-Aid, we likewise accept that the social constructions of humans are part of the tapestry that is nature, rather than separate from it. The human is neither slave to nor lord over nature; all things and species are part of the same mesh—the tulip, the bacterium, the bonobo, the soil, the human. As Karen Barad puts it in

Meeting the Universe Halfway, new materialism opens up "a *posthuman-ist* elaboration of the notion of performativity" that "calls into question the givenness of the differential categories of human and non-human" (66). Specifically, Barad deploys "a reworking of Butler's notion of per-formativity from iterative citationality [of human language] to reiterative intra-activity [of all phenomena]" (208), which argues for the perfor-matively quantum nature of all matter within which bodies less inter-act (a formulation that suggests that the bodies somehow preexist their actions) than they do co-constitute one another in a ceaseless move-ment of intra-action: "Matter is agentive, not a fixed essence or prop-erty of things" (137), and this intra-active, performative mesh is far from a mere human social construction—it has the status of the real.

However, this new materialist truism about the co-constitution of all things also evacuates the critical usefulness of the linguistic turn's fact-value distinction, because the "nature" of x or y body is no longer seen to be a ground for some kind of prescriptive formula for regulat-ing human relations. If nature is an intra-active performative force or flow running through everything, rather than a prescriptive essence that is unique to each being or species, it doesn't seem that anything at all concerning human political norms necessarily arises from that new materialist realization—there's no sociopolitical "ought" attached to that ontological "is." In short, that ontologically prescriptive sense of nature is itself a remnant of the linguistic turn and its demystifying, axiomatic social constructionism: ontological prescription (the way a being "really" is in its essence = the way it should be politically or socially) was in a nutshell why essentialism was "bad" in the era of the linguistic turn, and why realist essentialism was the privileged target to be unearthed and critiqued.

As we turn away from that linguistic-turn consensus concerning social constructionism, the Latour quotation above rehearses a per-formative point on which almost all recent new materialist thinking relies: once you posit that all living things are not cut off from each other (each staying in its own lane and obeying its own determining essence), but that "all living things . . . are interlinked, folded, and en-tangled in each other," and you accept the performative point that everything is doing things all the time, then the question of nature as lock-step determinism gives way to an understanding of the world as populated by performative agents, each interacting with and co-constituting the others. This of course doesn't necessarily imply a harmonious world of seamless cooperation (Latour's concern about the holistic mysticism of some Gaia-principle true believers); in fact, it doesn't imply anything at all about the relations among humans and the so-called natural world, other than we—along with everything else—swim in the same performative soup of endless co-constitutive activity, described differently in related insights like Deleuze and Guattari's cosmic refrains, Latour's actor–network theory, Stacy Alaimo's "trans-corporiality," Sara Ahmed's "situated bodies," Jane Bennett's "vibrant matter," Samatha Frost's "biocultural creatures," Fred Moten's performative riff on Édouard Glissant's "consent not to be a single being," or Barad's performative "intra-activity" of the quantum world.

In *Immaterialism,* Graham Harman offers a concise chart of what he calls the AXIOMS OF NEW MATERIALISM:

—Everything is constantly changing.
—Everything occurs along continuous gradients rather than with distinct boundaries and cut-off points.
—Everything is contingent.
—We must focus on actions/verbs rather than substances/nouns.
—Things are generated in our 'practices' and therefore lack any prior essence.
—What a thing *does* is more interesting than what it is.
—Thought and the world never exist separately, and therefore 'intra-act' rather than interact.
—Things are multiple rather than singular.
—The world is purely immanent, and it's a good thing, because any transcendence would be oppressive.[6]

Whatever else one might say about this list (and Harman offers it to juxtapose his object-oriented position from this brand of new materialism), it does seem recognizable enough as a summary of the complete and utter triumph and spread of performativity, taken initially as a linguistic description of speech acts and their forces (what something is or what it means is wholly beholden to how it acts or what it does), and exported to literally everything else. Perhaps the one axiom here that grounds all the others is the performativity 101 truism that "We must focus on actions/verbs rather than substances/nouns." In short, "What a thing *does* is more interesting than what it is," and all the other performativity upshots (about constant change and contingency, practices, co-emergence, immanence, multiplicity) follow from that initial axiom that *being* is a form of *doing*.

And Harman likewise foregrounds for us the extent to which these new materialist claims about the performative agency of everything are strongly—maybe even fiercely—ontological or realist ("Things are multiple rather than singular" is an ontological claim if there ever was one). Finally, as Harman's last axiom also highlights, there remain somewhat old-fashioned sociopolitical values attached to those new materialist ontological truths: "The world is purely immanent, and it's a good thing, because any transcendence would be oppressive." We will return over and over to this fact-value (or slippage between "is" and "ought to be") relation in new materialism as this book progresses, but it's worth noting here that, whether conceived as an older linguistic or a new materialist ontological category, there remains a very strong ethical or liberatory affect tethered to ontological claims about the performative. It is in fact this sociopolitical upshot—the idea that there's something emancipatory embedded in a philosophical position concerning performativity—that most obviously lives on in the shift from a linguistic understanding of performativity (the cornerstone of ideology critique, the idea that all seemingly inherent meaning is beholden to social actions of some kind) to a realist ontological one (all things are nothing other than what they do, so everything's connected to everything else, which for some reason is a "good thing").

In any case, this unlikely triumph of performativity (as the backbone of nothing less than a realist, "constative" ontology, the very bogeyman and despised "other" of the linguistic turn) allows us backtrack, and reexamine the genealogy of the two major paths that performativity took in the 1980s and '90s—those of Eve Sedgwick and Judith Butler. Despite their theoretical differences, each agrees that performativity or deconstruction needs to be taken into the realms where the Yale School was somewhat reluctant to go. As Sedgwick writes about her first-wave "linguistic turn" deconstructive teachers: "Deconstruction, founded as a very science of *différ(e/a)nce,* has both so fetishized the idea of difference and so vaporized its possible embodiments that its most thoroughgoing practitioners are the last people to whom one would now look for help in thinking about particular differenc*es.*"[7] In short, both Butler and Sedgwick looked to shift the debate on performativity, from the endless demonstration of meaning's undecidability to the political, ethical, and subjective questions posed to actual, material bodies (especially those labeled deviant) in the world: from reading literature (linguistic questions of meaning and its discontents) to talking about what cultural production (especially the production of subjective identity itself) does in the world; from questions of performativity as language to questions of performativity as force (linguistic for sure, but also social, scientific, global, economic, and so on); from the performativity 1.0 question of what things mean or don't mean to the performativity 2.0 question of what bodies, identities, and things do or are barred from doing in the world.

More accurately, on the linguistic-turn model, all that bodies, identities, and things can do is fail (that is, fail to "mean" univocally, to be essentially true, transhistorical, uncontestable), precisely because they're performatively, socially constructed within a world of disciplinary norms. The other or parallel sense of performativity as force looks at what things *actually or virtually produce,* rather than what they *can't produce* (a constative, final "truth"): in short, performativity 2.0 doesn't completely abandon the question of language, but emphasizes the myriad performative effects produced in the sociopolitical world, beyond the narrow linguistic concern with meaning and its impossibility. This, I think, is still where we've arrived today with the "performativity 3.0" affirmative sense of production that pervades new materialism, and why performativity is the subtending discourse for much current work in so many subfields of humanities enquiry. Or so a certain genealogy of the present might suggest.

But here's also where the two main paths of performativity in the 1980s and '90s (represented by Butler and Sedgwick) diverge—not around the question of whether to expand the terrain of theory outward from the question of textual meaning to engage political theory, queer theory, feminism, critical race theory, and the like; certainly Butler and Sedgwick agree on that necessity. The question of how to engage these sociopolitical questions, though, constitutes the two paths that performativity could go by—in the end, whether the demystifying of disciplinary social constructionism of the linguistic turn remained the primary grid of intelligibility for thinking about or responding to political issues (Butler's position in a nutshell, one that depends on a world of disciplinarity as its normative target) or whether the fields of force that exceed the grid of the linguistic turn are the primary foci for work going forward (Sedgwick's emphasis on the affective or reparative, rather than demystifying, forces of performativity, a biopolitical notion that largely abandons the idea that there is such a thing as a dominant, normative, disciplinary knowledge that organizes any given field). In short, Butler's work, it seems to me, lives and moves in a disciplinary world of normative knowledge and its subversion (demonstrated by what knowledge or bodies *can't* do), whereas Sedgwick's opens out onto a biopolitical world, one of multiplicities of modalities for living, and a concomitant emphasis what bodies *can* do.

It is of course well known that the central critique of Butler's work, even as it emerged in the late 1980s and into the '90s, was that it merely reduced all sociopolitical questions about identity, agency, politics, or biology into academic, disciplinary questions of language and signification. As Susan Bordo put it at the time, speaking for countless other critics in *Unbearable Weight*, "Butler's world is one in which language swallows up everything, voraciously, a theoretical pasta machine through which the categories of competing frameworks are pressed and reprocessed as 'tropes'. . . . Butler's analyses of how gender is constituted or subverted take the body as just such a text whose meanings can be analyzed in abstraction from experience, history, material practice, and context."[8] But here I'm not concerned centrally with the accusation of reducing everything to language in Butler's work on performativity—something like Bordo's implied charge that deploying language as a grid of intelligibility gives you no purchase on the social or political realm, which strikes me as flat-out wrong. Taken simply as a grid of intelligibility (a way to make sense of things), the turn to language on the Saussurean model is simultaneously a turn to the social: there are no natural languages or meanings "in abstraction from experience, history, material practice, and context" for Saussure, so to say that Butler's linguistic-turn model avoids, downplays, or trivializes the social realm seems a complete misunderstanding.

I am more narrowly interested in wondering about the "tragic" work of failure, negativity, or lack within a linguistic performative paradigm—understanding the world as remaining open to contestation primarily because it *lacks* inherent constative meaning, on the template of the material signifier that lacks the final stopping point of a transcendental signified. Language is on the face of it expensive as a universal sense-making grid for all the anthropomorphic reasons we've seen rehearsed above, but I think the real cost of linguistic performativity is not so much the danger of textualizing material bodies (Bordo's worry that the linguistic turn swaps out "real" sociopolitical problems for "merely" textual ones), but the linguistic turn's axiomatic sense of demonstrating the tragic impossibility of full "meaning" for any given social formation—and that demonstration of a ubiquitous lack in any given social formation then becomes the linguistic turn's primary social mode of critique (demystifying institutional, social, or disciplinary claims to essentialism).

That demystifying demonstration of the social construction of x or y disciplinary, political formulation has constituted a very powerful version of political critique, from Butler all the way to Marxist ideology critique and its attack on the manufactured hegemony of capitalist common sense. Language, for Butler, is then not a template of analysis that takes us out of the sociocultural realm (into the fanciful realms of fiction); rather, language as a grid of intelligibility actually gives us consistent purchase on the work of social critique. In Butler's hands, the critical work of the linguistic turn is the insistent demonstration of sociopolitical failure of totalized meaning: the meaning of a poem, for example, can never be exhausted because the material signifiers never simply mesh with a signified meaning, and reading is a theoretically interminable process because of that essential clause of signification's ongoing failure and reinscription. This is the linchpin of Butler's work on iteration and citationality—because identity (subjective, national, group, and so on) fails to be complete, these disciplinary notions of identity are always open-ended, necessarily open to critique and reart-iculation. Not because they're *excessive* in some essential or natural way (that would violate the Lacanian law of social construction), but because they *lack* completeness: all disciplinary formulations fail to be complete, on the template of linguistic meaning.

In the end, then, Butler doesn't simply reduce everything to language (suggesting that politics or science is primarily a language game), but she does continue to depend on normative, disciplinary meanings and the workings of signification and language (the question of mean-ing and the signified, and its necessary failure or return to the mate-rial signifier) as the primary grids for understanding, subverting, and mobilizing questions of identity, politics, biology, what have you. As Butler writes of her methodology in *Bodies That Matter*, the phrase "*Bodies that matter* is not an idle pun, for to be material means to mate-rialize, where the principle of that materialization is precisely what 'matters' about that body, its very intelligibility. In this sense, to know the significance of something is to know how and why it matters, where 'to matter' means at once 'to materialize' and 'to mean.'"[9] It's less the question of language per se than it is the linkage "mattering = mean-ing" that Butler finally can't give up, precisely because she's committed to the linguistic turn's social constructionist paradigm and its concom-itant dependence on disciplinary norms as a baseline or background to be disrupted by her deconstructive methodology. Nothing "matters," materializes or comes into social being, on Butler's account until it's subjected to the disciplinary grid of intelligibility represented by lan-guage. Because on that paradigm, if mattering isn't meaning (if it's "just" mattering, just the way things work, the real), then that's essentialism, and such an appeal to essentialism is both theoretically wrong and politically dangerous, because essentialism is inherently fascist or totalitarian in the political realm—my way or the highway. Though as we've seen with the rise of populist strongmen worldwide, totalitarian political ambitions no longer require (or seem to work well through) essentialist appeals to the really real, but through denials that there is such a thing, endless spin-doctoring and repetition of your version of events.

In any case, the drama of failure and reinscription so central to Butler's performativity goes like this: The determination of meaning (naming what matters as a social construction of disciplinary knowledge) strives to be whole or complete, to account for all cases; but it necessarily always fails, and the process of meaning-making inevitably starts over. This is the primary ethical component of linguistic-turn theory, demonstrating the necessary failure of the disciplinary drive for mastery and meaning. And this ethical imperative of meaning's failure has proven very productive around a whole series of disciplinary objects and sites of inquiry—this drama of striving and failure could shed light on everything from subjective identity questions to national political ones, and maybe everything in between, if you shoehorn it enough. A person or institutional group sets out to control the process of how something matters, to delimit its meaning and outcome; but that process inevitably fails because material social and disciplinary knowledge conditions never reach full metaphysical closure, so we have to start over every time, sadder but wiser.[10]

At that level, there is an ontological claim behind Butler's social constructionism: "We may seek to return to matter as prior to discourse to ground our claims about sexual difference only to discover that matter is fully sedimented with discourses on sex and sexuality that prefigure and constrain the uses to which the term can be put. Moreover, we may seek recourse to matter in order to ground or to verify sets of injuries or violations only to find that *matter itself is founded through a set of violations,* ones which are unwittingly repeated in the contemporary invocation" (29). Ironically, because the axiomatic social construction of x is

the primary insight of the linguistic turn, language as a grid of intelligibility gives you far-ranging access to critiquing all kinds of human
disciplinary endeavors, all of which on Butler's account come into being
(hence the ontology of the claim) only "through a set of violations."
As liberal political theory has long argued, the human political realm
works in and through the exercise of recognition—what and who matters (the citizen, the white man, the wealthy), and what or who doesn't
matter (everyone else). And Butler poses a series of questions to liberal
political theory concerning the supposedly benign act of recognition,
by asking after the moment of exclusion that grounds any moment of
political recognition. Recognition always fails to include everyone, so
must forever start over. As Butler writes, theories of identity "that elaborate predicates of color, sexuality, ethnicity, class, and able-bodiedness
invariably close with an embarrassed 'etc.' at the end of the list. Through
this horizontal trajectory of adjectives, these positions strive to encom-
pass a situated subject, but invariably fail to be complete. This failure,
however, is instructive: what political impetus is to be derived from the
exasperated 'etc.' that so often occurs at the end of such lines?"[11] In
questioning the limits of political recognition (demystified as anything
but universal, recognition is shown to be grounded on incomplete,
socially constructed violations), Butler eloquently speaks up for those
not recognized by disciplinary forms of exclusionary knowledge—for
every*one* else who's left not to matter.

But what about every*thing* else, all the other 99.999 percent of
nonhuman matter in the universe, which we'd have to account for if,
as Butler insists, "matter itself is founded through a set of violations"?
The linguistic turn exposes for us the fact that the disciplinary drive
toward the signified meaning that can never escape the material signifiers of social construction—there's a performative material process
whereby the meanings and values associated with the privileged term
are projected upon the abjected body. As Butler puts it, the disciplinary
call of interpellation "is formative, if not performative, precisely because it initiates the individual into the subjected status of the subject" (121); but of course that interpellation fails to be complete, fails
to control that body (on Butler's account, not because of something

inherently lively about the body, but because of a structural infelicity in the social, performative codes). "Here the performative, the call by the law which seeks to produce a lawful subject, produces a set of consequences that exceed and confound what appears to be the disciplining intention motivating the law. Interpellation thus loses its status as a simple performative, an act of discourse with the power to create that to which it refers, and creates more than it ever meant to, signifying in excess of any intended referent. It is this constitutive failure of the performative, this slippage between the discursive command and its appropriated effect, which provides the linguistic occasion and index for a consequential disobedience" (122), the iterative subversion of the dominant sociopolitical codes of normativity. As the mountain of interdisciplinary scholarship that she inspired attests, Butler's account of the political (mis)recognition that inheres to human identity categories remains convincing on the grid of intelligibility offered by social constructionism.

I think a lingering set of questions remains concerning whether you can apply that linguistic grid to understand, for example, the changing "performative" course of the Mississippi River or the workings of plant heliotropism and photosynthesis. Does the river change course on this template of human political and linguistic striving for completion and subsequent failure? On this tragic template of the human striving for meaning and its necessary failure, a lack of completion that in turn enables change and agency, can you understand the workings of human digestion or the mechanics of tissue cells (which require fluid, boundary-crossing contextual input, rather than attempting to repel it and remain sovereign)? You can maybe understand evolution as an old-fashioned "survival of the fittest" on this line of social-constructionist reasoning (the shorter-beaked birds fail to get nectar, so they evolve longer beaks or perish), but this drama of striving after dominance can't explain the emergent consensus that Darwinian sexual selection is in fact the driver of evolutionary survival (the now-dominant understanding that developing a capacity to be affected by surroundings trumps the sovereign survivor model for explaining which species survive and thrive).[12]

As many recent critics have argued, the new materialist understanding of imbricated, lively, co-constitutive life forms and objects renders obsolete the very nature/culture divide that is so central to social constructionist accounts of reality. As Barad notes, for example, the intra-active, co-constitutive nature of all bodies offers "a particularly effective tool for thinking about socialnatural [sic] practices in a performative rather than representationalist mode,"[13] which is to say that new materialist performativity offers us a way to think of nature and culture as intra-actively co-constitutive, rather than as separate entities. When it comes to Barad's notion of performativity, "subject and object do not preexist as such, but emerge through intra-actions."[14] Indeed, of all the hundreds of binary oppositions that got deconstructed over the years, probably none was more popular than the nature/culture binary—with hundreds of articles and countless classroom hours dedicated to showing over and over again that any conception of nature is at the end of the day a cultural linguistic construction, essentially a kind of fiction. To make this point in the literature classroom, you just have students read, for example, Hawthorne's "Young Goodman Brown" or Conrad's *Heart of Darkness,* and contrast the Puritans' or Victorians' menacing portraits of nature (including human nature) with today's loving embrace of all that is natural (including finding your inner child). Dutifully following Saussure, we can point out that the "referent" in the world may be the same (those "wild" spaces beyond the grid of the city), but different cultures and different historical periods bestow vastly different meanings on this thing called nature. And thereby we find that nature is socially constructed, as per the outline provided by performativity 1.0.

However, as Latour and Barad suggest above, the new materialist understanding of imbricated, lively, co-constitutive life forms may make obsolete the nature/culture divide that was so central to social constructionist accounts of reality. Once you accept that lively, new materialist rewriting of the nature/culture divide, there's a kind of inversion from the performative deconstruction of the nature/culture binary, which attempts to show that any appeal to nature is inexorably cultural. The 3.0 or new materialist performative rendering of that binary asks you to recognize not that nature was really culture all along, but asks you to wonder, as Vicki Kirby puts it, "What If Culture Was Really Nature All Along?" Within Butler's worldview of social constructionist performativity 2.0, language was thought to be the primary means by which human culture was barred from the realm of nature (on the Lacanian insight that once we fall into language we are forever cut off from the real). But if humans are understood as inexorably part of the mix of nature, actants among other actants, then language (the thing that seemed to distinguish us from mute, "natural" entities) is reunderstood as a continuous part of nature as well—a feature of one of the entities within the performative mesh of nature, much like the glaciers characteristic of the polar regions, the plumage of the peacock, or the acorns of the oak tree.

One might offer Kirby's new materialist insight concerning language in the form of a syllogism:

> Humans are part of nature (not opposed to it).
> Language is a distinguishing feature of humans.
> Ergo, human language is part of nature.

Or, more generally, if everything in nature is lively and connected, as we learn from new materialisms, then why must we banish language from the mix, as it is a lively form of connection, a marking apparatus that can be understood as far more generally utilized by all kinds of plants, animals, and ecosystems to "communicate" (about the existence of predators, sources of food, mating and pollination, and so on). Like Derrida's reading of intentionality in Austin, language doesn't disappear on such a rereading, but it does cease to rule the chain once you understand language as one element among a structurally more powerful set of others. Likewise, following everyone from Deleuze and Guattari, through Latour, to Barad's physics, once we realize that inert matter isn't so inert after all—that flesh and rocks and trees are lively and are part of a network of interconnection where they co-evolve with each other (the way we tend to describe "culture")—then it begins to look like a broad, posthuman sense of language or culture is integral to the workings of nature and the very physiology of our bodies. As Kirby writes, "the meat of the body *is* thinking material. If it is in the nature of biology to be cultural—and clearly, what we mean here by 'cultural' is intelligent, capable of interpreting, analyzing, reflecting, and creatively reinventing—then what is the need to exclude such processes of interrogation from the ontology of life?"[15] In short, a certain understanding of performativity—as the force of iteration and marking beyond the human—can, I think, assist us in chapter 1's project of rescuing deconstruction from its exile as a hopelessly linguistic-turn discourse that understands everything else in the universe on the world-building paradigm of human language. As Barad sums it up, "The move toward performative alternatives to representationalism shifts the focus from questions of correspondence between descriptions of reality (e.g., do they mirror nature or culture?) to matters of practices, doings, and actions."[16]

Performativity and/as Biopolitics

There are, then, two dominant versions of the performativity thesis. The first is the linguistic version in which language is shown to do things, to bring supposed constative truths and facts into being (rather than merely referring to a preexisting real). The uptake on this performative linguistic thesis has then not been any guarantee of linguistic or social success, but largely one of assured failure: all performatives will be unhappy, unsuccessful in the long run, because performativity requires constant repetition and recontextualization, and precisely because of that ironic "fact" of performativity, there is no final context, no truly constative meaning or phrasing. Concomitantly, there's no truth "out there" that remains untouched by the language game of human intervention, because mattering always implies meaning. On the linguistic grid, performativity guarantees only one thing: the failure of totalized, final, "real" meaning. This is essentially the performative road that Butler travels, and it depends on what I call a "disciplinary" understanding of the world, one where certain normative institutional diktats (established "truths") require endless subversive transgression or undermining from the position of the excluded term or other.

The second version of performativity is what I've characterized as the biopolitical, forceful, or maybe even "theatrical" one: the sense that everything acts (even objects or the earth itself) in a mesh of excessive, intra-acting co-constitution. Everything is, in some sense, "alive"—moving, performing, becoming—contrary to the linguistic performative, which suggests that wherever you may look, there's no there that's "really" there (only a disciplinary, socially constructed, and institutionally sanctioned consensus). On the biopolitical, forceful, or theatrical version of performativity, one might say there's a there there everywhere, a realist field of actant bodies and forces; and performative productions within that field produce excessive, momentary configurations along the continuum of that (largely nonhuman) field of affective forces. As Deleuze and Guattari put it in their work on the performative, even "I is an order-word."[17] Which is to say, an identity is not an always-failed attempt to totalize this thing called I, but is constituted by a marshaling of preexisting forces into this temporary, always-emerging, excessive smear called an I.

These new realisms or new materialisms are beholden to the performativity of the forceful, theatrical, excessive, sticky, bodies-as-forcefields variety (not the linguistic, lacking, bodies-as-spoken-into-being, social-construction-of-everything kind of thing). Taking stock of the two roads performativity could have gone by in the 1980s and '90s (Butler's disciplinary road or Sedgwick's biopolitical one), clearly the new materialism finds its roots in Sedgwick's notions of performativity, rather than Butler's—in the affects of stubborn, a-signifying, excessive biopolitical force, rather than in an understanding of bodies and forces marshaled on the template of the signifier and its lacks.

Most notably, we might recall that Sedgwick argues for a kind of affective, "reparative" (rather than "paranoid") style of performative engagement, one that looks to cultural productions for something other than subversions of disciplinary depth, hidden meaning, or large-scale significance. As Sedgwick puts it in the essay "Paranoid Reading and Reparative Reading," summing up Melanie Klein's work and the paranoid and the depressive, "the paranoid position . . . is a position of terrible alertness,"[18] always tasked with paying close attention so that one is not duped into playing the fool or making the same mistake over and over again. But Sedgwick (perhaps counterintuitively) finds a kind of queer potential not within that paranoid mindset but within a "depressive" aesthetic engagement: "By contrast, the depressive position is an anxiety-mitigating achievement" that opens "the position from which it is possible in turn to use one's own resources to assemble or 'repair'" (128) the paranoid space of constant subjective authenticity policing, or the contemporary overflow of way too many shiny objects vying for our attention as we try (and fail) to make meaning out of things.

Though of course here I can see the paranoid retort coming back again strong and arguing that an aesthetic space of involuted pleasure or mere escape is the *problem* rather than the *solution* in terms of the privatizing neoliberal imperatives dominant in contemporary capitalist life. The revolution can't come about if everyone's walled off in an isolated, individual, or small-group environment. To that dismissal, Sedgwick offers a very strong rebuff, which is worth quoting at length:

> Reparative motives, once they become explicit, are inadmissible in paranoid theory both because they are about pleasure ("merely aesthetic") and because they are frankly ameliorative ("merely reformist"). What makes pleasure and amelioration so "mere"? Only the exclusiveness of paranoia's faith in demystifying exposure: only its cruel and contemptuous assumption that the one thing lacking for global revolution, explosion of gender roles, or whatever, is people's (that is, other people's) having the painful effects of their oppression, poverty, or deludedness sufficiently exacerbated to make the pain conscious (as if otherwise it wouldn't have been) and intolerable (as if intolerable situations were famous for generating excellent solutions). (144)

If they are to function as politically compelling, everyday cultural practices of whatever kind have to function first as a biopolitical bridge from here to there, from one performative practice to another, rather than primarily being deployed as a cultural cover for the outsized demystifying disciplinary claims of tenure-line intellectuals. In short, you have to follow how cultural practices *function* before you can worry about what they *mean*, and the functions of cover and momentary escape constitute the nonconscious and collective bases for those things called individual and group agency.

And Sedgwick is likewise, as we noted above, somewhat suspicious of suspicion's unmasking move, not only because it's neo-imperialist—revealing the hidden truth pretends to be the only game in town—but likewise because the paranoid revelation of wholesale social constructionism masquerades as having some inherent (leftist) political or social content—the truth will set you free. Or will it? "That is to say, once again: for someone to have an unmystified view of systematic oppressions does not *intrinsically* or *necessarily* enjoin that person to any specific train of epistemological or narrative consequences" (127). Contra Butler, here Sedgwick argues that "mattering," either coming into being at all or making a difference in a sociopolitical context, does not have to go through the truth-discourse of "meaning": there are thousands of other affects and effects that make up a life, and reducing them all to the (linguistic) discourse of truth and falsity seems like a deeply comic move, but one that tends to have a lot of tragic consequences for the paranoid interpreter.

Sedgwick's biopolitical performative method is to take affects and bodies seriously, and not have to translate those performatives through a paranoid disciplinary apparatus of truth, which will somehow render up their subtending, masked meaning—as much for the discipline of psychoanalysis as for the discipline of literary theory. As she continues, "The reason I want to insist in advance on this move is, once again, to try to hypothetically disentangle the question of truth from the question of performative effect" (129), where the "truth" would be less the perlocutionary outcome of any given act or event (its truth or falsity confirmed or denied, say) than it would be found in the provocative, reparative, or more simply affective illocutionary forces unleashed on, by, or for a given local body or set of bodies. In short, Sedgwick opens up a path beyond language and its paranoid lacks, gaps, and demystifications—a path that leads to performativity 3.0 and its emphasis on bodies, forces, networks, and affects beyond language and meaning.

As Sedgwick insists in *Epistemology of the Closet*, "Repeatedly to ask how certain categorizations work, what enactments they are performing and what relations they are creating, rather than what they essentially *mean*, has been my principal strategy" (27). Which is to say, Sedgwick pivots from performativity understood primarily as a linguistic question about meaning to understanding performativity primarily as a series of questions about lives and identities. In terms of performativity as much as a series of other biopolitical shifts, the last quarter century has seen a move from the performative tragic to the performative comic, from language to social power, all this also caught up in a larger social phenomena that could be categorized under the transition from a disciplinary society to a biopolitical one: from the performative largely as a tool for deconstructing disciplinary identities and categories (man/woman, nature/culture, and so on) to an understanding of performativity as multiplying and consolidating biopolitical diversity of identities: from the truth or falsity of x or y to its life-effects, from the question of meaning to the question of force, from performativity as discipline to performativity as biopower, under a highly expanded rubric of what counts as bios or "life"—finally pointing to the performative, agential life of animals, plants, objects: everything under, over, and including the sun.

Building on Sedgwick's performativity 2.0, something like Barad's performativity 3.0 becomes a kind of operating system for the entire Gaian universe where all being is intra-active doing and everything is lively, if not outright alive—a posthuman world of teeming biopolitical life-forms wherein, as Barad puts it, "Matter is a dynamic intra-active becoming that never sits still—an ongoing reconfiguration that exceeds any linear conception of dynamics in which effect follows cause end-on-end, and in which the global is a straightforward emination of the local. Matter's dynamism is generative not merely in the sense of bringing new things into the world but in the sense of bringing forth new worlds, of engaging in an ongoing reconfiguring of the world."[19] I connect biopower to this sense of performative dynamism because the myriad performative claims made for everything in the age of new materialism (the sense that matter itself "never sits still," but is "an ongoing reconfiguration that exceeds any linear conception of dynamics," that it has a special connection to the "reconfiguring of the world") are statements that used to be reserved as the exclusive purview of the human. It used to be solely human life that was understood as agential, reflexive, self-overcoming, not bound by determinist causality. So when I say that performativity is the operating system of biopower, or performativity has become biopolitics, this is the case precisely because performativity 3.0 allows us—maybe even forces us—into a much more robust articulation of what "matters" in our ecosystems and what counts as the living "bio" in "biopolitics." Though as we shall see in the ensuing chapter, there may be good biopolitical reasons to wonder about the performative conception of ubiquitous, excessive life that we get from the new materialism: for all of its commitments to newness, there's something oddly familiar in the new materialist conception of vibrant matter.

3

The Bodacious Era

Thoreau and New Materialism; or, What's Wrong with the Anthropocene?

Thoreau jumps over the They, ascends to a heteroverse, crosses over into the Wild, heightens his days and nights, making them "more elastic, more starry, more immortal"—and then he is able to refuse to pay his taxes.

—JANE BENNETT, *Thoreau's Nature*

This chapter grows out of a writing prompt offered to me by Branka Arsić. She suggested to me that she was working on a collection on Thoreau and the Anthropocene, and given my work on *Plant Theory*, would I like to contribute something? Sure, I said, as these are still crucial topics to me (life, questions of nature, and the fate of the Anthropocene), though I confessed to her that I'm going to be something of an outlier in such a collection, as I have disliked the work of Thoreau ever since I was an undergraduate. Rereading a fair amount of his work has not really changed my assessment, but I do have to admit that today I hate something completely different about Thoreau. Back in college in the early 1980s, I disliked Thoreau for the (privileged yet lazy) hippie throwback that his work seemed to suggest—sticking it to the man by doing your own thing, which it turns out is producing prose that consists largely of smug, Hallmark card–ready sentiments like "Be it life or death, we crave only reality."[1] And presumably you can find that reality by camping out on Emerson's land for two years? A life of quiet desperation indeed. Rereading *Walden*, however, I find myself hating something completely different about Thoreau's work—the fact that most of those greeting-card aphorisms seem today more like things you could get out of Ayn Rand rather than Abbie Hoffman: "What a man thinks of himself, that it is which determines, or rather indicates, his fate" (263). Whatever else you might say about his corpus, there's no whining or asking the government for help in Thoreau: "However mean your life is, meet it and live it; do not shun it and call it names" (566). In this libertarian vein, one need only recall the opening line of his antitax manifesto, "Civil Disobedience": "I heartily accept the motto, 'the government is best which governs least.'"[2]

And then of course there's the MBA Thoreau, who disparages mere work for the sake of work, but admires the hard work of (some) individuals: as he writes in "Life without Principle," "All great enterprises are self-supporting."[3] But if by chance you do occasionally need some manure to be shoveled, "Do not hire a man who does your work for money, but him who does it for love of it" (635). (Tip: Look for the sign that reads "Acme Manure Services: We Love That Shit."®) Moving from the labor force to the administrative ranks of business, we recall that Thoreau is perhaps our most savage critic of money-grubbing businessmen, but in *Walden* he does admire an entrepreneur: "What recommends commerce to me is its enterprise and bravery" (370).[4] Unless of course you're a Native American trying to unload baskets on a gringo, and there you'll only get a marketing lecture from Thoreau, about how he's not buying any Indian baskets without a good reason—and certainly not just because they were made by someone who's experienced theft of his land and continuing discrimination at the hands of white elites. In *Walden*, Thoreau faults this "strolling Indian" entrepreneur for "thinking that when he had made the baskets he would have done his part, and then it would be the white man's [job] to buy them" (274). Not so fast, my Native American friend—you've got to *market* those things, Thoreau insists: "He had not discovered that it was necessary for him to make it worth the other's while to buy them, or at least make him think it was so, or to make something else which it would be worth his while to buy" (274). You've got to stay on message, be resilient and flexible (maybe "make something else" if the baskets don't sell?), and pay attention to demographics. In short, the Native merchant should have seen that rural consumers like Thoreau and his neighbors are likely not receptive to this multicultural branding. Maybe try peddling your Indian baskets to virtue-signaling cultural elites in liberal Boston?

I don't teach much C19 American literature, but those of you who do must, over the past decades, have become inundated with admiring essays on Thoreau written no longer by third-generation hippie wannabees but rather by Young Republicans celebrating the wit and wisdom of Thoreau—that flinty, fierce individualist (vehemently antipolitics and antigovernment), who was also an incel and (for a time at least) an off-the-grid antitax crusader. As Thoreau concisely sums up the neoliberal creed 130 years before the fact in "Civil Disobedience," "There will never be a really free and enlightened State until the State comes to recognize the individual as a higher and independent power" (130). Until we realize that enlightened State—where, perhaps, "there's no such thing as society, only individuals"—Thoreau confesses in "Life without Principle" that "I feel that my connection with and obligation to society are still very slight and transient" (636). Thoreau's even got a proleptic critique of "fake news" and the media: "The news we hear, for the most part, is not news to our genius. It is the stalest repetition. . . . Read not the Times. Read the Eternities" (646, 649). Like a Trump-era Fox News analyst *avant la lettre,* Thoreau intones: "the poor President, what with preserving his popularity and doing his duty, is completely bewildered. The newspapers are the ruling power" (654). And to think the failing *New York Times* was only twelve years old at that point. All in all, I can't shake the sense that Thoreau is primarily engaged in his own private competition: "Shall a man go and hang himself because he belongs to a race of pygmies, and not be the biggest pygmy that he can?" (564). Ok, Thoreau, the participation trophy is all yours.

Of course, reasonable people disagree, and I can foresee arguments and counterarguments concerning this Wildly ungenerous reading of Thoreau's corpus, wrenched out of its original context and made to play a role in a world that Thoreau could never have envisioned—a world of libertarian neoliberalism, rampant biopolitics, and the ecological

ravages of the Anthropocene. I think, though, we can all agree that
Thoreau offers an incessant critique of the stale banalities of C19 social
convention, social forces that Jane Bennett sums up under the heading
of "the They"—as Bennett explains, Thoreau's phrase for "the allure of
conventional wisdom and the comfort of conformity."[5] And this radically individualist project, against the social conformism of the mass,
may have done some useful work in a prior era of American history.
It certainly was an outlier 150 years ago to take up the Thoreauvian
project, which Bennett summarizes like this: "For the sake of the noble
self (the I), steps must be taken to disrupt the familiar self (the They)"
(5). For her part, Bennett shares Thoreau's suspicion of the They: "My
Thoreau labors most relentlessly to escape the They" (82). As I say,
this way of looking at the world may have done a tremendous amount
of against-the-day work 150 years ago, but today, in a world of neoliberal
individualism, that's just about the only project there is—outflanking
the They (the norms, the suits, the PC mainstream media) with your
own bodacious individuality.[6] Much more on this below.

   To cut to the argumentative chase, here I'm keen to argue that
Thoreau remains important to today's "new materialism" (Bennett's
founding text *Vibrant Matter* is Thoreauvian to the core) not so much
because his C19 works offer us *solutions* to the biopolitical problems of
our day ("become an authentic individual" is at present nothing other
than the most commonplace banality parroted by mainstream neoliberalism); rather, Thoreau remains important because he offers to today's
new materialists a diagnosis of the *problem* with modern (or postmodern) life in the era of the Anthropocene: to wit, the ways in which various
instrumental rationalities of the They (from the political and technological to the business-related and back to the personal) have dulled our
perceptions of the lively performative movements of things all around
us, and our entanglements within and among them. For the new materialist as for Thoreau, we (wrongly) see things and the world as a static
backdrop, and so our lives and experiences likewise become either
stale or, worse, imperialist—disconnected from the vitality that runs
through us and all matter. As Thoreau phrases it in *Walden,* in a brief
aside on hearing a robin for the first time in spring, we're disconnected

from the Wild becoming that runs through us and the bird; but we're also blinkered from engaging that Wild that runs through the twig on which the bird stands, and everything else under the sun (552). According to Bennett, Thoreau's "task will then be to locate and then regularly expose oneself to the Wild sites and sights, to maximize opportunities for shock and disorientation,"[7] to disrupt the tame verities of instrumentalism and see anew that the world is a place of vibrant connection.

Understood as such, Bennett's new materialist project in *Vibrant Matter* (2010) is a continuation not only of her *Enchantment of Modern Life* (2001) but even moreso an intensification of the insights garnered from her early work on *Thoreau's Nature: Ethics, Politics and the Wild* (1994). Indeed, Thoreau is a constant presence throughout *Vibrant Matter,* everywhere from the epigraph to the concluding remarks on the penultimate page. In Bennett's first example of what she calls "thing-power," she finds herself attending to the thingly agency of some particularly interesting detritus arrayed on the sewer grate outside a Baltimore bagel shop—"the items on the ground that day were vibratory"[8]—and she attributes the revelation to Thoreau: "I came up on the glove-pollen-rat-cap-stick with Thoreau in my head, who had encouraged me to practice 'the discipline of looking always at what is to be seen'" (5). In fact, it is Thoreau's "Wild"—"a not quite human force that addled and altered human and other bodies" (2)—that functions throughout as a kind of metonym for Bennett's vibrant matter, "stuff that commanded attention in its own right, as existents in excess of their association with human meanings, habits or projects" (2). Recalling her initial epiphany concerning the vitality of all things, Bennett notes, "I had achieved, for a moment, what Thoreau made his life's goal: to be able, as Thomas Dumm puts it, 'to be surprised by what we see'" (5). And it is this being surprised by what we see, jarred out of our conventional understandings of the world, that offers us the new materialist insight that we are imbricated with the things of the world, rather than masters of them—an insight directly related and attributed to Thoreau.

Outstripping simple connection or oneness with nature, Thoreau is a key source for seeing the things of the world as performatively *lively,* seething with their own powers of excessive enchantment. In other words, Thoreau helps us to mobilize the key new materialist insight that vitality is not a one-way street, from the living subject to the inert object, but names the very intra-active environment within which any encounter among bodies or things happens. As Bennett points out, this "Thing-power may thus be a good starting point for thinking beyond the life-matter binary" (20) precisely by taking the things that have been said in the modern period about human or animal life—it's characterized by excess, movement, becoming, performativity, self-overcoming—and extending those virtues to everything else, thereby deconstructing the "life vs. matter" opposition in order to unleash the overflowing wonder of life within what we thought were inanimate objects, or at least recognizing such excessive vitality at work within all things. As she restates the Thoreauvian stakes of all this near the end of *Vibrant Matter*, "The point is this: an active becoming, a *creative not quite human force capable of producing the new,* buzzes within the history of the term nature" (118; emphasis in original).

Indeed, a reading of Bennett's entire career trajectory reveals that the new materialist project of *Vibrant Matter* is really an extension of the concept of "microvision" that she finds in Thoreau: "Microvision, the deliberate and keen attention to the minutiae of the material world, where one restrains the urge to interpret or contextualize what one sees, is also crucial to the construction of a sojourner. Microvision enables one to live in doubleness, to refuse to see oneself as either objective or subject, or either as subject or object. It is a sensitivity to that robin, this twig, an immersion in the minutiae that issues in a distinctive sense of Wildness": "The practice of microvision upon nature is to transform it into Nature, beautiful, sublime and Wild."[9] If microvision and the Wild are crucial heightened affective states, concepts or practices to be cultivated for Thoreau and Bennett, then it's fair to surmise on the other side of the coin that something like "macrovision" (imposing a singular, overarching order on things) and what we might call the "Tame" (conventional ways of proceeding) are the primary problems to be addressed by the practice of microvision. The world requires aesthetic re-enchantment because it's fallen under the spell of a sinister instrumental rationality that mass produces experiences; so it's time to get back in touch with the nature of things, à la Thoreau, in whose work "the milk of Wildness flows freely, and this is, as we know, crucial to recrafting the self."[10]

Thoreau's mid-C19 project (throwing off the deadening qualities of habit and accepted social convention, in the name of reinvigorating the experience of everyday life to the human and beyond) went on to become the coin of the realm for aesthetic and philosophical modernism in the C20—in everything from existentialism and phenomenology (while it's very unlikely that Heidegger read Thoreau, Heideggerian *Dasein* does have a substantial beef with *das Man*, Heidegger's own version "the They"),[11] through pragmatism (in John Dewey's 1917 "The Need for a Recovery of Philosophy," he argues that we need philosophy "to project new and more complex ends—to free experience from routine and from caprice"),[12] all the way through the ruling ideology of aesthetic modernist writing (Virginia Woolf: "Life is not a series of gig lamps symmetrically arranged; life is a luminous halo, a semi-transparent envelope surrounding us from the beginning of consciousness to the end"),[13] to the new materialism of Bennett. None of these disparate movements shares a *solution* to the difficulties of modern life, but they do all diagnose a common *problem*: life, as we think we know it, just isn't bodacious enough—and if we could learn to see the bold audaciousness of all things, and participate in that bodacity, give ourselves over to it, then the Anthropocene world would be a better place. It is in this diagnosis of the problem where, it seems to me, Thoreau has most obviously lived on through the C20 and into the C21. Though, as you might suspect, in this chapter I want to question whether that diagnosis remains relevant or useful in naming the challenges before us today.

The Bodacious Era

When it comes to discussing the ethics of our current era, especially with reference to environmental issues, a question inevitably arises: what exactly should we call this sixth great extinction event that we're

ORIGIN

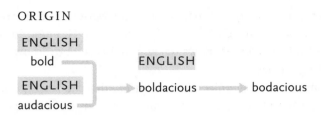

mid 19th century (in sense 'complete, thorough'): perhaps a
variant of SW dialect boldacious, blend of bold and audacious.

The Google etymology of the word *bodacious*. Definition by Oxford University
Press.

currently living though? This naming issue, it seems to me, is not
merely a question of semantics—as any quick tour through the popular
press treatment of climate change would confirm: do we say "andro-
centric climate change," for example, or is it the more seemingly neutral global warming? What you call the current era makes an ethical
difference, insofar as the name you choose tends also to "call out" (as
the kids say) a culprit or series of them: if you call our moment the era
of the Industrial Anthropocene, or the Capitalocene or the Plasticocene,
for example, that tends to put accusatory pressure on human industri-
alization, overproduction, and the instrumental rationality of the profit
motive as the drivers of global toxicity. Whereas if you call it merely
the Anthropocene or the late Holocene era, or the Biopolitical era, that
tends to cast less direct blame for current events—other than, of course,
locating the generalized rise of the human as the driver for what might
simply be some unintended environmental consequences or collateral
damage. Which is of course why climate deniers prefer the phrase
"global warming," as it's an overheating Gaia herself who's implied as
the agent there—rather than targeting what Nietzsche called the primary skin disease of the Earth,[14] human beings. And of course, any
given diagnosis of the problem also implies the efficacy of some potential solutions over others (or at least a robust diagnosis of the problem

marks certain practices to be avoided): in short, if you don't thematize or name the problem correctly, the reparative courses of action you recommend could end up making things worse.

Fully embracing the link between the name and the problem, I propose that we name our present phase "the Bodacious era." As you can see from the graphic above, the word *bodacious* was coined in North America in the middle of the C19, a fusion of the words *bold* and *audacious,* and the birth of the bodacious in the C19 is no mere historical coincidence. Nor is the major uptake in the word's usage in the era of neoliberalism over the past few decades. For those of you unfamiliar with the word beyond this etymology, allow me to let its primary linguistic facilitator gloss the word for you, Keanu Reeves from the *Bill and Ted* movies: "Bodacious is something that's, like, outstandingly outstanding . . . Bodacious is, like, a weird happening, an extraordinary happening . . . Almost like supernatural."[15] Most excellent, dude—and I'll particularly want to highlight that "weird," wondrous or mystical quality of the bodacious, which I think separates it from the common version of the word that suggests that bodacious describes primarily the spicy nachos available on Super Bowl Sunday at your local Buffalo Wild Wings.[16] Being "almost like supernatural," as Reeves puts, the bodacious foregrounds the ability for us to be surprised out of our everyday habits, to see the "outstandingly outstanding" vibrancy of things that bubbles just below their dull, everyday surface. However, lest you think that contemporary snowboarders or BMX bikers will be the primary theoretical touchstones of this chapter, let me backtrack for just a moment to fill in the strictly speaking theoretical justification for naming our moment (from the beginning of the C19 to somewhere near the present) as "the Bodacious era."

My sense that this nomenclature is both accurate and revealing is scaffolded on Michel Foucault's substantially more nuanced analysis of the rise of disciplinary power in early modern Europe, and discipline's slow intensificatory transformation into what he famously calls "biopower" in the C19, right up to the triumph of biopower in the C20's morphing from a disciplinary, factory economy (where we're all workers on the assembly line of the social) to a service and investment economy scaffolded on the entrepreneurial axioms of neoliberalism—where we're all enslaved not to the molding and confinement of the factory floor (or its disciplinary avatars the family, the army, the police, the prison, the bank), but to the performative project of becoming our own *Homo economicus,* constantly sculpting and resculpting our lives, which are in turn the very engine of biopower.

The basic picture of life that you get from biopolitical thinking is well summed up by Georg Simmel's *The View of Life* [*Lebensanschauung*] (essays composed in the early C20). Here, Simmel is specifically discussing the secret agreement between Nietzsche's and Schopenhauer's notions of the living, but I think it's a concise version of what life is (or better, what life does) throughout the modernist period. Simmel writes,

> life has two mutually complementary definitions: it is *more-life,* and it is *more-than-life.* The "more" does not arrive by accident to augment a life already stable in its quantity; instead, life is the movement that, for each of its parts, even when these are comparatively pitiful, at every moment draws something into itself in order to transform it into its life. No matter what its absolute measure, life can only exist in that it is more-life.[17]

So when *Blade Runner*'s combat robot Roy Batty tells his creator he wants "more life, fucker," he's not simply asking for a little bit "more" of this neutral substrate called "life"; rather, he's asking quite literally for "more life," for the life of vibrant excess, the only kind of life worth the name in the modern and postmodern periods in the West.

Simmel and Rutger Hauer are, of course, hardly alone in foregrounding this excessive, transcendental character of life, which would probably find its most robust articulation in Hegel's 1807 *Phenomenology of Spirit,* where life is rethematized as the overcoming and self-overcoming that is inherent in the vital, animal movements of desire: "self-consciousness is *Desire* in general," Hegel writes: "This simple infinity, or the absolute Notion, may be called the simple essence of life, the soul of the world, the universal blood, whose omnipresence is neither disturbed nor interrupted by any difference; but rather is itself every difference, as also their supersession." And thereby life becomes not a substrate that beings *possess* (say, on the model of a religious soul or rational human essence), but a movement—an excessive, quasi-miraculous, animal flow of consciousness that is life itself: as Hegel puts it, "Life in the universal fluid medium, . . . Life as a *process*. . . : Life as a *living thing*."[18]

From the C19 forward, life in most European and North American thought is only worth the name when it's what Simmel calls "more-than-life," when it's excessively desiring, (self-)overcoming, a nearly mystical process that's both bold and audacious. In short, life only qualifies as life, from Hegel onward, when and if it's *bodacious*. And this bodacious life doesn't take orders from anyone or anything—life has to transgress itself endlessly, to carve its own immanent path from and with this excessive desiring. Again, Simmel: we need to "conceive of life as something that *constantly* reaches beyond the bounds of its beyond and which finds its essence in this reaching beyond. It is an attempt to find the definition of life in general in this transcendence, to retain firmly the consistency of its individual form, to be sure, but only in order that it may be broken through by the continuous process. Life finds its essence, its process, in being more-life and more-than-life."[19]

And it is precisely this kind of animal, performative, excessive Thoreauvian "Wild" life that new materialism wants to export from the exclusive purview of the human and offer to all things: plants, the earth, trash on the street, even the structure of matter itself. As Diana Coole and Samantha Frost channel this "more-than-life" tradition in the introduction to their collection *New Materialisms,* a central tenet of the movement holds that "materiality is always something more than 'mere' matter: an excess, force, vitality, relationality, or difference that renders matter active, self-creative, productive, unpredictable. In sum, new materialists are rediscovering a materiality that materializes, evincing immanent modes of self-transformation."[20] On this point, let me just iterate here something I've argued elsewhere: this discovery of the secretly excessive life of everything in the C19, intensified throughout the C20, is likewise the exportation of a thoroughly "animal" conception of life to the whole of vitality itself.[21] It is, as Foucault limns out for us in *The Order of Things*, at the dawn of the C19 that animals take over from plants as the primary markers for those studying or understanding the life of plants, animals, and humans. On Foucault's account, it's with the rise of the transcendentals, in the era of the human sciences, that animals begin to take priority over plants as the privileged form or figure of life itself. In an era of natural history where knowledge was characterized by "the apparent simplicity of a description of the visible," "the area common to words and things constituted a much more accommodating, a much less 'black' grid for plants than for animals."[22] Most animals, simply put, have more hidden, interior space than plants, and thereby present a greater volume of "black" or blank space to the gaze of the classifying naturalist. As Foucault writes about this era of representation, "Because it was possible to know and to say only within a taxonomic area of visibility, the knowledge of plants was bound to prove more extensive than that of animals" (137), precisely because plants can be pulled up out of the ground, and thereby rendered fully visible, from the tip of the roots to the outermost edges of the flower or leaf.

At the dawn of the C19, however, Foucault traces a mutation of the dominant epistemic procedures—from a representational discourse that maps external similitude and resemblance, to the emergence of a speculative discourse that takes as its object hidden internal processes. In short, we see emerge a discourse that "opposed historical knowledge of the visible to philosophical knowledge of the invisible" (138): knowledge's privileged practices abandon the obvious surface of objects in order to plumb their bodacious hidden depths instead. And first and foremost among those transcendental "invisibles" was a little thing we like to call "life": "The naturalist is the man concerned with the structure of the visible world and its denomination according to characters. Not with life" (161), Foucault insists, because life is not representable. Life is in fact a kind of unplumbable depth, animating the organism from a hidden origin somewhere within.

In short, Foucault's work shows that animal life is not in fact jettisoned or abjected at the dawn of humanist biopower in the C19, but instead animality is fully incorporated into biopower as the template for life itself, for all life. As Foucault puts it:

> the animal, whose great threat or radical strangeness had been left suspended and as it were disarmed at the end of the Renaissance, discovers fantastic new powers in the 19th century. In the interval, Classical nature had given precedence to vegetable values . . . with all its forms on display, from stem to seed, from root to fruit; with all its secrets made generously visible, the vegetable kingdom formed a pure and transparent object for thought as tabulation. But when the characters and structures are arranged in vertical steps toward life—that sovereign vanishing point, indefinitely distant but constituent—then it is the animal that becomes the privileged form, with its hidden structures, its buried organs, so many invisible functions. . . . If living beings are a classification, the plant is best able to express its limpid essence; but if they are a manifestation of life, the animal is better equipped to make its enigma perceptible. (277)

In short, Foucault argues that with the emergence of the human sciences at the birth of biopower, the animal is not excluded or forgotten but quite the opposite: animality comprises the dominant apparatus for investigating both what life is and what life does. The living is no longer primarily vegetable (sessile and awaiting mere categorization) but understood as bold and audacious—vibrant, evolving, secret, discontinuous, mendacious, inscrutable, always on the prowl, looking for an opening to break free. As Foucault puts it, perhaps channeling Thoreau, "Transferring its most secret essence from the vegetable to the animal kingdom, life has left the tabulated space of order and become wild once more" (277). Following Foucault's reading, one might suggest that the role of abjected other has been played throughout the biopolitical era not by the animal but by the plant—which was indeed forgotten as the privileged form of life at the dawn of biopower. I can think of several dozen bodacious (or I guess they all them "charismatic") animals off the top of my head; I can think of only one such plant: the Venus Flytrap. Whatever else you might say about it, the sessile life of plants tends *not* to be "bodacious"—until and unless that C19 human-animal conception of vibrant, Wild vitality is engorged to the point where it characterizes everything else in the universe.

In any case, I'm arguing that this conceptual framework concerning life as more-than-life is the subtending ground of our biopolitical Bodacious era. But rather than celebrate or worry about the self-overcoming aspect of this transcendentalist horizon, I'd like to note, in a prior way, that this modernist, biopolitical understanding of life—the only life worth the name is excessive, more-than-*mere*-life—is scaffolded on a certain kind of disciplinary or repressive hypothesis. If more-than-life is authentic life, then this drama is of course based on an opposition to some sort of inauthentic life, that life of "quiet desperation" so unfortunately led by the "mass of men," as Thoreau's *Walden* would have it (263); or at least this whole discussion of the vital excess of things is subtended by something that is holding down or capturing life (which by its performative rights should be Wild and free), and trying to mold life into an enclosure of some kind, to make this vitality productive for some nefarious ends. To return to Foucault, this making-productive or training of life is of course the drama of disciplinary power. In short, Foucault shows us how the repressive hypothesis held over from disciplinary power is absolutely necessary for any positive valences to be attached to the excessive dramas of a re-enchanted everyday life—say, the idea of sexuality—to take on some kind of prized role in our liberation from disciplinary strictures. We, Other Romantics.

Again, from a sort of orthogonal angle, Simmel is very helpful on this point: he insists that the "other" or opposite of modern life is not *coercion* but *purposiveness* (in short, discipline—the harvesting of usefulness from life); which is why then for Simmel, and a host of other European thinkers of the modern and contemporary era, the only proper life is modeled on the work of art, a Kantian purposiveness without purpose.[23] In Simmel's terms, the creative life of desire becomes the "value" of the fact/value distinction, what he calls the "ought" of life, the driver and master over the (mere) facts of life.[24] Which is why the creative "ought" of life on Simmel's account never offers specific paths or instructions, in the manner that, for example, disciplinary training does. Rather, the excessive ought of life finds itself in the imperative to overcome actuality, to remake quotidian life: "Only when we understand the Ought, beyond all of its particular contents, as a primary mode in which individual consciousness experiences a whole life does it become understandable why one can never extract, from the fact of the Ought, *what* we ought, content-wise, to do."[25] Life is that which resists "actuality," the reductions of disciplinary training mechanisms, to focus instead on the ongoing performative process of biopolitical overcoming itself. And it is precisely this overcoming, excessive notion of "life" that new materialism wants to export from the exclusive purview of the human, to animate the entirety of matter in the universe.

At this point, you could of course say that the excessive, self-overcoming understanding of life in the West has always been such—as, for example, someone like Agamben does when he suggests that this tension between "the beautiful day of simple life" and the "great difficulty of political bios"[26] is the structuring opposition of all Western thinking over the past 2400 years. Though of course, Agamben also somewhat puzzlingly suggests, following Foucault, that this discovery of the "wild life vs. administered life" distinction is only a few hundred years old, leading to Derrida's humorous critique of Agamben on biopower. Derrida writes:

> In truth, Agamben . . . wants to be twice first, the first to see and announce, the first to remind: he wants both to be the first to announce an unprecedented and new thing [biopower], what he calls this "decisive event of modernity," and also to be the first to recall that in fact it's always been like that, from time immemorial. He is telling us two things in one: it's just happening for the first time, you ain't seen nothing yet; but nor have you seen, I'm telling you for the first time, that it dates from the year zero.[27]

Rather than limning out Derrida's comic dismissal of Agamben, here I'm going to cut to the chase, following Foucault, and suggest that this modern drama (excessive life and its dialectical relationship to myriad forms of constraint) is something that's maybe not born, but at least becomes widely disbursed into the realm everyday life within the disciplinary era in Europe and North America, alongside the uneven rise of capitalism and the waning of sovereign power. *To put it bluntly, the wild excessive animality of restive life (recognized in ourselves in the C19, and then in the objects around us in the C21) can only seem like an ethical response to the world if the primary problem is one of rigid confine-ment within a repressive, de-enchanting world of linked institutions or sti-fling social convention.* If we need more Wild, that's primarily because things have become overly Tame.

This is what Foucault is after when he says that life as we know it doesn't exist before the dawn of the C19.[28] What he means here is that this particular notion of life as excessive, hidden self-overcoming didn't exist before the C19 in a widespread and bedrock way—you won't find it in medieval thought, for example. But you will find it virtually every-where going forward from Hegel. Even if you say that excessive under-standing of life is clearly at work in Spinoza, Augustine, in a certain reading of Plato, Heraclitus, whomever, I'd say you're right (just as you could say there were homosexual acts before 1870, so Foucault's claim that homosexuality was invented in 1870 is nonsensical). But you would likewise have to admit, alongside Foucault, that the "artis-tic self-overcoming" version of subjectivity, whenever it was invented, got to be a *species* of subjectivity—a form of life or everyday life—only in C19 Romanticism, finding its earliest articulations in the English Romantics and American Transcendentalists. There are thinkers who embody that bodacious spirit throughout history, but that spirit of bodacity was something largely confined to the elite classes; the slaves of ancient Athens, or the vast majority of Roman plebians, or the serfs of the Middle Ages, or even the real denizens of Dickens's fictional London in the middle of the C19—none of those everyday folks thought of their lives as bodacious. (Hell, even my parents, both born to immigrant families in 1920s Chicago and thereby children of the Depression era, most assuredly did not think of life as an excessive, affective drama characterized by self-overcoming; though my children, both born in the C21, most assuredly do think of their lives that way.) Indeed, today so does every working-class Republican voter, Chick-fil-A lunch customer, and NRA member for life. As Foucault argues in "Lives of Infamous Men," the drama of everyday life—the understanding that it is an area of bearing and concern for power—is something that discipline discovers, and biopower intensifies. (The sovereign kings could not care less about the minutiae of peasants' sex lives, diets, or parenting skills; the disciplinary state cares about those things decisively, but not anywhere near as intensely as today's biopolitical attention capitalist at Google or Facebook does.)

Here of course, one could also quibble that all this misses the point, because it's not so much a matter of *life* than it is a matter of *capitalism* that's the primary issue in a world of ecological disaster—that we live not so much in the Anthropocene as much as it is a "Capitalocene."[29] But even when they call out capitalism as the primary problem of our era (not biopower or bodacious life, which on that reading are seen as secondary concerns), those critics can't, it seems to me, quite so easily dismiss the link between a certain strand of biopolitical, consumption capitalism and this "more than life" philosophical stance. In virtually all of this "more than life" work, it's the disciplinary capitalist who shamelessly shills for the uncreative instrumentality of "mere life," characterized by what Wordsworth derides as the too-busy "getting and spending" by which we "lay waste our powers" to be astonished.[30] Many theoretical diagnosers of the "problem" with the Capitalocene in the present (everyone from the late Mark Fisher in *Capitalist Realism* or *The Weird and the Eerie*, through various new materialisms, to the most extreme example of Bernard Stiegler's *The Re-Enchantment of the World*) suggest that life and experience are, at present, not bodacious enough, or they're not bodacious in quite the right way. The proper bodacity of responsive, aesthetic affect—make your life a work of art!—is contrasted to the faux bodaciousness of market run-ups and sell-offs or the mind-bending authenticity claims of various soda pops and sport utility vehicles.

Despite massive technological and social changes, this diagnosis of the "problem" with capitalism and everyday life has, since the C19, remained consistent through virtually the entirety of both American pragmatism and European existentialism, phenomenology, critical theory, and deconstruction: figures as disparate as Dewey and Husserl, Heidegger and Adorno, or Derrida and Habermas, all agree that there's a fundamental openness to possibility that has been blocked by the triumph of some form of technologization (instrumental reason, capitalist profit motive, the culture industry, the *Gestell* of technology, the deadening conformity of the They, new regimes of temporal presence). Thereby, it's the re-enchanting of everyday life that's offered as the high-culture solution by the critics of the capitalist *Gestell* of the Anthropocene: if that purposive alienation—the reduction of us all to disciplined, routinized robots—is the problem, then "more life, fucker" is just as certainly the solution. Which, if nothing else, suggests that much continental political theory today continues to offer a disciplinary, C19 or C20 solution to a decidedly C21 biopolitical problem. In short, much recent political theory ends up offering us more "excessive life" repackaged as the remedy for the supposed de-enchantment of modernity—and it's the solution not only for humans but for everything everywhere.

In *Vibrant Matter,* for example, Bennett does not reject and in fact doubles down on this project of attention enchantment leading to self-overcoming, but with the important caveat of extending the sense of wonder from the prison-house of human consciousness to the "vibrant" world itself, exporting the sense of wonder from the observing human subject and offering it up as an ontological insight into the impersonal vibrancy of everything. As she explains in *Vibrant Matter*:

> I continue to think of affect as central to politics and ethics [a truism that we may now consider a Trumpism], but in this book I branch out to an "affect" not specific to human bodies. I want now to focus less on the enhancement to human relational capacities resulting from affective catalysts and more on the catalyst itself as it exists in non-human bodies. . . . I now emphasize even more how the figure of enchantment points in two directions: the first toward humans who *feel* enchanted and whose agentic capacities may be thereby strengthened, and second toward the agency of the things that *produce* (helpful, harmful) effects in human and other bodies. (xii)

There are of course lots of things that one could say about this quotation, but let me zero in and argue for the thoroughgoingly anthropomorphic nature of the project outlined here. We used to think that a modernist understanding of authentic human life had an exclusive patent on enchanting the world around it, but now we know that everything in the universe works according to that C19 Euro-American biopolitical logic. The very stuff of the cosmos is at its core performatively "enchanting" and lively just like a stroll to get a bagel on a summer day. How, one might wonder, is such knowledge—that everything works the way we do—going to amount to a humbling of the human? Turns out, it's not that the enchanting Western bourgeois subject of the Anthropocene was all along a hubristic myth born with Romanticism, but far rather that everything in the universe was always already modeled on this C19 version of the modernist Western bourgeois subject who's bedazzled before it all.

So, if this new materialist diagnosis of the Anthropocene problematic seems suspiciously anthropocentric, so then is the prescription for treating the disease. In short, the problem isn't that there's a lack of bodaciousness characterizing everyday life under biopolitical neoliberalism, but that the bodacious has become pretty much the whole in the neoliberal world of ongoing transformation: at the lower ends of the class ladder, the constant precarity of looking for work in a gig economy that requires a kind of faux, bodacious enthusiasm—five stars for my Uber driver; man that greeter at Walmart was nice! All the way up to the endless iterations of the iPhone and the flood of new streaming TV shows at the top: it's all part of the same bodacious transformation of the socius and our everyday lives. When it comes to diagnosing what's wrong with the Anthropocene, the new materialist solution—"more life for everything in the universe, fucker"—seems like more of the (all-too-human) problem.

Finally, the idea that a re-enchanted or re-aestheticized relation to the everyday will save us from the ecological ravages of Anthropocene biopolitics is, I think, simply incorrect, or at least it too often partakes in a kind of unearned magical thinking: to wit, there remains this pervasive sense that if we see and confirm the blooming buzzing confusion all around us, we'll likewise see that the universe is based on openness and welcoming of the other, and that'll somehow make us better people. Because we're excessive and multiple by nature, and now we've even seen that things are as well (revealed for us by everything from new materialist thought, to actor–network theory, all the way through the quantum scientific discoveries about the performative nature of matter), then we will see that anthropocentric instrumental rationality is not the way of the world. And once we know or recognize that, then . . . Well it's the inexorability of the progressive "then" that seems magical thinking to me, a kind of unearned snug fit between scientific facts and social values that's summed up by no less a scientist than Neil deGrasse Tyson: "imagine a world in which everyone, but especially people with power and influence, holds an expanded view of our place in the cosmos. With that perspective, our problems would shrink— or never arise at all—and we could celebrate our earthly differences while shunning the behavior of our predecessors who slaughtered one another because of them."[31]

More pointedly, I suppose the question becomes something like this: while the reduction of everything to a kind of unbodacious, instrumental rationality was almost certainly the primary problem with C20 Fordist capitalism, and the disciplinary C19 before that, does that problem remain primary under the apparatus of contemporary biopolitical capitalism? As Fredric Jameson showed us more than three decades ago in *Postmodernism; or, The Cultural Logic of Late Capitalism*, "Make it new!" has become the mantra and dominant practice of neoliberal lifestyle capitalism, rather than the assured formula by which one could recognize its critics. As Jameson succinctly puts it, "What has happened is that aesthetic production today has become integrated into commodity production generally: the frantic economic urgency of producing fresh waves of ever more novel-seeming goods (from clothing to airplanes), at ever greater rates of turnover, now assigns an increasingly essential structural function and position to aesthetic innovation and experimentation."[32] Neoliberal finance capital runs on risk and uncertainty, on constantly modulated subject positions, not on the centralized, planned economies and unitary subject positions of the Fordist era of modernism. C21 finance capitalism has, to put it bluntly, fully weaponized the bodacious self-overcoming that was the central solution to the problem of disciplinary capitalism.

Neoliberal capitalism is about nothing but constant subjective transformation, endless movement, always being on the prowl for the new. That being the case, one would have to wonder whether this overflowing experience prescribed by the "more life" diagnosis presents much of an ethical or political challenge to our contemporary modes of social organization—a biopolitical capitalism that, while it is as sinister as the day is long, no longer quite so decisively pivots on disciplinary modes of standardization or massification (or, better, it standardizes us by coercing us all to become our own bodacious, attention-paying entrepreneurial individuals). You can always say that these advertising appeals to the bodacious are mere marketing ploys, not genuine commitments to excess and the necessity of everyday transformation (aesthetic, ethical, or otherwise), and I'll grant you that out of the box. But the bigger issue is the structural position of constant transformation within neoliberal capitalism—a world where a preexisting subject doesn't undergo disciplinary training transformations (from learning to be a daughter to a student to a worker to a mother to a patient, and so on). Rather, in the bodacious world of performative biopolitics, the subject is nothing other than 24/7, constant transformation and modulation. If that's the case today, that would leave us to wonder whether one could depend on affect and its excesses as an assured mode of resistance to what Heidegger called the *Machenschaft* of our day. The whole enchanting function of everyday attention or the valorization of Thoreauvian microvision would at that level hardly constitute an outside to the *Machenschaft* of neoliberal market capitalism, but would constitute one of its bleeding edges.

At this point in the Anthropocene era, then, it seems to me that everyday life is not primarily a site in need of excessive neo-aesthetic enhancement—if we could only see how bodacious everything is, we'd all be better people, and the planet would be enhanced as well. Rather, the everyday of the attention economy is a site of struggle within biopolitical capital, as attention becomes the primary commodity worth harvesting and financializing going forward in what Shoshana Zuboff calls *The Age of Surveillance Capitalism*.[33] In short, the question or problem is not how to re-enchant or return affect and wonderment to the everyday, through learning again to pay deep attention to the little epiphanies within our commodified lives. This is a widespread project that, for example, American poetry has lived on for the past seventy-five years, or at least since Frank O'Hara, who coined what may be the catchphrase for the biopolitics of the bodacious: "attention equals life."[34] As I argue throughout, this project of re-enchanting the everyday, of hesitating and paying enough conscious attention in order to find the excessive vitality otherwise lost within the fallen quotidian realm, remains to this day the central project of a dizzying array of European and American cultural thought as well: surely this is the project of phenomenology, implicit in Husserl's work (on bracketing distractions to focus on presencing) and quite explicit in Heidegger's work (on a kind of attunement meant to break through the industrialist and capitalist *Machenschaft*). Habemas's communicative rationality (buried under instrumental rationality), Derrida's trace structure (making the fetish of presence both possible and impossible), the Austinian performativity of language all the way to Bennett's vibrant matter and Barad's performativity of all space-time and matter: these disparate movements all suggest that there's some lively, bodacious force underneath or alongside the quotidian everyday. And if we could glimpse it or live it, there's a political or ethical upshot that's built into that realization—we could see, as Barad would have it, that the universe bends towards justice.[35]

Perhaps the strangest thing about *Vibrant Matter* is its belief in, or emphasis on, the (human) political realm being somehow necessarily connected to a series of ontological claims—as if there were a strong, almost seamless, relation between facts and values. So, for example, the animating query for Bennett's book is stated in the preface: "A guiding question: How would political responses to public problems change if we were to take seriously the vitality of (non-human) bodies? . . . My aspiration is to articulate a vibrant materiality that runs alongside and inside humans to see how analysis of political events might change if we gave the force of things more due" (viii). Notwithstanding the anthropomorphism of our deciding (or not) to give nonhuman things or forces more recognition, the logic on which this kind of question depends is not "new materialist" at all, but follows a really very recognizable version of the "old" (dialectical) materialism known as ideology critique: if you can show people the way things really work in the world, that demonstration or revelation will inevitably change their beliefs and behaviors. This at least is the logic behind Bennett's stated guiding assumption:

Why advocate the vitality of matter? Because my hunch is that the image of dead or thoroughly instrumentalized matter feeds human hubris and our earth-destroying fantasies of conquest and consumption. It does so by preventing us from detecting (seeing, hearing, smelling, tasting, feeling) a fuller range of the nonhuman powers circulating around and within human bodies. . . . . My claims here are motivated by a self-interested or conative concern for human survival and happiness: I want to promote greener forms of human culture and more attentive encounters between people-materialities and thing-materialities. (ix–x)

Any discussion of how argumentative "claims" about the nature of matter might be said to "promote" anything at all politically is left untouched here, but we are presented with a very C19 understanding of the relation between such ontological claims and their relationship to (human) behavior: the "hunch" is that truth about the vitality of things will set you free. We'd at least have to hesitate here and note that most C20 work on ideology—the relationship between values and facts, or as Althusser famously puts it, the "imaginary relationship to real conditions"—has primarily dwelled on the fact that there isn't a kind of base–superstructure relation within the subject, wherein superstructural "beliefs" are determined by any "base" of rational knowledge about the world. Not only Althusser, but Antonio Gramsci and Birmingham thinkers like Raymond Williams and Stuart Hall have all had a go at this complex question, but all of them agree that what someone does can't primarily be indexed to or explained by what that person believes about the nature of things.

Bennett is well aware of this, arguing flatly against the hermeneutics of suspicion and its hubristic sense that ideological "demystification presumes at the heart of any event or process lies a human agency that has illicitly been projected into things" (xiv). So if rationalist demystifying isn't the game we're playing here, what's the mechanism by which Bennett translates the relation between a set of highly abstract theoretical claims about the nature of reality and the idiosyncratic realm of human behavior? In short, the bridge is not a critical but a kind of aesthetic consciousness—which depends not on the rationality of "facts" serving as the basis for human action (a political theory that's been out of favor for quite some time, though as we've seen in earlier chapters, has new life on the American left in the era of posttruth); rather, the political heavy lifting in Bennett, or the primary way the theoretical claims find an upshot in the human world, is accomplished by the aesthetic movement of what her 2001 book calls *The Enchantment of Modern Life*. There, as she recalls in the preface of *Vibrant Matter,* the "focus was on the ethical relevance of human affect, more specifically, the mood of enchantment or that strange combination of delight and disturbance. The idea was that moments of sensuous enchantment with the everyday world—with nature but also with commodities and other cultural products—might augment the motivational energy needed to move selves from the endorsement of ethical principles to the actual practice of ethical behaviors" (xi). In short, it's not rational choices or moral imperatives but aesthetic affects that can bring about liberatory worldly effects, and the obligatory references to Foucault on the care of the self work to bolster this theoretical move concerning the ways that affect can or may help us to twist free from the rationalist cage of instrumentalism.

Of course, as I've also emphasized above, these appeals to excessive life or making your life a work of art performed a great deal of work from their birth in the C19 all the way through O'Hara's or Heidegger's native moment in late disciplinary capitalism—whose commitments to mass production called for a certain re-enchantment of reified life. However, I think you'd be hard-pressed to find any Capitalocene villains at contemporary high-end tech or culture firms who would disagree with this picture of life as excessive self-overcoming in the everyday. Indeed, the project of contemporary capitalism (of advertising, social media, and data aggregation on purchases and internet searches) is sutured by the supposed re-enchanting of everyday life through harvesting the value-producing focus of human attention: while you're using Google Maps to find the best route to that hot new restaurant you researched on Yelp and reserved on OpenTable, catching virtual Pokémon along the way, why not follow the prompt that just came on your cellphone screen, and stop to try on a pair of shoes you Googled earlier in the day?[36] Which is to say that the everyday, and the distributed attention of all of us, is better understood as a site of conflict than it is as a site for a potential re-enchantment of our fallen quotidian experience. And if nothing else, all this suggests that the least-new thing about the new materialism is its founding commitment to making it new: that new materialism is, in essence, another (I hesitate to say the last) gasp in the transcendentalist tradition of the C19, and its Romantic obsession with the re-enchantment of the universe, for which the work of Thoreau is a quite intense shorthand.

Here I'm not arguing that Bennett (or Barad, Latour, or other new materialists) are *wrong* concerning these ontological claims about how matter actually works—I'm not really in a position to know. But I am saying that, for better or worse, in a post–linguistic turn environment (where the "nature" of x or y body is no longer understood as a prescriptive entity to be followed, critiqued, or escaped), it doesn't really make any sociopolitical difference whether the new materialists are or aren't correct about the performative, vibrant, co-constitutive workings of all life and all matter in the universe. In other words, after the new materialist turn, the ontological status of performativity, interesting as it is, becomes largely evacuated of axiomatically resistant sociopolitical import: after the linguistic turn, the way things are no longer contains any special "meaning" directed at humans and our exceptional, rational logos. As Simmel reminds us, the excessive, overcoming version of life's "is" by definition doesn't carry with it a necessary series of prescriptive "oughts," and likewise the intra-active "facts" of the new materialist world don't carry with them determinant social "values"—again, at least partially because that iron fact–value connection was among the things floating in the bathwater that was tossed out with the human-exceptionalist, social-constructionist baby of the linguistic turn.

And I should note that not all so-called new materialists share Bennett's or Barad's enthusiasm for translating realist ontology into the human political realm. In *Biocultural Creatures,* for example, Samantha Frost cautions against positing any particular sociopolitical upshot for these scientific or ontological claims: "Although it might be tempting to try to attach an alternative ontology [of force, movement, and energy] to political worlds, political hierarchies, or visions of collective action, I want to caution against it. . . . Even if we rewrite or re-vision an ontology for the moment of post-humanism, politics conceived broadly as an effort to organize collective life cannot be thought as a necessary logical or conceptual entailment of an ontological claim" (159).

Let me also be clear that I'm not interested in reanimating nostalgia for the linguistic turn or returning to the late disciplinary era of cordoned-off knowledge domains; and I agree that the Bodacious era is something that's here to stay. But having looked at the ontological status of performative biopolitics in the first half of this book, and having come to a series of questions about its diagnostic usefulness in our (dire) global political climate, I turn in the second half of this book to looking at the possibility of biopolitical, performative engagements against the day (I'm happy to dub them "critical" performative engagements, even though that word has bizarrely become something of a kill-switch for academic work) in relation to our current Bodacious era—where, for better or worse, things like climate change denial, the return of oligarchical strongman and their cults of personality, and assaults on the university (more specifically, the humanities and arts) are also part and parcel of the bodacious, performative, biopolitical turn. So I pivot from the ontological performative to looking at three specific sites of potential against-the-day biopolitical investments or performances, trying to make good on my opening sense that performativity at present is more of a way of doing critical work (looking at "living," biopolitical relations rather than ossified terms, while refusing demystification as a critical mode, and remaining suspicious of "bodacious" ontological prescriptions for the political realm). So in the second half of the book, I'll look at the recent history of capitalism (with Piketty and Negri), university teaching and research (with Foucault), and the potentially resistant roles of literature (more specifically, Kenneth Goldsmith's infamous conceptual poetry) "after" meaning and signification, in a world thoroughly soaking in bodacious performative biopolitics. Going forward, I'm not going to attempt anything as clumsy as an "application" of some shiny new performative "method" that I've somehow distilled from these opening chapters, but more deploy a way of doing critical work that seems to me to be the fate of the performative—attending to bodies of whatever kind in motion, rather than to the questions that surround some overflowing (and finally reassuring) sense of multiple meanings (whether those meanings might be engendered by the new materialism's originary, ontological excess or the linguistic turn's epistemological, socially constructed lack of final closure). Indeed, as my primary performative throughline within an emergent biopolitics, I'll continue prosecuting these opening chapters' critique of meaning (linguistic or otherwise)—or its flipside, lamenting meaning's tragic failure—as constituting the primary dead end for performative interventions in the C21. Performativity in the tragic mode of undermining truths is dead; long live the comic performative mode, one that returns again and again to sites of emergence and transformation, without offering itself the enchanting reassurances of the Bodacious era.

Performativity and/as/into Biopolitics

4

Biopolitics, Marxism, and Piketty's *Capital in the Twenty-First Century*

> Throughout this book, when I speak of "capital," without
> further qualification, I always exclude what economists
> often call (unfortunately, to my mind) "human capital,"
> which consists of an individual's labor power, skills,
> training, and abilities.
>
> —THOMAS PIKETTY, *Capital in the Twenty-First Century*

> The philosophers of rue d'Ulm at the École Normale
> Supérieure (ENS) in the 1950s and 1960s . . . faced
> the problem of reproduction by tracing the relations
> of production back to a series of anthropological
> equivalents, mainly the claim that everything, in society,
> is productive.
>
> —ANTONIO NEGRI, "At the Origins of Biopolitics"

There's a lot for humanities scholars to like about Thomas Piketty's *Capital in the Twenty-First Century*. First of all, Piketty actually takes Karl Marx seriously, which is damn close to treason for mainstream thinkers commenting on capitalism and its discontents today, inside or outside the academy. Precious few economists would be caught dead furthering the notion that "the very high level of private wealth that has been attained since the 1980s and 1990s in the wealthy countries of Europe and in Japan . . . directly reflects the Marxian logic"[1] about class inequity, accumulation, and finance capital that was already laid out for us in the C19.

In telescopic shorthand, Piketty's primary formula for understanding capitalism's history is quite simple: capitalism is an economic regime that, absent external intervention by a global war or other large-scale disaster, is defined by the formula $r > g$ (where the return on capital investment "r" is greater than the rate of increase in the output of goods and incomes "g"). As he explains, "When the rate of return on capital exceeds the rate of growth of output and income, as it did in the C19 and seems quite likely to do again in the twenty-first, capitalism automatically generates arbitrary and unstable inequalities that radically undermine the meritocratic values on which democratic societies are based" (1). In short, Piketty shows that capitalism's baseline formula "$r > g$ implies that wealth accumulated in the past [and invested] grows more rapidly than output and wages" (571), suggesting in turn that capitalism is less a system characterized by egalitarian, class-mobile possibility (as it may have seemed in capitalism's golden era after World War II in the West) than it is a system that inevitably fosters the increasing power and influence of entrenched old money (as capitalism had functioned for the better part of its history, from the early modern period until the mid-C20).

In short, left to its own market devices, Piketty argues that capitalism in the C21 will look more like it did in the C19 than the C20, and as such capitalism going forward will favor political oligarchy rather than the democracy we tend to associate with mid-C20 Euro-American nation-states (a notion of meritocratic consumption capitalism that ideological pundits have, at least since the fall of the Berlin Wall, tended to associate with "freedom" itself). Given the various authoritarian, crony capitalisms that have come to political power in the United States, Russia, and China (not to mention Hungary, Brazil, Poland, and dozens of other places around the globe), and the gutting of worker protections worldwide, I think we already have a pretty good glimpse of Piketty's dark vision of capitalism's future being more like its pre-1945 past than it will be akin to the widespread (though still uneven, to be sure) economic growth we in the West saw after World War II.

As Piketty reminds us, without really unpacking the connection, this state of affairs (where big capital inexorably accumulates more capital, with scant "trickle down") was already foreshadowed for us in Marx's analysis of credit and finance in *Capital*—where in his own formulaic gambit, Marx explains how capital investment in commodity production (M-C-M') differs from financial investment, which requires no commodity (C) to be produced in order for invested capital (M) to be transformed into profit (M'). As Marx famously puts it, finance capital's formula is M-M' (invested capital M directly begets profit M', without the intervention of working-class labor power required to manufacture a commodity C). As such, finance and credit capital largely turns its back on Piketty's "*g*" or the potential for higher rates of growth in the wider economy, and in the concomitant possibilities for income gains by the working class. In short, one could translate Piketty's $r > g$ formula for capitalism into Marxist terms like this: M-M' > M-C-M'. Or in a kind of commonsense shorthand, both Marx and Piketty show us that, when it comes to rates of return, Wall Street > Air Conditioner Factory.

However, Piketty's sideways nods to Marx are hardly the only things to like about this surprising book that comes squarely from within the dismal science of economics. For any academic who's ever been on a committee with an arrogant, loudmouth supply-sider, Piketty's takedowns of the discipline are themselves worth the price of admission. He speaks of economists on both sides of the Atlantic in terms of "their contempt for other disciplines and their absurd claim to greater scientific legitimacy, despite the fact that they know almost nothing about anything" (29). His specific smackdown of North American economists is worth quoting at length:

> To put it bluntly, the discipline of economics [in the United States] has yet to get over its childish passion for mathematics and for purely theoretical and often highly ideological speculation, at the expense of historical research and collaboration with the other social sciences. Economists are all too often preoccupied with petty mathematical problems of interest only to themselves. This obsession with mathematics is an easy way

of acquiring the appearance of scientificity without having to answer the
far more complex questions posed by the world we live in. (29)

Despite such entertaining broadsides against many economists' "highly
ideological" conservative pandering (economists consistently shill for
the "scientific" dogma of necessary tax cuts for the wealthy and the inherent evil of government intrusion on the free market), Piketty clearly
continues to consider a numbers-based social science thinking as the
only brand of thought that can offer us a proper handle on describing
the workings of capital in the past and into the C21. Which is at least
partially to say that in both the form and content of Piketty's analysis,
any humanities contributions to the project of understanding capitalism are left largely confined to the aesthetic sphere, narrowly understood as a kind of supplement to social science thinking—specifically
through offering representative examples of the existential or personal
toll of large-scale changes in economic rationality. For example, Piketty
notes the ways in which Balzac's or Jane Austen's novels can show us
the fine grains of class stratification in the C19.

In short, while Piketty offers us a clear critique of the worst tenden-
cies in the social sciences, his faith for understanding and responding
to the dangers and possibilities of capital in the C21 remains rooted
in his calls for a more robust application of those very social science
methodologies (bigger data sets, clearer math, less dogma concerning
the role of government, fewer simplistic translations of numbers to
policies).[2] This is certainly both understandable and highly productive,
and I realize that I risk mimicking the know-it-all economist's bluster
if I simply feign indignant surprise that there's a lack of philosophical or
aesthetic consideration in a book on economics (just as an economist
could object that there are no charts, graphs, and mathematical formu-
lae in Derrida's work, and thereby he can't be saying anything worth-
while). To be clear, my desire in writing this chapter is not to chide
Piketty for being an economist (rather than a philosopher or cultural
critic) but rather to ask whether some conceptual tools from recent
philosophical and cultural theory might enhance, supplement, or even
extend his fine-grained analysis of the numbers and their history.

Specifically, my question or thought experiment in this chapter is simple: what can an examination of biopolitics (a genealogical and conceptual apparatus born in Foucault's work, which finds its most robust contemporary formulations in the neo-Marxist corners of humanities disciplines like philosophy and literary-cultural studies) add to Piketty's big-data social science analysis, or how can a consideration of biopolitics cut across his work in some ways that would offer a potentially enriching humanities foothold within the terms of his work? I'm simply suggesting here that, when it comes to understanding the workings of capital in the C21, methods and concepts born in the humanities can offer quite a bit to the economic analyses performed by Piketty.

To telegraph the argument, I'd begin by noting that one of the highly provocative upshots of Piketty's work, translated into a Marxian idiom, is that *Capital in the Twenty-First Century* gives us the numbers and the *longue-durée* analysis to back up the genealogical and social claims about class and worker discontent that autonomist Marxists have been making for decades: namely, that the Fordist compromise of the middle of the C20 in the overdeveloped world was a blip in the development of capitalism, a rare and forced capitulation of the capitalist class to the demands of the workers. As Piketty writes, "In the twentieth century, it took two world wars to wipe away the past and significantly reduce the return on capital, thereby creating the illusion that the fundamental structural contradiction of capitalism $(r > g)$ had been overcome" (572). In short, the so-called golden age of capitalism in the C20 was a hiccup in the history of capitalism, a postwar period of widespread economic growth that constituted not an evolution of capitalism into a more democratic and worker-friendly form, but a brief interregnum or respite from the long-term accumulative rules of capitalism. And Piketty is likewise clear that capitalism's unegalitarian $r > g$ nature is due *not* to market manipulations or imposed externalities of any kind. As he insists, "It is important to note that the fundamental $r > g$ inequality, the main force of divergence in my theory, has nothing to do with any market imperfection. Quite the contrary: the more perfect the capital market (in the economist's sense), the more likely r is to be greater than g" (27).

Along a parallel track to Piketty's analysis, Marxists have long argued that the post–World War II period in Europe and the United States signaled not the inevitable dawn of a new and more equal distribution of wealth, offering average workers a living wage and retirement stipend in return for their work in saving Western capitalism from the scourge of fascism in Europe. Rather, the Fordist compromise was a short-lived truce with the working class, a pact that was destined to be rolled back by global neoliberalism once Europe had been rebuilt and the memories of those world wars had waned (by the 1970s, to be exact). Marco Revelli puts it starkly: through the neoliberal revolution of the late C20, "Capital sought to take back—with interest, we could say—what had been won by labor, in terms of income and rights, during the previous cycle of industry and conflict, in the 'social twentieth century.'"[3] As Antonio Negri narrates that history, the golden years of unions and workers' rights led to a centrality of the working class and its labor power in retransforming Europe from rubble to prosperity, but the capitalist class couldn't abide that acknowledgment of workers' centrality for too long. Negri writes that, by the 1970s,

> To respond to the threat of workers' centrality, capital decided to bring down the centrality of industry and abandon, or revolutionize, the industrial society that had been both the reason for and the means of its own birth and development. This it did to the extent that it turned itself from industrial into financial capital. . . . . What was left of direct production started being "put out" of the factories, processes of "outsourcing" proliferated, and gradually and eventually, the company became computerized and placed under the control of financial capital. Enter *post-Fordism*.[4]

As Negri narrates it, what Piketty calls capitalism's natural tendency to "undermine the meritocratic values on which democratic societies are based" was staved off for some part of the C20 only through a forced Fordist compromise between labor power and capital (a détente made necessary by the devastations of World War II). And for Negri the remnants of that labor power, in a post-Fordist world, are characterized less by what Foucault calls the "disciplinary" power of the factory (and the Marxist labor theory of value) and more inexorably a kind of "bio-power" spread across the surface of everyday life in the late C20 and early C21. (Much more on this below.)

It is, interestingly enough, precisely this biopolitical form of capital—what economists call "human capital"—that Piketty strictly excludes from consideration in his analysis. Any book on *Capital in the Twenty-First Century* begs a simple question about the definition of Piketty's terms, which he takes up like this:

> But what is capital? . . . First, throughout this book, when I speak of "capital," without further qualification, I always exclude what economists often call (unfortunately, to my mind) "human capital," which consists of an individual's labor power, skills, training, and abilities. In this book, capital is defined as the sum total of nonhuman assets that can be owned or exchanged on some market. (46)

While Piketty acknowledges that "there is also the idea, widespread among economists, that modern economic growth depends largely on the rise of 'human capital'" (42), he rejects that case entirely, choosing instead to bracket any consideration of human capital in his analysis of what capital really is or how it really works. Piketty goes on to enumerate all the things that count as capital for him: "To be clear, although my concept of capital excludes human capital (which cannot be exchanged on any market in nonslave societies), it is not limited to 'physical' capital (land, buildings, infrastructure, and other material goods). I include 'immaterial' capital such as patents and other intellectual property. . . . More broadly, many forms of immaterial capital are taken into account by way of the stock market capitalization of corporations. For instance, the stock market value of a company often depends on its reputations and trademarks" (49); and at the end of the day, such immaterial or biopolitical notions of capitalizable innovation, brand loyalty, reputation, and confidence are "reflected in the price of the common stock" (49) and thereby obliquely measurable as "real" capital. But human capital itself remains unmeasurable for Piketty—precisely what attracts the attention of someone like Negri.

However "clean" this exclusion of human or biopolitical capital may prove to be methodologically (it's notoriously difficult to place a concrete price or value on interests, skills, and capacities, especially of individuals), when Piketty defines capital tout court in this way (as held, priced, and tradable assets), he virtually guarantees the truth of his thesis—essentially, that the C20 rise in factory-worker Fordism (the building boom made necessary by the ravages of the two world wars in Europe and the Pacific) contradicted the economic energies of the late robber-baron era in the C19, where the greatest returns were not to be found in the production of goods or services but in the returns on investment itself. And going forward, if you cut human capital out of the picture (even an old-fashioned labor-theory-of-value version of human capital—where the worker's only asset is the labor power she can rent to the capitalist), then in the future there seems no real hope for capital to entertain the interests or well-being of the everyday person, other than through the faux-benevolent golden-shower trickle-down generosity of the corporation, the wealthy investor, or the government. None of these deep-pocketed entities will, I expect, be forthcoming in sharing their assets with the vast majority whose economic lives will stagnate under the $r > g$ dictates of capitalism that Piketty presages as coming for us all in the C21.

Hence my interest in looking at what a consideration of human capital or biopower could add to Piketty's analysis. Following the Derridean training of my youth, it seems to me axiomatic that it's worth looking at those concepts or practices that a given theory excludes or remains unwilling to deal with—what an analysis sees as a marginal, uninteresting, or parasitic case is oftentimes the skeleton key to understanding the strengths and weaknesses of that theory. If nothing else, it would seem to me that one needs, in classic deconstructive fashion, to account for the excluded cases if one wants a robust recent history of economic activity in the West. In any case, the rise in C20 human capital (everything from the cultural capital made more widely available by the GI Bill to the endless remaking of subjectivity that has become the home terrain of the C21 culture industries) would have to be taken into account somehow in Piketty's diagnosis—other than suggesting, as true as it is, that one end of the human-capital spectrum (the wealthy, investing top of the capitalist food chain) that has innovated the cellphone, the GPS, or robotic technologies has all but ravaged the human capital at the bottom (excising or outsourcing the jobs of the telephone operator, the cab driver, or the assembly-line worker).

In short, I'm going to want to argue that the biopower of human capital today saturates not only or even primarily the supply side of the economic situation, but rather the demand side—through the attention economy necessitated by the rise of cognitive capitalism. Most commentators who want to discuss human capital tend to understand it in terms of the service economy (health care, repair services, information technology), and suggest that it's in the so-called affective industries that human capital became central (and measurable economically). And while the service economy is hardly disappearing, I think we only need to look at what robotics did to service jobs like factory worker, bank teller, and travel agent, or what automation is about to do to those employed as truck and taxi drivers (as well as Amazon package handlers), and you can see that the service economy on the production side is not necessarily where the human-capital gains or transformative powers are to be found in the near future. In the end, this double-edged sword of biopolitics and/as human capital may offer a bit more hope on the "workers" side of the class struggle, as we're all workers now, involved in the work of performatively sculpting and resculpting our identities, and indeed our lives.[5]

Adding Biopolitics to the Mix

The C20 was an era that, to borrow some terminology from Michel Foucault, saw a decisive shift in the individual's relation to the social whole, a shift that Foucault diagnoses as the movement from a society of "discipline" to one of "biopower," a distinction that we can initially translate like this: discipline functions within and depends on a Fordist understanding of factory society (where the individual is understood as a cog within the larger social machine, and thereby has a series of disciplinary roles to fulfill—daughter, student, doctor, patient, tinker, tailor, soldier, spy). Contrast that with the laissez faire, neoliberal consumer society in which we presently live (where everyone's primary job is to become him- or herself, hopefully without external intrusion by the government), and you can see the disciplinary idea of fitting in within a larger social whole (or merely working on the assembly line of the social, for the greater good of all) is now looked upon as dangerous, totalitarian even. In a world where everything is filtered through an individual's life or lifestyle (rather than through larger disciplinary questions about configuring an optimal social cohesion), biopower has become the dominant logic: everything in a society of biopower gets filtered through the lens of the individual subject.

In Foucault's career, there is a well-known shift between his work on disciplinary institutions and power (culminating in 1975's *Discipline and Punish*, an exhaustive history of the prison as the central institution of disciplinary power), and his late work on sexuality, wherein he introduces a mutation in modes of modern power: according to Foucault, a new form called biopower (with its primary operating system of sexuality) is born in C19 Europe and gradually becomes dominant in the C20. Just to begin with the most obvious opening example of this mutation from discipline to biopower, think of the shifts in Western economic production over the past hundred years or so—from a factory economy of discipline (everyone trained to master his or her segment of the mass-production process), to the supposedly creative capitalism of our day, which is all about individual innovation and niche markets (lifestyles, innovation, creativity and identity). Today, the dominant mode of economic production entails producing any given person's life and lifestyle, not mass-producing identical objects; in fact, niche-market consumption is oftentimes ideally refined to a market of one: "Welcome to amazon.com, Jeffrey. We have some suggestions for you." Lifestyle purchasing is the primary economic driver in a neoliberal finance economy, and that form of hyper-consumption is dependent on constant biopolitical innovation. (This for example explains why China is relocating masses of its population, around 250 million people, from the rural countryside into prefab cities: to unleash the power of the Chinese consumer.)[6]

In his lecture courses touching on the concept of biopower (*Society Must Be Defended* and *The Birth of Biopolitics*), Foucault discusses the ways in which an emergent biopower might differ from the disciplinary mode of power (which aims at modifying individual behaviors and is always mediated through institutions). As Foucault explains in his 1975–76 lecture course *Society Must Be Defended*, biopower comprises

> a new technology of power, but this time it is not disciplinary. This technology of power does not exclude the former, does not exclude disciplinary technology, but it does dovetail into it, integrate it, modify it to some extent, and above all, use it by sort of infiltrating it, embedding itself in existing disciplinary techniques. This new technique does not simply do away with the disciplinary technique, because it exists at a different level, on a different scale, and because it has a different bearing area, and makes use of very different instruments. Unlike discipline, which is addressed to bodies, the new non-disciplinary power is applied not to man-as-body but to the living man, to man-as-living-being.[7]

As Foucault insists, this new form of biopolitical power doesn't simply replace discipline, but extends and intensifies the reach and scope of power's effects by freeing them from the disciplinary focus on "man-as-body" through the "exercise" of training carried out within various institutions.

Biopower, one might say, radically expands the scale of power's sway: by moving beyond discipline's "retail" emphasis on training individual bodies at linked institutional sites (family, school, church, army, factory, hospital), biopower enables an additional kind of "wholesale" saturation of power effects, saturating these effects throughout the entire social field. What Foucault calls this "different scale" and much larger "bearing area" for the practices of power make it possible for biopower to produce more continuous effects, because one's whole life (one's identity, sexuality, diet, health) is saturated by power's effects, rather than power relying upon particular training functions carried out in the discontinuous domain of x or y institution (dealing with health in the clinic, diet at the supermarket and the farm, sexuality in the family and at the nightclub, and so on). Hence biopower works primarily to extend and intensify the reach of power's effects: not everyone has a shared disciplinary or institutional identity (as a soldier, mother, nurse, student, or politician), but everyone does have an investment in biopolitical categories like sexuality, health, or quality of life—our own, as well as our community's.

Discipline forged an enabling link between subjective aptitude and docility: as Foucault concisely puts it in *Discipline and Punish,* the disciplinary body becomes "more obedient as it becomes more useful."[8] For its part, biopower forges an analogous enabling link, but this time between the individual's life and the workings of the socius: one might say we become more "obedient" to neoliberal, biopolitical imperatives the more we become ourselves, insofar as the only thing that we as biopolitical subjects have in common is that we're all individuals, charged with the task of creating and maintaining our lives. And that biopower-saturated task is performed not solely at scattered institutional sites (as it was for discipline), but virtually everywhere, all the time, across the entirety of your life. That being the case, the major difference between discipline and biopower is that in a biopolitical society, power no longer primarily has what we might call a "mediated" relation that is aimed at confining or rigidly defining individuals (which is to say, power is not primarily doled out through institutional training as much as it is a question of direct access to one's life or lifestyle). Foucault describes the biopolitical society as a world "in which the field is left open to fluctuating processes, . . . in which action is brought to bear on the rules of the game rather than on the players, and finally in which there is an environmental type of intervention instead of the internal subjection of individuals."[9] The bearing area of disciplinary power is what you can do, and it's primarily invested in training at a series of institutional sites. Through a kind of intensification of discipline, the bearing area of biopower has morphed into your entire life, and thereby biopower's relation to any given individual tends to be less mediated by institutional factors, and instead constitutes a more "environmental," diffuse, engulfing—one might even call it "ambient"—form of power.

Which brings us back to Negri's specifically economic, Marxist version of this biopolitics story, the story of post-Fordist capital that was outsourced from factories in response to worker activism and power in the so-called first world. Recall that, for Negri, this shift occurs precisely because such a biopolitcal lifestyle capitalism (which emerged out of Fordist credit regimes and the increasing necessity of a skilled service workforce) offered too much power to the worker, or the ordinary person, and thereby necessitated the move from a disciplinary capitalism of factory production to a biopolitical capitalism of everyday consumption. As Negri writes, "Here the *biopolitical* entered the scene: biopolitical as life put to work, and therefore as politics mobilized to organize the conditions and control of the social exploitation of all realms of life. As we said in Marxian terms, capital 'subsumed' the whole of society."[10] In the biopolitical world of our era, your life is your job and vice versa—no longer can you clock out at the factory and get at least some distance from your job before you return the next day. When your primary job is constantly creating and updating your subjectivity (at work as well as at home), life has been decisively put to work. As Negri writes, once there's a complete biopolitical subsumption of the socius,

> There is no longer a realm "outside" production. Whether it critiqued or denied the centrality of workers' labor, [this] was not an anti-Marxist stance; quite the contrary, because it emphasized the importance of labor understood as a social activity. . . . Production and reproduction are one, a whole. A refusal, contra the tradition of orthodox Marxism, of any possibility of mediation that is external to the movements, of any recourse to a dualist model, including the claim to the truth of the Party, thus became possible. (52–53)

For Negri, the total subsumption of everyday life by capital is less a lamentable cage that imprisons the worker and negates the importance of her work than it is a possibility for the living power of labor (here, reunderstood ultimately as the power of subjectivity to remake itself) to be finally brought front and center, rather than merely disappearing into the mediations of factory labor (the finished product of the commodity, as it does in the labor theory of value) or the mediations of the Communist Party (as "representing" the interests of the working class).

As Negri insists, "If there is no 'outside' of production, and knowledge, ideology, and the concept are found in the process of reproduction, then the whole of powers is organized autonomously, or rather structurally" (53); and subsequently, the new question becomes, "how to *reestablish subjectivity* and situate it *within* a new framework that was solidly and fully immanent? To this challenge rose Foucault's thought, which confronted it [the problem of reestablishing subjectivity] by turning the structuralist perspective into a *biopolitical one*" (53). In short, for Negri, the whole of life becomes saturated with the face-off between the "biopolitical" everyday actions of everyone, and the top-down "biopower" deployed by the parasitic, ideological state and corporate apparatuses of capture that are built upon those everyday creative actions (everything from the race-baiting policing tactics of the nation-state—See something, say something!—to the culture industries of celebrity and the ubiquity of advertising, which depend completely on harvesting creative attention from subjects).

In short, the grounds of class contestation shift as the dominant modes of power shift, in Negri's world, from the primary contestatory site of the factory strike (in the era of Foucauldian discipline) to the surface of each of our everyday lives, our subjectivity itself comprising both the stake and the driver of biopolitical capitalism:

> the transition from the "disciplinary society" ("government") to the so-called [biopolitical] "society of control" ("*governance*") was being registered. An analysis developed to recognize that, in the society of control, production and resistance are organized into "modes of life." This operation amounted to a total reversal of the structural field and thus to an articulation of the "field of immanence" as a biopolitical terrain. There is no "outside," *dehors*; the *bios* is that "inside" wherein each one is entirely enveloped. Resistance thus exemplifies acting in this contradiction, but the contradiction one is immersed in is a biopolitical reality. The collective body lives there because it produces everything, because it

works, but most of all because it resists, and in this resistance it configures reality. (55)

Like the transformative power of labor in its day, in a biopolitical field,
something like human attention and creativity comes *first* and bestows
value, rendering all of us—the disbursed working class that Negri re-
dubs the global "multitude"—as the creative and value-generating power
of biopolitical capitalism.

Attention Deficit

In fact, Jonathan Beller argues that attracting and managing human
attention has become *the* hot commodity of the C21, and a quick Google
search will concur—as one website puts it straightforwardly, "attention
is now the ultimate commodity." In her article "I Attend, Therefore I
Am," philosopher and cognitive scientist Carolyn Dicey Jennings goes
as far as to redefine human subjectivity not in terms of its reasoning or
language-using abilities, but as the being capable of paying attention:
"the self comes into being with the first act of attention, or the first
time attention favours one interest over another."[11] (One is tempted
here to insert a comment about the Lacanian mirror stage relocated to
the clothing-store fitting room.) Behind this turn to attention economics is a larger biopolitical harnessing of the productivities of everyday
human life, including the body and the senses, within an expanding
world-media system. Just to take the most obvious example, in a disciplinary society the workday was pretty much over when you clocked
out or left the office. Not anymore, as smartphones, email, texts, Face-
Time, Skype and a hundred other web- and app-based intrusions make
it clear you can never escape from your job—both your actual job (what
you do for a living) and the ancillary job you have as a productive consumer who's in charge of endlessly remolding his or her life.

With a relatively inexpensive smartphone and a wifi or data connection, you can pay attention—that is to say, you can buy things, answer
email, read reviews, track a delivery, hail a ride, or update Facebook—
from virtually anywhere, at any time. As Beller puts it in his article
"Paying Attention":

we have entered into a period characterized by the full incorporation of the sensual by the economic. This incorporation of the senses along with the dismantling of the word emerges through the visual pathway as new orders of machine–body interface. . . . All evidence points in this direction: that in the twentieth century, capital first posited and now pre-supposes looking as productive labor, and, more generally, posited atten-tion as productive of value.[12]

Beller's argument revolves around cinema as an intense site of train-ing in the early C20. In his view, the movie theater constituted a kind of factory for training spectators to extract value from their attention, as a kind of testing ground for the biopolitical expansion of capital-ism into everyday life. In *The Cinematic Mode of Production: Attention Economy and the Society of the Spectacle,* Beller goes as far as to call this new form the "attention theory of value": "What I will call 'the atten-tion theory of value' finds in the notion of 'labor,' elaborated in Marx's labor theory of value, the prototype of the newest source of value pro-duction under capitalism today: value-producing human attention."[13] And this attention theory of value constitutes an experimental R&D operation within each of us, a biopolitical niche market of one wherein "New affects, aspirations, and forms of interiority are experiments in capitalist productivity."[14]

In the hundred years since the disciplinary era of the cinema's emergence (Beller talks largely about early modernist film, Vertov and Eisenstein), we've seen a decisive intensification and general spread of such attention labor, into your home through television and into your everyday routines through the near-ubiquity of computer and smart-phone screens today, where it seems everyone's always looking at some-thing. In short, modes of focusing our distributed attention are the hot advertising and business commodities of our time. As Beller reminds us, "perception is increasingly bound to [value] production"[15]—think of the way the stock market fluctuates with changing perceptions about the future, or the ways that brands are managed not by making changes in the products but largely through influencing consumers' feelings about them. And most obviously, various forms of clickbait on the internet are vying for attention as value: you have to click through for someone to get paid, and before you can click through, something first has to draw your attention. Beller convincingly shows us how the movie theater was a visual factory for mass training in disciplinary capitalism, and watching remains an important pedagogical practice for the intensification of subjective attention in the move from discipline to biopower (from the theater to the home TV and finally to the portable ubiquity of the smartphone screen). Thereby popular culture, as Adorno shows us in his "Culture Industry" essay, becomes a mode of production in its own right—finding its end-product not in songs or films or TV shows but in the form of subjects, consumers who produce their whole lives out of their consumption patterns.[16]

Just in passing I'd note that one could construct a similar argument concerning the cash value of attention and the senses, not only for film or TV but in terms of Euro-American museum art in the C20. Virtually everything having to do with "artfulness" (and concomitantly with economic value) from Dada forward shifts art's value from the object (and from the question of representation) to the kind of attention paid to the object once it's brought into a museum or gallery space: from Hugo Ball's performances and Duchamp's urinal through Jackson Pollock's splatter works, Jean-Michel Basquiat's layered semiotic universe and Cindy Sherman's movie stills, all the way to conceptual art, whose anticommodity stance barely conceals the ways in which the high art scene over the past few decades has constituted an immense economics seminar in Beller's "attention theory of value." Which is to say, we learn from contemporary art the invaluable lesson that drawing attention to an object or practice, then manipulating or even merely holding that attention, has become the most highly-prized marker of cultural "value" in our time.

This turn to the biopolitical subject as producer of artistic value also reveals for us the mistake continually made by the exasperated parents in the museum, looking at a Duchamp hat-rack, a Paul Klee painting, or a Jenny Holzer scroll of banal phrases on a pixel screen, shaking their head and saying "My kid could do that." For the expert, of course, this kind of comment immediately rebounds onto the person making the judgment, who seems not to realize that the artfulness isn't in the object, but in the kind of attention that the object asks you to pay to it: the way the artwork invites *you* to infuse the work with artfulness, and thereby to separate it from the common mass of artless things. This move to elevate the everyday is of course the holy grail of the attention economy, and we can thereby see how the high-art markets of the C20 were the attention-grabbing proving grounds for the click-bait advertising and endless Facebook posting of today, desperate to draw a certain kind of attention in order to add value to an otherwise worthless practice or object.

Pierre Bourdieu points out that modern art requires much from its consumers, as it is the beholder's attention (not the objects themselves) that must finally articulate the "artistic" quality of otherwise mundane objects in a gallery:

> never perhaps has more been asked of the spectator, who is now required to "re-produce" the primary operation whereby the artist (with the complicity of his whole intellectual field) produced this new fetish. But never perhaps has he been given so much in return. The native exhibitionism of "conspicuous consumption," which seeks distinction in the crude display of ill-mastered luxury, is nothing compared to the unique capacity of the pure gaze, a quasi-creative power which sets the aesthete apart from the common herd by a radical difference which seems to be inscribed in "persons" . . . . The new art is not for everyone, like Romantic art, but destined for an especially gifted minority.[17]

What Bourdieu describes in the 1960s as a class-mobile striving (to accumulate cultural capital, to allow the artist or art lover to break out of the class strictures inherent in Bourdieu's mid-century, Fordist, disciplinary society) has intensified and spread to become the central pillar of the logic of everyday identity in the biopolitical era—where no one is comfortable being ordinary, and everyone is charged with the task of infusing his or her life with meaningfulness, making your life a work of art. However, this mission of personal branding, of not disappearing into the crowd, is no longer merely the purview of the upper classes and the striving artist class, as it is in Bourdieu's disciplinary analysis. This manufacturing and updating of identity, this constant performative remaking of your life, is the daily job of each and every one of us in a biopolitical world.

In terms of a Marxist analysis, what changes historically over time is not so much any given theory's imbrication with the economic imperatives dominant in its moment of historical emergence; rather, what changes are those dominant economic imperatives themselves and how they bear upon individuals. Likewise, theory as well as modes of subjectivity must evolve to respond to those economic shifts. And this is most clearly where Negri the Marxist and Piketty the social scientist differ: for Piketty, there seems to be one iron law of capitalism ($r > g$) and even very intense, revolutionary shifts in human subjectivity or technology have little to no effect on that properly and autonomously *economic* law. However, what counts as a properly economic question or field within the mid-century, disciplinary, essentially Fordist capitalism will not be the same as what counts as an economic question within the biopolitical finance capitalism of our era. It's no longer possible, to put it bluntly, simply to pit "proper" economic questions (of the tradable, productive economic base) against fanciful questions of social identity (superstructural questions of human capital), precisely because social questions of identity fuel the economic imperatives of our biopolitical day.[18] What's changed from disciplinary to biopolitical capitalism, in other words, is the very intense becoming-economic of what used to be thought of as merely cultural questions about identity or personal tastes and desires. Within the attention economy of biopower, these "inside" questions about personal identity or desire have met up with "outside" questions of economic class and finance. As Foucault puts it, in a biopolitical world, "the class struggle still exists; it exists more intensely,"[19] distributed across the surfaces of our lives and identities, rather than being enforced from above or below everyday life by the various ideological state apparatuses that train and constrain us.

To circle back to Negri, it is this wide distribution of the new class struggle, into the saturated level of everyday life, that makes the biopolitics of something like attention less an individual whimsy to be manipulated and more of a distributed site of contestation to be negotiated. Negri flat out asks a question that many Marxists have struggled with in recent years:

> Where is *class struggle* today? How does critical Marxism work as a movement practice rather than a philosophy? There are two possibilities that follow what has been said thus far. By the end of the 1970s, evidently dogmatic Marxism was over, but it seemed obvious that historical materialism invaded the *entire* field of political thought. One can no longer escape class antagonism. Second, and this is very important, the concept of class, without losing its antagonistic characteristics, had profoundly changed as a social subject. The working class had changed its *technical* composition via a process that it itself had set in motion—*from the factory to society.* Against the ontological backdrop of these transformations of the relations of production and political struggle, the working class thus reappeared as a *multitude,* as a collection of singularities that built the common. (56)

While Piketty clearly wants nothing to do with this kind of revolutionary Marxism, much less with the very strong—even excessive—emphasis that Negri puts on the transformative power of the multitude's "human capital," Negri's sentiments about the potentials of biopolitics at least share Piketty's realistic sense that the terrain of capitalism can be (and has been) transformed, so our tools for understanding or reshaping it will have to be refashioned as well. As Piketty writes, "Capital is not an immutable concept: it reflects the state of development and prevailing social relations of each society" (47), which is a simple historical claim that we can trace: "the nature of capital itself has changed radically (from land and other real estate in the eighteenth century to industrial and financial capital in the twenty-first century)" (42). And as the nature of capital continues to mutate today, so must our responses to it. In a biopolitical world, performative subjectivity or human capital finds its charge not through making products and commodities but in the on-going project of making ourselves. So aesthetics and the concerns of the humanities are not merely epiphenomenal, reflective, representational, or superstructural discourses (as Piketty understands them); but the arts and humanities remain a crucial linchpin for understanding the workings of (and against) capital in the C21. And this finally is where Piketty and Negri may find some uneasy but common ground, a convergence that Piketty sums up when he writes, "I do not see any genuine alternative: if we are to regain control of capitalism, we must bet everything on democracy" (573). Which is finally betting everything not on benevolent government intervention through taxation (Piketty's reformist suggestions), nor appeals to corporate charity on our behalf, but on a more robust biopolitics, understood as a redirected emphasis not on the bankrupt politics of the nation-state but on the radically democratic, transformative power of the multitude.

In closing this chapter, though, I would note that much of the work on capitalism in the C20 took the horizon of disciplinary, liberal democracy as the (inevitable, if unevenly developing) horizon of modern capitalism itself, capitalism's preferred and most efficient form going forward (think most obviously of Fukuyama's "The End of History"). However, as has become clear in the last decade, it's not at all obvious that representative liberal democracy is the preferred state form we'll see in the future of capitalism, but rather a kleptocratic oligarchy model, pivoting on a right-wing strongman—the sort of stuff that we've seen recently represented (in varying ways) by Trump's United States, Putin's Russia, China's Xi, Turkey's Erdogan, Hungary's Orban, as well as a global junior varsity arising in Poland, Brazil, Italy, the United Kingdom, the Philippines, et cetera. As Vladimir Putin put it succinctly in 2019, with the worldwide rise of populism, political "liberalism has become obsolete."[20] This too is, unfortunately, aligned with the rise of performative biopolitics.

While there's quite a lot of discourse dedicated to explaining the rise of the new populism, and average citizens' declining faith in liberal democracy, there remains a fairly clear Marxist explanation for the uptick in populist xenophobia over the past decade: since the 2008 global crash, Western democracies have seen an already-large wealth disparity grow to enormous proportions. As Revelli insists, the new populism is perhaps best grasped as an old-fashioned class war: "the exponential growth in inequalities across the whole globalised West between 2005 and 2014 opened up an outright social chasm, and . . . in twenty-five advanced economies between 65 and 70 percent of citizens had seen their incomes flatline or fall: which is to say, a mass of between 540 and 580 million people who feel themselves being pushed to the margins or losing their class position. Of these, just 10 million—a tiny 2 percent—had reported in 2005 that they had remained at a standstill or become poorer over the previous decade, between 1993 and 2004."[21] When 70 percent or more of the Western democracies' populace— more than half a billion people, most of those working class—see their incomes flatline or fall over the last fifteen years, while only 2 percent had reported such declines in the decade prior, it's not clear to me that you need to go hunting for psychological explanations for the alarming rise in global xenophobic populism. The greater the income stagnation in any given country, the more intense the populist backlash against immigrants and other "outsiders." Revelli reminds us that

> the great freeze has not hit everyone in a homogeneous way—that some countries have been hit more violently, and that Italy is by far the worst case, with the largest proportion of the population having become im- poverished [since 2005], some 97 percent of families, followed by the United States with 81 percent and the United Kingdom with 70. France is doing a little better, with 63 percent *déclassés*. . . . This map of malaise, which takes account of the reduction in both "disposable income" and "market income," can almost entirely be traced onto the map of the insurgent phenomena classified as "populism."[22]

The more income stagnation, the more populist sentiment—and inso- far as neoliberal income stagnation for most of the working populace seems here to stay, we'd better brace ourselves for more pitched battles with those angry displaced workers who fuel it—folks who only a few decades ago were our neighbors and seemingly natural comrades in the fight against neoliberalism.

And while this is maybe another topic altogether, a difficult one to bring up at the end of a chapter, let me just say that I'm not sure the present fashionability of just calling this "the return of fascism" is quite accurate, as these are seriously capitalist, neoliberal, or biopolitical projects; Brexit or Italy-First are of course nationalist phenomena of a seemingly old-fashioned disciplinary kind, but their drivers are more neoliberal economics ("me first!") than anything else—though racist xenophobia is of course a close second, followed by a nostalgia for the very Fordist compromise years that their neoliberal heroes have systematically eviscerated. While many in the white working classes can be brought behind these nationalist economic policies, largely through combining them with race-baiting rhetoric, it's protecting the narrow interests of 1% hyper-capitalism that finally drives these policies, and turning poor, working-class populations against each other along racial and ethnic lines is a proven tactic to keep said poor folks from banding together to eat the rich. That being the case, the ways in which biopolitics functions within these regimes will need to be rethought again, from the ground up, as most of our thinking about biopolitics and capitalism works itself out in terms of a liberal democracy model of the state that is quickly fading from hegemony.

There are of course forms of a brutal neofascist social discipline that we're seeing reemerge on the horizon—most disturbingly, the continued racist and anti-immigrant diatribes that fueled Trumpism's ascendency and Brexit, all the way to the detention and reeducation of up to a million Muslim Uyghurs in China; but all of that is undertaken, as I note above, while hundreds of millions other Chinese citizens are being moved from the countryside into prefab cities, to become biopolitical lifestyle consumers that will fuel China's economy in the C21. And large-scale disciplinary manufacturing jobs are not coming back to the United States. But whatever state form emerges as the preferred delivery system for capitalism in the future, Piketty importantly shows us that a corrupt inequality has been baked into the capitalist cake from the beginning—from the tulip bulbs of early modern Holland to the Coronavirus recession of 2020 and beyond.

5

What Is a Lecturer?

Performative, Parrhesia, and the Author-Function in Foucault's Lecture Courses

> When philosophy becomes a teaching profession,
> the philosophical life disappears.
>
> —FOUCAULT, *The Courage of Truth*

Exactly what kind of performative situation characterizes the act of teaching, or giving a lecture? Teaching and lecturing are of course things that most of us who write articles and books end up doing a whole lot, but never really theorize very much. When another academic asks you how your work is going, you almost always recognize that's asking about the writing, not the other stuff. Though recently, for many long-deceased capital-a Authors (Foucault, Derrida, Heidegger, Adorno, and the like), those teaching or lecturing moments have found their way into print as well as into scholarly debates, and become full-fledged theoretical statements worthy of academic commentary in their own right. The English translation of Foucault's *Birth of Biopolitics* lectures, for example, has garnered more than ten thousand scholarly citations since its publication in 2008, which was already twenty-four years after Foucault's death. This chapter will wonder, at the most basic level, about the relationship between the performative act of lecturing and the consolidation of that performance into a constative form as the published lecture course. What happens to a discourse or a series of statements when it slides from having being (merely?) lectured into the category of having been authored (organized into coherent book form and published along-side other such works by the same author)? Much more on this below.

But I'd first like to transition into this chapter by pointing out that, of all the myriad topics introduced into Foucault scholarship by the publication of his lectures, the status of Foucault's late preoccupation with the ancient question of "parrhesia"[1] (the courage of truth-telling) has become of special interest. And that's not surprising, insofar as Foucault spends hours and hours in his lectures of 1983 and again in 1984 wondering over the status of parrhesia, and such courageous truth-telling's relations to the modes of veridiction that one sees in contemporary philosophy. In the 1983 *Government of Self and Others*[2] lectures, Foucault points out that, contra philosophical modes of telling or assessing the truth, parrhesia can't finally be unearthed from the content of the speech acts, but remains exterior (or maybe even anterior) to the truth or falsity of the claims made: "if we want to analyze the nature of parrhesia, I do not think we should look to the internal structure of the discourse, or the aim which the true discourse seeks to achieve vis-à-vis the interlocutor [the realm of rhetoric], but to the speaker, or rather to the risk that truth-telling opens up for the speaker. . . . Parrhesiasts are those who undertake to tell the truth at an unspecified price, which may be as high as their own death. Well, this seems to me the crux of parrhesia" (56). Parrhesia, then, is finally concerned with the uncertain risks of speaking, and the (potentially dangerous) force of such speaking a forceful provocation which is not of the "constative" (true or false) variety. So on the surface at least, Foucault's late concern with parrhesia can make it look a lot like Foucault also took a late interest in the performative as a form of speech that doesn't merely refer to preexisting truths, but makes things happen or moves things around.

As early as 1969's *Archaeology of Knowledge,* Foucault shows a keen knowledge of, and interest in, the performative "speech act spoken of by the English analysts":

> This term does not, of course, refer to the material act of speaking (aloud or to oneself) or of writing (by hand or by typewriter); nor does it refer to the intention of the individual who is speaking . . . ; nor does it refer to

the possible [perlocutionary] result of what he has said . . . ; what one is referring to is the operation that has been carried out by the formula itself, in its emergence: promise, order, decree, contract, agreement, observation. The [performative] speech act is not what took place just prior to the moment when the statement was made (in the author's thoughts or intentions); it is not what might have happened, after the event, in its wake, and the consequences that it gave rise to; it is what occurred by the very fact that a statement was made.[3]

He goes on in the *Archaeology* to contrast this notion of the performative utterance with his own developing concept of "the statement," suggesting in the end that the statement is more of primitive function that traverses language, a kind of anonymous murmur that makes sentences and speech acts possible, but is not reducible to them: "one finds more statements than one can isolate speech acts" (84). For example, "a graph, a growth curve, an age pyramid, a distribution cloud are all statements" (82) rather than grammatical sentences or performative speech acts.

Early on in his late lectures examining parrhesia, Foucault specifically brings up the performative as a point of contrast. In his January 12, 1983, lecture in *Government of Self,* he compares the performative to parrhesia (largely unfavorably, or at least suggesting they're two distinct entities or modes of veridiction).[4] Here Foucault takes up

a form of enunciation which is exactly the opposite of parrhesia, and which has been called for some years now the performative utterance. You know that a performative utterance requires a particular, more or less strictly institutionalized context, an individual who has the requisite status or who is in a well-defined situation. Given all this as the condition for an utterance to be performative, [an individual] then makes a statement. The utterance is performative inasmuch as the enunciation itself effectuates the thing stated. (61)

Foucault adds in the manuscript of his lecture: "The performative is carried out in a world which guarantees that saying effectuates what is said" (61). In a nutshell, performative statements aren't (automatically or primarily) parrhesiast for Foucault largely because performative statements don't entail any risk, and their possible outcomes are already encoded within the social and institutional situations wherein they function: when the boss says, "this meeting is open," thus the meeting is open. "I now pronounce you to be married," said after the proper affirmations by the parties, in the proper context, and uttered by a person sanctioned to conduct marriage ceremonies, simply moves the participants from one socially recognized category (single) into another socially recognized category (married). This is what Foucault characterizes as the "major and crucial difference" between the performative and the parrhesiast speech act:

> In a performative utterance, the given elements of the situation are such that when the utterance is made, the effect which follows is known and ordered in advance; it is codified, and this is precisely what constitutes the performative character of the utterance. In parrhesia, on the other hand, whatever the usual, familiar, and quasi-institutional character of the situation in which it is effectuated, what makes it parrhesia is that the introduction, the eruption of the true discourse determines an open situation, or rather opens the situation and makes possible effects which are, precisely, not known. Parrhesia does not produce a codified effect; it opens up an unspecified risk. (62)

In short, Foucault highlights the conventional nature of both the performative locution (someone has to be authorized to open the meeting or marry the couple) and the perlocutionary effect (it's easily recognizable to the participants what an open meeting or marriage ceremony entails). (One could note here in passing Foucault remains largely silent on the illocutionary force that moves things into a category or creates new ones, which has been our primary focus in this book.) On Foucault's analysis, the performative is less a deployment of force than it is a chess game with players able to make certain moves; parrhesiasts on the other hand make up the rules as they go along, binding the risky truth of the statement only to the speaking subject and not to an institutional or social context. And even more importantly, anyone can in principle be a parrhesiast (can risk telling the truth to power), whereas only certain eligible individuals within recognized institutions can effectively wield the power of the performative—if you get married to another actor during the performance of a play, you're not "actually" married, at least partially because the actor playing the minister isn't legitimately empowered to marry anyone. "What characterizes the parrhesiastic statement, on the other hand, is not that the fact that the speaking subject has this or that status. He may be a philosopher, the tyrant's brother-in-law, a courtier, or anyone whomsoever. So status is not important or necessary" (65): "To that extent, it is not the subject's social, institutional status that we find at the heart of parrhesia; it is his courage" (66). Those words, as you can imagine, function like crack cocaine for all those department-meeting radicals who want to see their work as sticking it to the man; and on a more sober, scholarly assessment, there are myriad very fine books and articles arguing that such parrhesiastic truth-telling is Foucault's final word on his own philosophical practice.[5] Most of those texts follow the groundbreaking summary of the lectures offered by Thomas Flynn in 1987, under the title (also the article's thesis) "Foucault as Parrhesiast: His Last Lecture Course at the Collège de France."[6] In short, the argument is that Foucault's books and even his lectures were all along engaged in the risky business of telling the unpopular truth to power. As Michael Hardt summarizes that line of thinking straightforwardly in "The Militancy of Theory," when Foucault works "through the notion of parrhesia in ancient Greek thought," specifically "in the work of the ancient Cynics" on dangerous truth-telling, "he discovers a biopolitical militancy that can serve as a model for theory today beyond critique."[7]

But Foucault himself quickly walks back that emphasis on personal "courage" in his next lecture, suggesting that parrhesia is a characteristic of a democratic political system more than it is the product of idiosyncratic subjective courage. In fact, Foucault will go on to question whether such courageous truth telling has any relation at all to the modern practice of philosophy, and he is throughout his career a particularly savage critic of the pedagogical or philosophical mistake of thinking that someone merely saying something, however provocative, has any political upshot whatsoever. As he suggests as early as 1978's *Security Territory Population* lectures, "the imperative discourse that consists in saying 'strike against this and do so in this way' seems to me to be very flimsy when delivered from a teaching institution or even just on a piece of paper. In any case, it seems to me that the dimension of what is to be done can only appear within a field of real forces, that is to say within a field of forces that cannot be created by a speaking subject alone and on the basis of his words."[8]

And in the end, this whole history of parrhesia is not so much a redeployment in the present as it is a genealogy that's largely of antiquarian interest—despite what commentators like Flynn or Hardt want to suggest. As Foucault clearly states in *Government of Self*, "Modern Western philosophy, at least if we take it as it is currently presented as an object of academic or university study, has relatively few points in common with the parrhesiastic philosophy I have tried to talk about. This ancient, perrhesiastic philosophy . . . should not be understood as a system of truths with regard to Being itself. Throughout Antiquity philosophy is really lived as the free questioning of men's conduct by a truth-telling which accepts the risk of danger to itself" (346). Near the end of the 1983 lecture course, Foucault sums up his interrogation of parrhesia like this: "I think we can also do the history of philosophy, neither as [Heideggerian] forgetting nor as the [Enlightenment] development of rationality, but as a series of episodes and forms—recurrent forms, forms which are transformed—of veridiction. The history of philosophy, in short, as movement of parrhesia, as redistribution of parrhesia, as varied game of truth-telling; philosophy envisaged thus in *what we could call its allocutionary force*. This, if you like, was the general theme I wanted to develop in this year's lectures" (350, emphasis added).

If we recall that "allocution" names a formal speech giving advice or a warning—hortatory, exhorting discourse—then it's clear that Foucault does sum up his engagement with parrhesia by decisively foregrounding the question of force (rather than meaning): not the immaterial force of the performative illocutionary, but the "allocutionary force" of histories of "truth-telling," treating the force of philosophy as a series of ways of speaking the true, rather than the project of uncovering, representing, or understanding some preexisting reality or truth. An emphasis on modes of veridiction exhorts us to recall that you have to be "in the true" (within the proper mode of veridiction) in order to "speak the true"; the allocutionary force is a provocation always to recall that the games of truth are not transhistorical. In the end, however, that allocutionary force of the parrhesiastic regime remains very close to the immaterial force that is the illocutionary engine of performativity—or at least the emphasis for both parrhesia and the performative remains on force rather than original meaning or eventual outcome, keeping the focus on doing as a form of being.[9]

And insofar as his last lecture course is titled *The Courage of Truth*,[10] it's tempting yet again to think that here at the end Foucault offers us a way to understand the entire itinerary of the lecture courses themselves as a parrhesiast exercise in biopolitical veridiction. As Flynn argues, "If his hard-fought battle against anthropologism kept him from idealizing Hellenic culture, he nevertheless admired and, indeed, practiced the kind of ethical parrhesia whose roots he uncovered in Plato but whose flower he savored among the 'good' Cynics. . . . If Habermas failed to find in Foucault the unity of his theory and practice, it is perhaps because he overlooked the parrhesiast."[11] But Foucault takes away that potential interpretation almost immediately, reminding his audience that delivering a lecture course is a *tekhnē* or a procedure, not a form of courageous truth-telling: for

> someone who has received knowledge and must pass it on, there is the principle of an obligation to speak which is not found in the sage but is found in the parrhesiast. But clearly, this teacher, this man of *tekhnē*, of expertise and teaching, does not take any risk in the truth-telling he has received and must pass on, and this is what distinguishes him from the parrhesiast. Everyone knows, and I know first of all, that you do not need courage to teach. . . . This truth-telling establishes a filiation in the domain of knowledge. Now we have seen that the parrhesiast, to the contrary, takes a risk. He risks the relationship he has with the person to whom he speaks. (25)

As Foucault continues, he points out that "The parrhesiast is not a professional. And parrhesia is after all something other than a technique or skill, . . . akin to a virtue, a mode of action" (14).

Rather than seeing this work on parrhesia as a recovery operation, to make the courage of truth a valuable "mode of action" again in the biopolitical present, Foucault argues instead that parrhesia is a thing of the distant past.[12] He straightforwardly says that "the parrhesiastic modality has, I believe, precisely disappeared as such" (30), so Foucault's work on this mode of veridiction is not really the recovery of a road not taken. Whereas according to Foucault "teaching ensures the survival of knowledge" (25), "the parrhesiast's truth-telling risks hostility, war, hatred, and death" (25)—outcomes which, however bad your student evaluations may have been last semester, lie far outside the modern teacher–student relation, which is more strictly speaking a performative one (with preexisting institutional roles set out for the student and the professor) rather than a parrhesiast one. After all, the teacher is precisely a "professional," and so at this point is the philosopher, who in Foucault's case is called to perform a lecture course on his research each year as part of the terms of his appointment.

In any case, it's the status of those lecture courses, their relations both to their spoken and later written forms, that will interest us here. If we've gotten from Foucault a pretty good handle on the constative question "What is an Author?," here in this chapter we'll wonder over the performative question, "What is a Lecturer?"

What Is a Lecturer?

So the primary task I set myself here is relatively straightforward, and I'm sorry to admit, maybe even a little pedantic: it's to see what Foucault's 1969 essay "What Is an Author?" might have to say about the posthumous entry into philosophical discourse of his lecture courses, and to wonder whether Foucault's concept of the author-function has anything to say about the immense amount of critical attention recently paid to Foucault's lecture courses, and indeed to myriad other authors' lecture courses throughout the disciplines of theory and continental philosophy? Recall that all of Heidegger's lecture courses have been published, as will Derrida's be eventually, as well as Adorno's, Merleau-Ponty's, and so on. Following the standard posthumous editorial practices that brought us, for example, both Hegel's *Philosophy of History* and his *History of Philosophy*, even Kant's *Lectures on Ethics* have recently been reconstructed from student notes. Alain Badiou's 1986 lectures on Nicolas Malebranche have not only been published but translated into English, leading one reviewer to wonder "if there is anyone who has been desperately curious about the relationship between Badiou and the 17th century philosopher, this book must be a welcome surprise. For the rest of us, there are some obvious questions surrounding it. What drove Badiou to dedicate a seminar to Malebranche? And which one was Malebranche again anyway? Wasn't he the occasionalism guy? That Modern Philosophy course was so long ago."[13] The only major figure who's an exception to lecture-course publication fever is probably Deleuze, and from what I understand it's mostly the Deleuze family getting in the way there.

Today, most of the major "authors" of recent continental thinking have their lecture courses flooding the book stalls of large humanities conferences; and that fact is, it seems to me, worth thinking about in its own right, because a lecture isn't exactly or always something that an author has decided to offer to the published archive. So what exactly are we doing when we lean heavily on philosophical evidence gleaned from a lecture course, material that oftentimes an author had the opportunity to publish, and thereby to attach a prized mode of author-ity, but decided otherwise? Likewise, if the author-functions that are connected to lecture courses comprise, in Foucault's words, "projections . . . of our ways of handling texts,"[14] what, if anything, does the disproportionate amount of attention these days lavished on lecture courses—rather than more straightforward published books and articles—tell us about our contemporary disciplinary ways of handling texts?

The author-function is tied up first and foremost with archival guarantees of meaning and value, the most obvious way a figure designated as an "author" is different from someone who writes or speaks something; in short, the author-function is a guarantee of the work's textual "depth" and archival significance. Given that fact, I'll also want to speculate a little bit about the changing author-function in at least some contemporary humanities discourses. For example, I wonder what becomes of the author-function in recent attempts to decolonize the discipline of philosophy through rethinking its canonical, race-based, and geographical biases? Or what happens to the author-function in data-driven forms of discourse analysis (say, Franco Moretti's "distant reading") or in emergent forms of literary theory that largely eschew altogether the depths of hermeneutics—say, various kinds of historicism (where Shakespeare, for example, is read as a symptom of social changes in England rather than a visionary poetic text)? Or for that matter, what happens to the author-function in conceptual apparatuses like "postcritical reading," or evolutionary and neuroscientific accounts of reading, all the way to various forms of what some humanities commentators call "descriptive" or "surface reading"?[15] If the author-function attached to a text is at least to some degree a guarantee of profundity, what happens when and if our "ways of handling texts" no longer require notions like hidden depth and enduring significance (let's just call it "meaning") from an author or her works? (And here, just to telescope the argument, I think there's a growing disciplinary divide between literature departments and philosophy departments—ironically, philosophy as a discipline clings much more strongly to the author-function than does literary theory these days.) Finally, straying from Foucault's texts a bit, while I hope remaining true to his commitment to think about the question of "today," I want to wonder in conclusion about the performative question "what is a lecturer?" in our era of dwindling humanities tenure-line job prospects.

So, first, what is a lecture course? There are a lot of different answers to this question, but if you go looking to the recent flood of lecture courses published in continental philosophy, you might come away with the idea that, at least for the people producing them, a lecture course is primarily a chore rather than a joy. First of all, there's a wealth of comic material having to do with the logistical hassles involved in performing such lectures—we get to witness towering philosophical giants like Theodor Adorno, for example, consistently grumbling about the room temperature or the microphone cutting out, or we get a front row seat for Foucault's frustrated attempts to manage the crowds at his lectures. But then of course there's the window we get into the simpler frustration of having to prepare and deliver the lectures each week. Foucault, for example, admits in an interview to having performance anxiety before his weekly lecture at the Collège de France, and one only has to follow out the immense number of loose ends strewn throughout his lectures (moments where Foucault says, "we'll continue this next week," and then never returns to the topic at hand) to see that the lectures have to be arduously sculpted from week to week, rather than planned out in meticulous detail beforehand. As Foucault admits to his seasoned audience during his final lecture course on *The Courage of Truth*, "you know that I never really know what I will be doing from one week to the next" (31n).

Like our more mundane classroom lectures, we may know what's coming up on the syllabus, but we probably don't know exactly what we're going to say about it, or how we're going to connect it to the weeks before and after. That performative, connective tissue all has to be produced on the fly. Though in the more classroom-oriented seminar, even if you're primarily lecturing, you have texts to help you focus the room's attention. In that way, it's important to recall that Foucault's lecture courses are not exactly "teaching" situations—his strict requirement is to offer a report on the *research* he's doing, rather than cover material as one would in a course on, for example, Nietzsche or phenomenology. However, packaging up that "research" for general consumption nevertheless takes time—more time frankly than would a text seminar, where as we all know, when everything else fails, you can let loose the close reading machine on a particularly dense paragraph, and watch the minutes fly by. And here we could note in passing that someone like Derrida performs this kind of close reading quite often in his lecture courses, but Foucault much less so—at least up until 1982, when he abandons the smaller research seminar that had met in addition to the lecture course, and begins performing some of that seminar work of close reading within his lectures.[16] Along these lines, it's maybe symptomatic that the opening lecture of Foucault's first Collège de France course, 1970–71's *Lectures on the Will to Know*, consists

of just such a reading of a paragraph from Aristotle; it's clear in retrospect that he's still making the transition from the seminar room to the
lecture hall.

In any case, all this is perhaps to say that the primary problem presented by the lecture course is the amount of time that lecturing takes
away from performing other "research" work. Most economically put,
giving lectures takes away from the writing of books and articles, published material that has an author-function attached to it. This is the
primary frustration that Foucault voices in his exasperated introduction to his January 7, 1976, lecture, the opening salvo from the "Society
Must Be Defended" course: "The problem for me was—I'll be quite
blunt about it—the fact that I had to go through this sort of circus
every Wednesday was really—how can I put it?—torture is putting it
too strongly, boredom is putting it too mildly, so I suppose it was
somewhere between the two. The result was that I was really preparing these lectures, putting a lot of care and attention into it, and I
was spending a lot less time on research in the real sense of the word
if you like."[17] He then goes on to outline his strategy to cut down the
circus—moving the meeting time for the lectures from late afternoon
to 9:30 in the morning as "a way of getting our Wednesday conversations and meetings back into the normal pattern of research" (3). In
closing out his opening rant on the status of the lecture courses themselves, Foucault muses, "So what was I going to say to you this year?
That I've just about had enough" (3).

In addition to the raw time-sink of the lecture course, there's also
the question of the idiom of a lecturer, which is not exactly the same
idiom deployed by an "author" of philosophical texts. In a lecture, one
is forced to condense, simplify, and make consumable material that
one might treat very differently—usually in a more complex fashion—
in an authored book or article. As Foucault puts it, "I do not regard
our Wednesday meetings as a teaching activity, but rather as public
reports the work I am, in other respects, left to get on with more or less
as I see fit . . . These are suggestions for research, ideas, schemata,
outlines, instruments; do what you like with them" (1). Research, as
Foucault somewhat idiosyncratically defines it, is not the reportage of

conclusions; rather he suggests that research consists of "the interesting but somewhat incoherent things I could have been saying" (2) in his lectures, if he did not have to occupy his time crafting a kind of finished script to perform each week. Foucault wonders, "How, in the space of an hour, an hour and a half, can I put something across in such a way that I don't bore people too much, and that they get some reward for being kind enough to get here so early to hear what I have to say. . . . I got to the point where I was spending months on it, and I think that the reason for my presence here [at the Collège de France], and the reason for your presence here, is to do research, to slog away, to blow the dust off certain things, to have ideas" (2). As such, for Foucault research is characterized by the productive qualities of uncertainty, while the lecture form demands a certain kind of, if not exactly certainty, at least a consumable packaging of what Foucault ironically dubs his "'feverish laziness'" (4), his daily research into "the great, tender, and warm freemasonry of useless erudition" (5). And packaging up your still-nascent thoughts constitutes, maybe, the essence of the lecture course, at least that's what it seems to be for Foucault.

Foucault's lecture courses are, then, in the end not designed to be thought of as "research" but as "suggestions for research, ideas, schemata, outlines, instruments; do what you like with them." But among all the myriad things one might do with Foucault's lecture courses, one of the major things that's been done with them in recent years is to produce commentary on them, as if they were full-blown "authored" research texts, right alongside the published books and articles. For the most spectacular version of this interpretive enterprise that's sprung up around the lecture courses, see Columbia University Law School's "Foucault 13/13" online archive, which houses extensive commentary by academic theorists (with some provocative interventions by folks who aren't primarily Foucauldians, such as Seyla Benhabib and Linda Zerilli, alongside more predictable fare penned by the Foucault brand managers); in any case, each is brought to Columbia to assist local faculty in unpacking Foucault's thirteen lecture courses.[18] Much of this secondary work gives us a preliminary handle on the trajectory of the lecture courses; but this intense attention paid to explicating Foucault's lectures should also give us pause—insofar as in his inaugural lecture at the Collège de France, "The Order of Discourse" (published in French as *L'Ordre du discours*, translated into English as "The Discourse on Language" and published with *The Archaeology of Knowledge*), Foucault states in a concise fashion his critique of commentary. As he puts it, "Commentary averts the chance element of discourse by giving it its due: it [commentary] gives us the opportunity to say something other than the text itself, but on the condition that it is the text itself which is uttered and, in some ways, finalized. The open multiplicity, the fortuitousness, is transferred, by the principle of commentary, from what is liable to be said to the number, the form, the masks, and the circumstances of repetition" (221). Throughout his early archaeological work on the ordering of discourse, Foucault routinely savages the idea of finding or revealing hidden or excessive meaning in an author's text, and likewise consistently questions the enabling power of commentary, which enables the critic to mime the voice of the master, to hear the secret rumblings beneath or beside the text. As Foucault summarizes these concerns in his inaugural (1970–71) course, *Lectures on the Will to Know*:

> I have never tried to analyze the text on the basis of the text itself. As far as possible, I have tried to get rid of the principle of exegesis, of commentary; I have never tried to know the non-said which was present or absent in the texture of the text itself. I have tried to get rid of textuality by situating myself in the dimension of history, that is to say locating discursive events that take place, not within the text or several texts, but through the fact of the function or role given to different discourses within a society.[19]

In the *Archaeology*, Foucault follows out a line of questioning that to my knowledge remains unexplored in terms of his own lecture courses: "The analysis of statements, then, is a historical analysis, but one that avoids all interpretation. It does not question things said as to what they are hiding, what they were 'really' saying, in spite of themselves, the unspoken element they contain, the proliferation of thoughts, images or fantasies that inhabit them; but, on the contrary, it [archaeology] questions them as to their mode of existence, what it means to them to have come into existence" (109). There has, in short, been plenty of commentary on Foucault's lecture courses, and a good deal of unearthing the hidden or latent content within them; but there seems to have been relatively little Foucauldian hesitation concerning "their mode of existence, what it means to them to have come into existence" in the first place, in published form at the present academic moment. If, as Foucault insists over and over again, his practice "is not an interpretive discipline: it does not seek another, better-hidden discourse" (139), one might then begin to wonder: just how "Foucauldian" is the interpretive boom in academic commentary surrounding Foucault's lecture courses?[20] As Foucault lays out his methodology for treating discourse, "Before a set of enunciative facts, archaeology does not ask what could have motivated them (the search for contexts of formulation); nor does it seek to discover what is expressed in them (the task of hermeneutics); it tries to determine how the rules of formation that govern it—and which characterize the positivity to which it belongs— may be linked to non-discursive systems" (162) such as the disciplinary workings of institutions or academic fields. Maybe the question surrounding the posthumous Foucault publication boom is less "what do these texts mean?" but rather "what disciplinary and institutional 'rules of formation' govern their emergence in the first place?" In a related set of questions, we might wonder what became of Foucault's explicit ban on posthumous publications, now that his fourth volume of the *History of Sexuality* has been published, against his explicit wishes: "Don't pull the Max Brod-Kafka trick on me," Foucault pleaded shortly before he died.[21] Which is a plea that has provoked little to no scholarly response, as far as I can tell. Our right to know, and thereby to comment, publish, or opine endlessly, apparently trumps both the content and the provocation of Foucault's thought.

While we might hesitate then in producing either author-functions or commentary around Foucault's lecture courses, given that he is an excoriating critic of those practices, the dissemination of his lecture courses does find a certain warrant elsewhere in Foucault. Specifically in "What Is an Author?" where he asks:

Assuming we are dealing with an author, is everything he wrote and said, everything he left behind, to be included in his work? This problem is both theoretical and practical. If we publish the complete works of Nietzsche, for example, where do we draw the line? Certainly, everything must be published, but can we agree on what "everything" means? We will, of course, include everything Nietzsche himself published, along with the drafts of his works, his plans for aphorisms, his marginal notations and corrections. But what if, in a notebook filled with aphorisms, we find a reference, a reminder of an appointment, an address, or a laundry bill, should this be included in his works? Why not? These practical considerations are endless. (1478)

Working alongside Deleuze several years later, Foucault did indeed help prepare Nietzsche's complete works for publication, so there is no knock-down, drag-out prohibition in Foucault against publishing "everything" (whatever that might entail) once someone's been designated as an "author" (whatever that might entail).

Perhaps we might say when it comes to publishing everything, once the author-function is secured for any given proper name, you then merely have a genre question on your hands (the author-function guarantees the shift of reading attention from author to work and as Foucault notes; one can then endlessly quibble about the minor or major works, the status of interviews, or the generalized importance of certain genres within an author's oeuvre). For example, say that someone famous for other things—Herman Melville or for that matter Martin Heidegger—also writes poetry or keeps a diary. That would be a somewhat minor genre vis-à-vis their author-function (known primarily for narrative fiction and philosophy, respectively), but still valuable or interesting, something to publish, if only for the ways that it illuminates more central lines of inquiry in an author's itinerary. Melville for example wrote an aesthetically unspectacular poem about the Manhattan draft riots during the Civil War, but it's important largely because the poem is highly unsympathetic to the resisters—calling upon "wise Draco" to bring the protesting "wharf rats" into line—and thereby gives some insights into Melville's critique or embrace of democracy in *Moby-Dick* or *Billy Budd*.²² Heidegger's *Black Notebooks* have of course served a similar function, illuminating and transversally connecting to the major works, especially around the vexing question of Heidegger's anti-Semitism and his support (however short-lived) for the Nazi regime.²³ And one can imagine (if not recall having read) structurally similar kinds of arguments around Foucault's lecture courses, looking for example about how his treatment the infamous Charles Jouy incident in the *Abnormal* lecture series of 1974–75 may differ from or otherwise change our understanding of that incident's scandalous usage in the first volume of the *History of Sexuality*.²⁴

But it's at least worth hesitating to wonder if Foucault's lecture courses are really designed to be "major" works, fodder for commentary on their own terms? I'm not saying it's illegitimate to write books explaining, expanding on, applying, or otherwise providing commentary on Foucault's lecture courses (we're all doing it), but wondering why there's so little hesitation concerning this massive interpretive enterprise surrounding the lecture courses. Quite simply put, in recent disciplinary practice (especially within philosophy) the explosion of lecture courses has not found these texts designated as minor works or supplements to the major texts—quite the opposite. I would venture that, for example, there's been more work published recently on Heidegger's 1929–30 lecture course (the one that famously argues the stone is worldless, the animal poor in world, and humans are world-building) than there has been on the little tome he published two years before, *Being and Time*. My general sense is that one could say similar things about Foucault scholarship and its relation both to his late parrhesia lectures and his *Birth of Biopolitics*, even more specifically Foucault's thoughts on neoliberalism—which seem to be everywhere in the adolescence of the C21, even though I don't really know that Foucault's analysis, produced at the dawn of neoliberalism in the late 1970s, has much new or startling to say to people like us, who've been living with full-blown neoliberalism for four decades.²⁵

Which is maybe only to say the author-function helps us to understand the rush to the lecture courses, as they offer commentators new texts from the same old sources, and thereby new ways to double down on the security of the author-function in the discourse of philosophy and humanities theory more generally. As Foucault himself puts it in 1969, "While all this [talk about the end of the author as a guarantor of meaning or value] is familiar in philosophy, as in literary criticism, I am not certain that the consequences derived from the disappearance or death of the author have been fully explored or that the importance of the event has been appreciated" (1478). If nothing else, the commentary industry that's sprung up around Foucault's (and others') lecture courses is proof positive that, a half-century after Foucault pointed out we were not yet done with the author as an organizing guarantee of philosophical or literary value, we in the humanities are *still* not done with the author.

Maybe that's changing somewhat in the present, however. For example, the discipline of literary studies has, since the eclipse of deconstruction as the "last reading method" in the early 1990s, been subsumed largely as a brand of historicist cultural studies. So work on Melville is less concerned with producing new readings of *Moby-Dick* than it is dedicated to understanding *Moby-Dick* in certain historicist or culturalist ways—as a bellwether for social changes of some kinds, or looking at the text as a historical symptom (what it has to say about social unrest in the mid-C19 or the decline of the whaling industry or as an early example of globalization, how it fits in with other narratives penned by career sailors, and so on). There are very few critics still talking about what *Moby-Dick* means as a formalist artifact, offering explanatory commentary on it, or celebrating the genius of Melville, though of course maybe that's just another example of Foucault's "ways of handling texts" that reconfigure how authorship functions. In the end, though, I think it is true to say that C19 American literature, as it's presently configured as a disciplinary and scholarly research field, could get along just fine without the hyper-author-functions of Melville, Whitman, Dickinson, et al.—because it's largely become a historicist enterprise, wherein literature is one thing among a series of other cultural productions.

And of course the canon wars of the late C20 added to the literary studies syllabus substantial new layers of authors (Native Americans,

African Americans, women, ethnic writers) and topics (moving away from the formalism of meaning and toward social questions). When I was an undergraduate student, American literature was the nearly exclusive purview of dead white men who produced supposedly "universal" works of genius-tinged "greatness." In any case, I think it's fair to say that over the past quarter century, literary studies has in the main become historicist, and thereby has put considerable mutating pressure on the author-function as a guarantee of something like lasting meaning or enduring literary-historical-philosophical significance.

Philosophy, or at least the continental wing of philosophy departments wherein Foucault is seen as a major figure, is a bit more stubborn in its holding onto the author-function. For example, at present, I don't see any way that the scholarship on modern continental philosophy could do without Kant—and certainly the job ads that I see in philosophy look surprisingly similar to ones you would have seen thirty years ago. To my astonishment, there are still actual things called "Kant jobs," advertised specifically for specialists in some aspect of Kant's thought. Philosophy is probably the humanities discipline with the most stubborn and heroic version of author-function, precisely because, for the most part, the history of philosophy remains a highly constricted field of authors. By and large the modern philosophy course today remains uncannily similar to the course I took (admittedly, in a "continental-friendly" department) in the early 1980s, dominated completely by a handful of European proper names: Descartes, Hume, Kant, with a few other figures treated along the way (say, Leibnitz, Berkeley, or Spinoza—maybe even Malebranche), depending on time or interest.

Most specifically, the disciplinary problem in philosophy returns us to the problem of commentary, which is what 99 percent of us are doing when we write an article on Foucault. Indeed, as Foucault makes clear, our commentary is in fact what makes or bestows a continuing author-function on any given figure (a way of handling texts that constructs the object "worthy of commentary"); and what is philosophy as a discipline if it's not a discipline dedicated to producing commentary on "great" texts? As Foucault points out in "What Is an Author?," the death of the author has in practice added up to little more than the prolific rise of the commentator—and here he's particularly targeting Derrida and deconstruction, which on Foucault's account constitutes an attempt "to reintroduce in transcendental terms the religious principle of hidden meanings (which require interpretation) and the critical assumption of implicit significations, silent purposes, and obscure contents (which give rise to commentary)" (1479).

There are of course heartening signs of an opening up of the author-function in the recent and much-needed calls to "decolonize" philosophy as a discipline in the United States (to take it beyond its narrow focus on Euro-American philosophy, which is to say in practice, to take philosophy beyond commentary on a handful of Euro-American writers who have a strong, almost hyper-canonical author-function attached to their works). On the face of it at least, there seem two obvious ways to go about decolonizing philosophy: you can expand the author-function— as many in philosophy are calling to do—to proper names and traditions from other continents, national and geographic locations outside Europe and America, and other time periods. For example, you can run courses on ancient Chinese thought, Vedic traditions, contemporary Buddhist thinking, or Caribbean political philosophy from Toussaint Louverture to Sylvia Wynter. While this ongoing canon expansion of the author-function at the disciplinary level is a welcome shift toward more inclusiveness and rigor (can you really talk about "late C19 thought" without any attention to what "thought" looks like at a time when well over 70 percent of the people on the planet lived outside Europe and the United States?), a certain kind of Foucauldian intervention might also wonder whether simply expanding the canon—as necessary a task as that may be—may mask its own kind of colonializing move, the colonizing of Western European knowledge-producing practices onto traditions far and wide from those forms of explanation and commentary. Simply shifting the hermeneutic practices from authors x to authors y does not seem up to the task of radically rethinking the colonial practices of Western thought. Though on the other side of the coin, one can always worry about the author-function waning just as peoples from non-Western cultures get within its reach (perhaps as feminism worried over the deconstruction of the autonomous subject just as women were haltingly reaching something closer to such subjective autonomy in the larger political and social arena).[26] In any case, it seems clear that the author-function (and its discontents) will constitute one of the principle problematics going forward in attempts to decolonize philosophy as a discipline.

Though I'd note that the author-function may be under even deeper siege from new approaches that eschew author-based commentary altogether (which a decolonized philosophy may or may not end up doing). There are I think two main strands in this post- or antihermeneutic vein today, both of them most intensely represented in literary theory: the first set of approaches would follow what Rita Felski calls "postcritical reading": rather than looking behind a text for hidden causes, meanings, and motives, Felski argues that scholars should place themselves in front of it and reflect on what it suggests and makes possible.[27] Postcritical readings of this kind are no longer quite so hung up on what a text "means," and become more interested in what that text can allow us to do—what interesting lines of engagement it opens up for the reader. This type of criticism tends to downplay reading as a recovery (of the author's experience or the text's hidden meanings), and to valorize reading as opening up new destinations for thinking about x, y, or z cultural or political project (in the present, or in the historical present of the literature itself)—so, for example, the question would be less "what do these lines from *Paradise Lost* mean," and more a matter of "how do these lines from *Paradise Lost* help us to think about the relations between politics and religion (either in early modern England, or in contemporary America)?" To sum up this first "postcritical" brand of thinking, Christopher Nealon calls it moving from a "hermeneutics of suspicion" (what meanings are hidden in this text?) to a "hermeneutics of situation" (what does this text allow us to say about its sociopolitical situation, or ours?).[28]

A second, and more radically antihermeneutic brand of contemporary criticism, comes out of the so-called digital humanities (probably *the* talismanic phrase for the present), mostly answering a desire to use the tools of big data within the humanities—which has of course been resistant to such scientizing. The most famous of these projects is

Moretti's "distant reading," which eschews close reading of individual
texts altogether, and attempts to look instead at global sociological patterns surrounding the historical archive of literary production. As
Moretti puts it, "the trouble with close reading (in all of its incarnations,
from the new criticism to deconstruction) is that it necessarily depends
on an extremely small canon . . . At bottom, it's a theological exercise—
very solemn treatment of very few texts taken very seriously—whereas
what we really need is a little pact with the devil: we know how to read
texts, now let's learn how not to read them."[29] As Moretti points out,
there's a constant bait and switch on display in much literary criticism—
when for example one reads a few exemplary scenes from a Thomas
Hardy novel and then makes sweeping claims about Victorian literature. The problem is that there were tens of thousands of Victorian
novels published in England, more than any one person could possibly
read in a lifetime. This scale problem becomes much, much more pressing if you attempt to decolonize or globalize reading, and talk about the
global volume of literature produced in the C19, where the issue of what
Moretti calls "the great unread" becomes completely overwhelming.

Instead, Moretti set about harnessing Stanford's considerable com-
puting power (and its large supply of graduate student labor) to digi-
tize this great unread (the 99 percent of literature produced since
Gutenberg that hasn't become canonical—that has no author-function
attached, and no one reads anymore). Moretti runs these texts through
computer programs that "read" the literature to produce not interpretations but graphs, maps, and trees that chart the rise and fall of various genres, types of characters, literary topics, and so on: a distant or
topological reading, rather than a close or hermeneutic reading. Such
digital mapping eschews traditional reading's focus on the sentence
and embraces instead patterns and rules engrained in the language
itself. For example, instead of attempting to provide commentary on
the shifting lexical meanings of "love" in Goethe's *The Sorrows of Young
Werther*, data-driven critic Andrew Piper has pointed out that usage of
the word "love" in that text is "equivalent to 0.00109 (the percentage
of times it appears relative to all of the words in the novel)" compared
to "0.00065 in Faust (or about half as likely)."[30] Fascinating . . . or

maybe not, insofar it's not really clear what you know when you know this; and even the most guileless freshman probably could have surmised this by reading plot summaries on Wikipedia: love is likely to be paramount among the "sorrows" of a Romantic protagonist like Young Werther; while Faust's cutting a deal with the devil isn't as likely to be suffused with the language of love. But for their part, critics like Piper and Moretti have produced a wealth of graphs, maps, and charts (of everything from *Werther*-words in Goethe to maps of genre fiction— the rise and fall of the hunting novel in the C19, for example), material that begins, maybe fifty years after the fact, to finally have done with the author-function, and usher us further toward attending to what Foucault called "the order of discourse."

For most of my friends in both literature and philosophy departments, for whom close reading has for a long time been the only game in town, this antihermeneutic streak in recent theory comes as very bad news indeed. But I'm not here to suggest that the hermeneutic sky is falling, just because textual exegesis has become unmoored from the dictates of close reading or the search for "meaning," because I'm not sure that a suspicious stance toward literary or philosophical meaning is something all that new. Or at least it's not hard to see how Foucault is completely on board with favoring a hermeneutics of situation over a hermeneutics of suspicion (again, think of his life-long critique of depth and commentary). For that matter it's not much of stretch to suggest that Foucault's itinerary finds him engaged in a kind of distant reading before the fact—think of all the proper names that circulate through his books on madness, the clinic, the birth of the human sciences, and/or sexuality: Foucault displays for us less a commentary practice (revealing meaning or sense) than a kind of mapping procedure. As he writes in "What Is an Author?": "For instance, my objective in *The Order of Things* had been to analyze verbal clusters as discursive layers which fall outside the familiar categories of the book, a work, or an author" (1475). Indeed, we live in a world where textuality is exploding in unprecedented new ways: aside from all the material "authored" on Facebook, Twitter, Snapchat, Wechat, Instagram, Weibo, or TikTok, for example, there were 1.7 million self-published books released in 2018.[31] Given this textual explosion, it seems clear that mapping rather than reading will be the only way to deal with the question of authorship going forward.

In any case, while it's not entirely clear to me what a distant, or post-critical, or data-driven reading of philosophy might look like (other than taking Foucault as a template—a philosophy not dominated by commentary on a handful of proper names), these are nevertheless more arrows in the quiver of decolonizing philosophy as a discipline, of breaking up the very, very narrow canon of those bestowed with an author-function, and thinking about discursive and archival practices in a series of different, more global, ways.

What Is a Lecturer, or an Author, in the Present?

As I said at the outset, I want to wind down this chapter by thinking about the question "what is a lecturer?" in the present—maybe moving away from Foucault's texts somewhat, but I ask the question in the spirit of Foucault's commitment to thinking about "today." At the present moment in the United States, "lecturer" is the proper name for growing sector of non-tenure-line positions created by university administrators in a kind of frontal assault on tenure and faculty governance: today, more than three quarters—a staggering 76 percent—of all college classes are staffed by adjunct lecturers nationwide. A lecturer in the United States is a non-tenure-line faculty member, and as such someone who has important pillars of academic freedom withdrawn from his or her intellectual itinerary. (When you have to be reappointed each and every year, or every three years, it's hard to roll with Kant's Enlightenment imperative, "Dare to know.") But of course along with tenure, the most obvious thing subtracted from a contemporary lecturer is access to a kind of author-function: if you look at the AAUP literature on academic freedom, some of it penned by John Dewey, you'll see that said academic freedom applies only to university research, which is to say, it applies to authored and published work that pushes the boundaries of knowledge for a discipline. And this correlate of the author-function (absolute freedom to publish your findings) is precisely what is denied to lecturers—who may produce fantastic research, but are not rewarded for it, and instead strongly encouraged to concentrate on teaching endless sections of the 101 course. Lecturers are encouraged to *transmit* knowledge, not so much to *produce* it, and as such they have not only job security but academic freedom withdrawn from their job titles and responsibilities. Simply put, today a university lecturer is someone without access to an institutionally sanctioned author-function.

This is especially pressing not merely because it's exploitation pure and simple in the present, but because if the needle keeps trending the way it's going in the American humanities, within a few generations there may be nothing but lecturers—faculty without any kind of potential author-function attached to their names—and that I think paints the author-function, its potentials and pitfalls, in a somewhat different light going forward. We, for excellent reasons, may want to say good riddance to the author-function at the overarching, canon-forming, disciplinary level, but there are good reasons to want to hang onto something like the author-function at the local level of protecting tenure-line jobs in the humanities, insofar as promotion and tenure evaluations really do at some level come down to whether any given faculty member has a kind of small-a author-function attached to his or her name. These recognizable promotion-and-tenure questions (have you written a well-received book and a number of refereed articles, have other scholars cited your work, have you been invited to referee others' works, or to contribute essays for volumes?) are really questions about whether you've attained a kind of author-function, and if we give up too easily on that small-a author-function, I think with it goes both tenure and academic freedom.

At the macrolevel of the disciplines, we probably can and should learn to live without the meaning-guaranteeing author-function and the concomitant practice of academic commentary as unearthing an author's "meaning," a largely unmet provocation that Foucault challenged us to take up a half-century ago. But at the local level of teaching and research jobs, academic freedom, and the fate of tenure, I think we need to shore up—and in fact insist on—a version of the author-function, or else we risk relinquishing the very research function of the humanities, so key to Foucault and all the other authors whose lecture courses we're presently obsessed with. On that point, you might wonder, "Ok, but how do you square that circle—don't we need commentary on capital-a authors if we're to have research work to publish in order to secure our small-a author-function as tenure-line faculty?" Well, if there is an available blueprint for what it looks like to do research in the humanities that's not primarily commentary on a narrow canon of authors, in an attempt to unearth what they really mean, I can think of no better toolbox going forward than that body of scholarly provocations attached to that author-function called Michel Foucault— who, in his inaugural lecture at the Collège de France, characterized his work going forward at that august institution not as commentary or fodder for shoring up the author-function, but as a "slender wedge I intend to slip into the history of ideas," a lever or tool that "consists not in dealing with meanings possibly lying behind this or that discourse, but with discourse as regular series and distinct events."[32] Ironically, Foucault's provocation to abandon the work of commentary remains largely unheeded all these years later.

But this still leaves us to grapple with Foucault's central question in "What Is an Author?" (a question borrowed from Samuel Beckett): "What does it matter who's speaking?" My students today almost always take that as a rhetorical question—because to them, almost nothing matters *but* who's speaking, at least among the "woke" students of the biopolitical C21. Though Foucault is, in the wake of Barthes's "Death of the Author" (1967), re-posing Beckett's question in the context of an avant-gardist dream of having done with the author ("the man and his work") as an organizing principle for knowledge, or at least to wonder about unearthing buried authorial intention as a primary "mode of veridiction" for knowledge production (the utopian dream of discipline, perhaps, is to reduce the author from an animated subject to a code that could be deciphered?). As Foucault recalls in *Hermeneutics of the Subject*:

we can say that we enter the modern age (I mean, the history of truth enters its modern period) when it is assumed that what gives access to the truth, the condition for the subject's access to the truth, is knowledge (*connaissance*) and knowledge alone. . . . That is to say, it is when the philosopher (or the scientist, or simply someone who seeks the truth) can recognize the truth and have access to it in himself and solely through his activity of knowing, without anything else being demanded of him and without him having to change or alter his being as a subject.[33]

This disciplinary "modern age" of knowledge doesn't appeal to the authenticity of the author's experience, and in fact it only requires the author's name for editorial reasons as an umbrella under which to organize the work. In principle, within the disciplinary game of knowledge, the work should stand for itself (even though Foucault worries over the status of the "work" of an author as a replacement for the person and her deeply interior inspiration) and not require grounding in the life story of the individual who conceived or wrote it.

However, once we come out the other side of the biopolitical world that Foucault limns out for us a decade after "What Is an Author?" in his late lectures (and forty years later that biopolitical world has in fact arrived as a full-blown cultural dominant), such an "objectivist" disciplinary sense of knowledge, or what's left of it, has gradually given way to other modes of veridiction that find their ultimate warrant in the lived experience of the agent. In short, in the world of biopolitical performativity, the author (as an individual who possesses a trove of experiences that bolster the validity of her works) is back, at least in some sectors of the humanist knowledge-production machine; but that postdisciplinary or biopolitical sense of the author functions not so much in terms of literary profundity or disciplinary greatness (in short, not so much as the depth of infinite meaning) but in terms of the value of a life-knowledge, rendered in its own terms or in its #OwnVoices—for example, a life specifically gendered, raced, classed, disabled, aged, and so on.

Knowledge, in order to count as such in the biopolitically performative present, must in many sectors of humanities inquiry also be tied to a specific body, and not merely to the general norms of disciplinary thinking. This discipline versus biopower split, for example, helps to explain the disconnect—some would call it a war—today in the discipline of philosophy around gender and trans identities. Without attempting to adjudicate this very volatile issue, I would simply note that the two sides are talking past each other when it comes to "modes of veridiction": in short, the "gender critical feminists," as Kathleen Stock puts it, question whether trans women "qualify" to be women—in her words, Stock wonders "whether self-declaration alone could reasonably be the only criterion of being trans."[34] These gender-critical (or "trans-exclusionary," as they're also known) folks inhabit a still-disciplinary world, where topics like gender need to be debated and validated institutionally around their constative truth-value. In sharp contrast, most trans scholars and activists live in a decidedly biopolitical universe, where questions of identity and recognition are simultaneously questions of life and death, and those life-concerns are far more important than questions of disciplinary mastery or sanction (which can easily be indexed at the end of the day to a kind of white institutional privilege—counting the numbers of "prestige" books and articles on someone's CV while downplaying or ignoring the lived experiences of marginalized groups).

This debate, of course, takes place far outside of what young people call my biopolitical or performative "lane" (as a cisgender heterosexual white guy who's a named professor at a research university), and I realize I run a risk of merely reducing this nuanced field of lived experiences and exclusions to a philosophical example within my developing argument about discipline and biopower. But in the hopes of maybe taking this disagreement someplace else, beyond the name-calling, I'm merely pointing out that this battle is subtended by vastly different modes of veridiction for sex and gender identities: one is disciplinary (we should be able to debate the "validity" of these topics within accepted institutional norms and categories) while the other is biopolitical (the trans "issue" can't be "debated" because someone's very life is on the line, and the outcome of the debate might well eradicate the very biopolitical legitimacy of the other person engaged in this supposedly objective disciplinary exercise).

One could point out a similar disconnect in modes of veridiction surrounding the anti–Wall Street protests in Zuccotti Park several years ago. Several prominent theorists—among them Žižek—at first criticized the protestors for having no concrete lists of concrete demands or policies that they wanted to see implemented. Occupy Wall Street was unrecognizable as a protest movement without such specific demands, or so it would seem if you have a disciplinary, proceduralist understanding of protest movements. But as the organizers and participants said time after time, they were calling for a different way of life, and were directly protesting the (capitalist) mode of life itself. Theirs was, in short, a biopolitical protest, not a disciplinary one of incrementally adjusted normativity. Similarly, the Black Lives Matter movement decisively leads with its uncompromising commitments to honoring Black lives and identities and calling for a complete transformation of American society.

In a biopolitical sense, then, it makes all the difference in the world who's speaking, insofar as our contemporary modes of veridiction hold that knowledge can no longer speak for itself, or no longer speaks in the voice of noninterested, normative disciplinary authority: biopolitically, knowledge necessarily speaks for and from a life (which, after the performativity of all things, could be the life of anything, not just humans). This contemporary biopolitical linkage of life and truth does not, it seems to me, suggest that we've finally or fully recovered the lost, ancient world of parrhesia as the dangerous life of truth-telling; today's modes of veridiction are quite different from Foucault's study of ancient parrhesia, insofar as Foucault constantly reminds us that we cannot simply import yesterday into today.

One can always decry this new biopolitical performativity as neoliberal, utopian, mere identity politics, or the coddling of the American mind, as many critics nostalgic for disciplinary norms routinely do;[35] but in a Foucaultian sense what you see here is neither the wholesale abandonment of norms nor a return to ancient modes of truth telling, but a decisively changed relation between what counts as "knowledge" and its "mode of veridiction." The triumph of biopolitics forges a new knowledge connection between an author and value, and I think goes a long way to explaining why philosophy (or at least continental philosophy) remains stubbornly attached to a series of recognizable names:

those proper names still carry a great deal of disciplinary importance, in a world where doing philosophy for many teachers and students will still primarily entail being familiar with the canon of "great" thinkers. But even in a thoroughly biopolitical world, those canonical figures continue to have currency—both among those stubbornly hanging on to a disciplinary understanding of philosophy and even among those who have a biopolitical view of the project—precisely because canonical philosophers have a mode of veridiction (an author-function) attached to them that intensifies in the transition from disciplinary knowledge to biopolitical knowledge: hence, in a biopolitical sense, it's less a question of producing endless commentary on the meaning of Foucault's lectures, but rather looking at how Foucault may help us to treat certain problems concerning life—Foucault and the university, Foucault and health care policy, Foucault and animal studies, Foucault and climate change, and so on.

In the end, I'm hoping that revisiting Foucault's 1969 provocation, specifically in terms of his later lecture courses, helps us to see some things more clearly about the life of research and teaching in the humanities today, without simply shoehorning his arguments into a snug fit with the present. The author-function at present remains quite literal in scientific discourse: Einstein is not a guarantor of enduring value that enables endless interpretations of his work (as Shakespeare perhaps remains for English departments) but a set of testable hypotheses (turns out Einstein was right about black holes!). And once figures like Newton and Galileo have been proven incorrect in their hypotheses about the world, they're largely defunctioned within the disciplinary logic of physics. The scientific author, in the modern period, is not fodder for commentary or meaning, but the name for understanding or resolving a series of problematics: the ways that a scientist's work rebounds on questions of "life" (intervening among problems like climate change, health care, politics, cell biology) becomes more important than what the scientist's work "means." This is where Foucault's 1969 provocations concerning the author are on the same page as his late work on philosophy and its connections to biopolitical questions of life: philosophy going forward is not primarily a hermeneutic discipline, dedicated to unearthing textual "meaning" in either its teaching or research formats. Which is why "What Is an Author?" is worth revisiting more than fifty years after Foucault's initial provocation to have done with the work of unearthing meaning through textual commentary: to help us in the humanities to move on with various social "problematics" as organizing grids for humanities teaching and research.

6

Literary RealFeel

Banality, Fatality, and Meaning in Kenneth Goldsmith's The Weather

Right now it is twelve degrees, mostly sunny in Central
Park, northwest wind at eleven, that makes the RealFeel
temperature zero.

—KENNETH GOLDSMITH, *The Weather*

I've deliberately saved what's maybe the thorniest question for last:
what's the fate of literature in the biopolitical Bodacious era, where
everything is in a state of performative intra-action all the time? Certainly, contemporary literature is much more patient than, for example, the excessive rush of superfast and -loud images you see in what
Steven Shaviro calls "post-cinematic cinema,"[1] such as *The Fast and the
Furious* franchise or any given Marvel superhero flick. These are movies that largely dispense with cinematic plot development or narration,
and are instead characterized by a loosely related collection of over-the-
top, totally bodacious action sequences. As I note in chapter 3, literature
in the modern and postmodern era has dedicated itself to producing
some version of that overflowing affect or charge of the new, brought
on by sustained attention to textual detail within the context of everyday
experience. In short, at least since the English Romantics and American
Transcendentalists, literature has aspired to its own brand of the Bodacious. But once capitalism catches up—and surpasses—that project of
re-injecting everyday experience with an intense, startling originality

(seeing the everyday anew), then whither the project of literature? If
literature through its modern and postmodern periods was dedicated
to a subversion and reinvention of quotidian biopolitical experience,
then does post-postmodern literature maybe have to dedicate itself to
something else? That will be my question in this chapter: what newer,
resistant roles might literature—specifically the seemingly marginal
formation of contemporary experimental poetry—play in the Bodacious era?

Though it's probably worth wondering about the question of poetry
here at the outset: why take as your topic what is surely the most marginal form of contemporary (American) writing? Of the "New York
Times 100 Notable Books for 2018," for example, only three were poetry
volumes—one penned by the year's poet laureate of the United States
(Tracy K. Smith), one by the director of the New York Public Library's
Schomberg Center for Research in Black Culture (Kevin Young), and
one by Homer (*The Odyssey,* in a new translation by Emily Wilson). The
category of "fiction" (among a series of genres like nonfiction, essays,
history, sports, biography, current events, and the like) for the year boasts
a collection of forty-eight notable books (one of them, oddly enough, is
The Odyssey, in a new translation by Emily Wilson, so we really are down
to two poetry volumes for 2018). The 2019 list showed about the same
ratio—three poetry volumes and forty-seven works of fiction. All of this
of course suggesting that there's much, much more "notable" fiction
than poetry being produced today, and that overall only 2–3 percent of
noteworthy titles published in 2018 and 2019 can be classified as contemporary poetry (and 100 percent of those poetry titles in 2018, it
turns out, were penned by African Americans). So it seems we live in
a golden era for African American poetry (which I actually think is true);
but on the whole, it's fair to surmise that poetry as a cultural form is
not seen as much of a significant driver when it comes to assessing the
wider, more "notable" literary world. Poetry enjoys polling numbers
akin to those tallied for John Hickenlooper's Democratic 2020 presi-
dential bid on the day I write this sentence (in late July 2019).

And if fiction, or more narrowly the novel, rules the roost at the
popular end of the literary spectrum in places like the *New York Times,*

it's worth noting that fiction enjoys similarly hegemonic prestige and saturation within recent academic literary criticism and theory—much of which has come to equate "fiction" or "the novel" with "literature" itself: for example, Amy Hungerford's influential *Making Literature Now* concerns itself exclusively with fiction writers; Mark McGurl's history of creative writing's rise in the university, *The Program Era,* also looks solely at fiction (subtitle: *Postwar Fiction and the Rise of Creative Writing*). In either case, "literature" or "creative writing" each respectively becomes synonymous with "fiction." For my narrowcast purposes in this book, however, fiction is by far the least interesting literary genre, insofar as the novel as a form boasts the least obvious or necessary connection with the extralinguistic performative forces of illocution, the through line that connects up the disparate threads of this book on the biopolitical fate of the performative. In contrast to narrative fiction, both drama and poetry have long drunk deeply from the spring of extralinguistic performativity, the deployment of illocutionary force experienced in the performance of a play or at a poetry reading, an immaterial force deployed among the words but not reducible to a drama concerning their "meaning." It's settled law that "A poem should not mean / But be,"[2] whereas the novel, on the other hand, seems completely beholden to the unfolding narrative time of solitary reading, which depends decisively on the question of sorting out linguistic "meaning," in the first and last instance.

Why the novel matters going forward as a linchpin cultural form, or why it matters so decisively and uniquely in recent criticism, remains a bit of a mystery to me, because I see narrative fiction not as the future of literature after the linguistic turn but far rather as an anachronistic form leftover from that era. Which is to say in a cryptic shorthand that I see the novel as completely beholden to the linguistic question of figuring out (or frustrating) meaning, and I simply don't see that question as a driver of much emergent cultural significance in the present—though of course the novel's traditional functions, keeping alive the temporality and immersive attention of reading, as well as the empathy effects of seeing the world from other perspectives, obviously remain important functions of narrative fiction. But these novelistic functions are, on Raymond Williams's terms, residual rather than emergent artistic affects and effects. And as the rise of long-form "binge-watching" television attests, the novel is no longer the primary owner—and far from the most intensive affective purveyor—of narrative empathy or *longue-durée* attention as artistic endeavors.

And while Hungerford would undoubtedly disagree with my somewhat dismissive critique of fiction in the present, or might agree but suggest that close reading does not make a network of fiction producers and consumers, she does decisively suggest that things are changing in the world of writing fiction. She argues, in her lauding of various writing "scenes" (the McSweeney's crowd in San Francisco, for example), that "making literature now" has moved away from the modernist or postmodernist drama wherein a solitary genius tries to innovate his or her way out of a cloistered drawing room into a cutting-edge global book market—on the figure most intensely of David Foster Wallace, whom Hungerford argues we should not-read, largely because of his misogyny. Rather, Hungerford suggests that, going forward from now, writing has become a kind of local cottage enterprise, one that tends to be situated in a particular place, scene, and aesthetic.

As she writes about Dave Eggers and his involvement with various McSweeney's projects, thinking about any given book's meaning tends to make us "misunderstand the ways that buying books—or more generally, reading—is related to the social scenes from which Eggers's various ventures arise and to which they often seem to return."[3] Though of course some writers (like Eggers) within any particular scene will have a chance of becoming more widely known, much of making literature going forward, Hungerford suggests but doesn't come right out and say, will be somewhat akin to being a popular musician: there's a scene that your band grows out of, a local vibe that conditions your initial sound or style, and at first you have local fans, play local gigs. If you're a local-scene musician, you of course have some chance of going viral (or going national or producing a megahit song), but the vast majority of solo performers or people in bands will never be able to quit their day jobs and make a living playing music. So, Hungerford suggests between the lines, it will likely go with writing fiction—not a matter of national or international fame and fortune, but a local ethics of care and recognition: "In McSweeney's publications and its reader networks[,] love and friendship is the affective tenor of the interpersonal links that McSweeney's calls into being."[4]

As provocative as Hungerford's analysis proves, in addition to my skepticism about the novel being a producer of much widespread cultural significance going forward, or at least any moreso than fiction or drama, I likewise don't see the novel as a particularly promising niche-market, "scene-produced" literary form—insofar as either writing fiction or reading it remains largely a solitary exercise that takes place within language and the narrative time of unfolding meaning in an internalized, solitary reading or writing practice. The novel has a performative dimension, to be sure, but that dimension takes place largely on the level of a plot's unfolding in language, a narrative line that is gradually revealed by a highly individualized reading practice—it's just me and the novel, on the bus or in the easy chair at home. And while the picture of "novelist as solitary genius" is undoubtedly a holdover that requires demystification, even today we still don't tend to think of the great novelists as having been produced by a school of writing or an artistic scene: from what school would James Joyce or Toni Morrison have arisen?

On the other hand, C20 American poetry remains to this day routinely understood, written about, and taught as a series of just such schools or scenes—the Imagist Pound Era, the Harlem Renaissance, the Objectivists, the Confessional Poets in the Lowell lineage, the Beats, the New York School (part 1 of O'Hara and Ashbery and part 2 of Ted Berrigan and Bernadette Mayer), the San Francisco Renaissance, the Black Mountain writers, the Black Arts movement, "Language" poetry, Nuyorican poetry, Conceptual Writing, and so on. As McGurl points out, there's maybe a school of minimalist short fiction that grows out of Raymond Carver's writing, but it would be hard indeed to pinpoint much beyond that as a "scene" in the canon of C20 modernist and postmodernist fiction. There are of course myriad after-the-fact categories and imposed distinctions that we teach by—the modernist split between Hemingway's minimalism and Faulkner's maximalism (reworked for the postmodernism course as the DeLillo–Pynchon divide); the Black postmodernist grouping of Ishmael Reed, Morrison, Amiri Baraka, or Toni Cade Bambara; Latin American Magical Realism; and so on—but we tend not to understand these movements as having been generated by people consciously aware of honing a movement or sharing the concerns of a particular local scene, in contrast to the way that O'Hara and Ashbery were united in foregrounding an ironic attention to the everyday in New York School poetics, or Language poetry's deliberate imbrication of fractured verse with contemporary literary and cultural theory.

If nothing else, folks like Ashbery and O'Hara are going to the same poetry readings, bars, and art openings in and around New York—in short, they're participating in the same scene, as are many of the Black Arts, San Francisco Renaissance, Beat or Black Mountain poets. Fiction writers like DeLillo and Pynchon, as far as we know, not so much. Indeed, many of the lesser-lauded middlebrow fiction writers from the C20, for example Dorothy Parker or Norman Mailer, are well-known largely as scenesters, but that's one of the primary reasons that academic critics have not taken their fiction seriously—because their work is *not* seen as a sui generis product of lone artistic genius. Or just consider the inordinate amount of time that today's Program Era academic fiction writers spend distancing themselves from the workshop aesthetic, and we I think can see where this lone wolf theory of authorship continues to be hegemonic, despite Hungerford's best efforts to dislodge it going forward.

In any case, however narratively driven any given poem or play might be, poetry's and drama's preferred (though by no means exclusive) delivery systems—which is to say, the performed play or the poetry reading—depend crucially on a kind of performative context and "scene" (the local in-crowd at the bookstore, the theater, the bar) in a way that fiction does not. So it seems odd to suggest, if "scenes" are what "making literature now" is all about, that we pay absolutely no attention to poetry or drama (the collectivity of poetry reading or community theatre production anyone?). Even long-form narrative television is, on the face of it, a collective enterprise—the screen is crowded with actors, the shots composed by armies of technicians, online fan sites allow hardcores to swap theories, and so on. It may well be that fiction writing is becoming more like contemporary poetry or other scene-driven artforms in this way, as Hungerford argues; but it seems to me if that's the case, then historically speaking American poetry, rather than fiction, should be the template discourse for "making literature now."

In fact, poet David Antin made such a project (quite literally making literature in and of the now, literature as a series of actions rather than as a consumable product) into his life's work: not reading or writing finished poems to be consumed, but giving improvised "talks" to live, responding audiences—talks that would later be published in lines, as talk-poems: Antin's whole itinerary for his poetry corresponds quite closely to what Hungerford wants to claim for fiction today, the care and maintenance of lively writing scenes rather than a focus on finished works being read by strangers in isolation. For his part, Antin sums up his aesthetics like this: "theres a situation and you respond to it": "even if i write i dont come to read / i come to talk." As Antin expands on his method for making literature in the now:

> when
> i went somewhere i wanted to make things happen because
> it seemed to me that the art of poetry was the act of making
> poetry not distributing it[5]

In short, there are several available ready-to-hand models for what a scene-based (rather than lone genius–based) concept of making literature looked like in C20 American poetry (in addition to Antin, Jack Spicer's commitment to the local would be the other obvious poetics to examine); but somehow today fiction remains completely hegemonic in our discussions of literary production, virtually synonymous with literature itself, both in the writing outlets and in literary criticism.

Part of fiction's hegemony in literary critical discourse is, I think, to be found in the continuing belief in fiction's cultural impact (the sense that nobody reads poetry and very few people attend plays, especially new ones, whereas novels sell briskly and are widely read, and thereby function as an important and widespread cultural bellwether or influencer). While it's demographically true that more people read fiction than poetry, in the end I think this idea of fiction's cultural relevance is magical thinking. Contemporary fiction is less akin to popular music, as Hungerford's analogy about local scenes might suggest, than it is like classical music—a nostalgia form for the well-educated (which is already, truth be told, how drama or poetry function in the present). Perhaps my only point in this long-winded introduction is that, in a new materialist world of immaterial flows of force, it's not fiction but poetry or drama that hold out the possibility of emergent, transformative literary force going forward—precisely because drama and poetry scenes (both in terms of production and reception) are more local, collective, and performative than fiction's will ever be.[6]

Following out the spirit (though not the letter) of Hungerford's provocation to think about literature through looking at particular scenes, I'll concentrate on the poetry circuits that I've been most familiar with—largely the experimental poetry world in New York City and Washington, D.C., in the 1990s (centered mostly around the Ear Inn and St. Mark's in NYC, and Bridge Street Books in D.C.) and beyond. Most specifically I'm interested in the "conceptual turn" that has taken place in recent experimental poetry, which eschews the bodacious excesses of overflowing expression and the transgressive fragmentation of language, and turns instead to copying out or collaging existing materials. Most people find conceptual writing tedious, but that's exactly where I want to locate a strange potential literary power in this project—locating its "against the day" potential in the fact that it's about the farthest thing from bodacious you can find. It's almost completely banal.

The Fatality of Banality

There's nothing more banal than the weather. In fact, the weather often functions as a privileged figure for banality itself, the lingua franca of everyday phatic speech. The weather constitutes a pervasive, nearly contentless discourse that we can all safely engage—connecting with others on a superficial level, without running the risk of offending anyone. "Nice day. Looks like rain. Hot enough for you?"

In her classic essay "Banality in Cultural Studies," Meaghan Morris argues that much of the news industry works to ping-pong its consumers between the binary poles of banality and fatality—between comforting repetition of the obvious and wild speculations about impending disaster. As one of her primary examples of this banality/fatality coupling, Morris not surprisingly has recourse to the weather. She recounts an anecdote from her youth when communication was lost, for the better part of a day, with the news bureaus of Darwin in her native Australia. Of course, everyone expected (and hyped) the worst: a disaster, man-made or natural, had stricken the outpost city. The banality of communication lines being down gets instantly translated into the fatality of Armageddon; as Morris recounts, "people panicked, and waited anxiously for details."[7]

Morris here lays out a dialectic that's familiar to anyone who's ever watched the Weather Channel: sharply dressed men and women stand calmly in front of brightly colored maps, pointing out movements and temperatures, completely in control. Then comes the abrupt shift to the live report from an announcer in a drenched slicker, standing in a driving hurricane-force rain on the beach; or a brave correspondent sporting a parka, standing in hip-deep snow, watching cars slide out of control in some Midwestern city. These reporters inform viewers of the severe danger of the situation, urging them to stay inside and stay tuned for updates: which is to say, please enjoy the fatality of this situation through the banality of television coverage. And this banality/fatality rollercoaster is likewise the upshot of Morris's anecdote about the city of Darwin. When it's finally established that the entire town wasn't nuked or invaded, but that "Darwin had merely been wiped out by a cyclone," the normal news cycle can continue: "We went into the 'natural disaster' genre of TV living, and banality, except for the victims, resumed" (122).

Morris's ultimate prey in her essay, however, is not so much uncovering the banality/fatality dialectic at work in the culture industry (the imperative to keep the customers scared, then soothed, so they keep watching) but uncovering the work that banality and its secret partner fatality perform in the discourse dedicated to critical unmasking of the culture industry, cultural studies itself. As Morris points out, cultural studies scholars often find themselves in the uncomfortable structural position of the TV weatherperson, standing before the colorful banality of grocery shopping, NASCAR races, or Cineplex films, calmly breaking them down; and then explaining in some breathless way why these formations are important—why we should pay attention, stay tuned, and worry over these cultural formations as if they were an incoming tornado. In short, Morris argues (quite persuasively), that while cultural studies pretends to be enamored of the banal "everyday" (advertising, pop music, cookbooks), at the end of the day cultural studies tends inexorably to transmute that banality into a kind of fatality, something with a hidden (and usually sinister) cultural "meaning."

Morris uses Jean Baudrillard's work as an example of the premises behind such work, wherein a feminized "banality is associated, quite clearly and conventionally, with negative aspects of media—overrepresentation, excessive visibility, information overload, an obscene plenitude of images, a gross platitudinousness of the all-pervasive present" (124–25); and Baudrillard thereby functions as a metonym for the familiar movement in countless cultural studies essays wherein a banal everyday practice—answering email or walking the dog—is injected with "meaning": wherein the banal is baptized in the waters of a compelling fatality. "Baudrillard's theory merely calls for an aesthetic order (fatality) to deal with mass cultural anarchy (banality)," as Morris puts it (125). She points out that the terrain of cultural studies research on the practices of everyday life is populated by scholars who are ironically circumventing the study of the everyday precisely by inventing or celebrating any given banal practice's secret, hidden, fatal side. Which in turn leads to the familiar picture of cultural studies as "a field of study which—surprisingly, since 'everyday life' is at issue—often seems to be occupied only by cheerleaders and prophets of doom" (130). We've all read articles like those Morris alludes to here, those that crisscross their reader between boosterish optimism and impending doom. The internet: does it portend a sunny, revolutionary rhizome of democracy-to-come? Or is the internet the final closing of the iron cage of panoptic surveillance? But of course, if one really wanted to treat the internet as a series of everyday practices, it would seem more likely that such articles should have titles like, "The Internet: A Place to Buy Stuff, Find Directions to Poughkeepsie, or Look at Naked People?"

Morris's essay, in the end, is not so much a denunciation of the banality/fatality dialectic in popular culture as it is an exploration of how cultural studies partakes of and extends this very same cultural logic: biking in the city and listening to the songs of Shania Twain aren't interesting practices because they're banal and everyday but because they contain a secret. Being a fan of *Star Trek* is, it turns out, not banal at all, but is in fact secretly fatal to the banality of existing order. All of which is to suggest that cultural studies can remain, on Morris's reading, still too hung up on what everyday practices "mean"—an almost-complete emphasis on their fatal significance, as opposed to an exploration of their banal ubiquity as a series of useful cultural practices.[8] As Morris insists, following Michel Foucault, practices themselves don't "mean," but rather they function—they produce effects (which may or may not in turn "mean" something). Oddly, though, the banality of everyday practices themselves—studying the "how" of practices as practices, outside of "what" they supposedly signify—remains a kind of ungrasped and seemingly even tarnished brass ring for academic work on literature and culture, decades after Morris's provocation to take banality seriously. If Kant's provocation for the Enlightenment was the bodacious "Dare to know," perhaps the unmet performative challenge today remains "Dare to be banal."

Banality without Fatality: Kenneth Goldsmith

By his own admission, there's nothing more banal than Kenneth Goldsmith's work. As he writes, "I am the most boring writer that has ever lived. If there were an Olympic sport for extreme boredom, I would get a gold medal. My books are impossible to read straight through. In fact, every time I have to proofread them before sending them off to the publisher, I fall asleep repeatedly."[9] Goldsmith is associated with a loose amalgam of contemporary poets who produce what they call "conceptual poetry," and Goldsmith's work is in turn paradigmatic of this movement.[10] Goldsmith doesn't so much create (in the sense of inventing new forms or expressing anything in particular) as he does transcribe, quite literally: "Over the past ten years," he writes, "my practice has boiled down to simply retyping existing texts."[11]

For example, Goldsmith's magnum opus American trilogy, *The Weather* (2005), *Sports* (2008), and *Traffic* (2007), consists of straight transcriptions of daily New York radio weather reports (a year), a baseball game (every word of a single Yankee game radio broadcast), and traffic reports (a full day of traffic reports, "on the 1s").[12] He's also published works that consist of retyping every single word in the *New York Times* for a day (which becomes the 900-page book *Day*), every movement made by the author over a thirteen-hour period (*Fidget*), every utterance for a week (*Soliloquy*), and what is to my mind his masterpiece, *Head Citations,* a list of more than eight hundred slightly misheard popular song lyrics (like "Killing me softly with Islam" or "This is clown control to Mao-Tse-Tung"). For those with an even more musical bent, he has a series titled "Singing Theory," which consists of MP3 sound files where Goldsmith sings classic theory essays (belting out Fredric Jameson accompanied by John Coltrane, for example, or Roland Barthes sung to the tune of an Allman Brothers song).[13] Goldsmith remains most (in)famous for his (completely inappropriate) reading from the autopsy of Michael Brown, the unarmed African American teenager gunned down by Missouri police in 2014, at a poetry event shortly after that tragedy.

The point of all this repetition, you ask? Goldsmith thematizes his writing practice like this:

> In 1969, the conceptual artist Douglas Huebler wrote, "The world is full of objects, more or less interesting; I do not wish to add any more." I've come to embrace Huebler's ideas, though it might be retooled as, "The world is full of texts, more or less interesting; I do not wish to add any more." It seems an appropriate response to a new condition in writing today: faced with an unprecedented amount of available text, the problem is not needing to write more of it; instead, we must learn to negotiate the vast quantity that exists. I've transformed from a writer into an information manager, adept at the skills of replicating, organizing,

mirroring, archiving, hoarding, storing, reprinting, bootlegging, plundering, and transferring.[14]

Goldsmith's poetics puts him squarely within the everyday of the internet age—what does "expressing yourself" look like when a searchable database of nearly everything ever written is easily within reach of anyone with an internet connection? If postmodernism played to endgame the thematics of innovation born in modernism (can you really "make it newer" in the C21?), then the problems of writing shift to negotiating, through the vast archive of ubiquitously available information, the creative powers that might be chemically released by combining or juxtaposing preexisting language practices, rather than hoping through force of individual will or genius to add something novel to that archive. As Goldsmith puts it succinctly, referring both to the conceptual poetry he's aligned with and Flarf, a rival but related movement dedicated to writing poems through internet searches: "With so much available language, does anyone really need to write more? Instead, let's just process what exists. Language as matter; language as material."[15]

When pressed to explain further, Goldsmith likes to quote Brion Gysin's mid-C20 observation that writing is fifty years behind painting, and certainly his project owes much to the cut-up, as well as the antisubjectivist collage and splatter methods of modernist visual art: what do sculptors do but take blocks of given material and carve something out of them? What does Jackson Pollock foreground but the basic practices of painting—movement and oil paint, that's all there is. Ditto someone like Mark Rothko, using color and shape not so much in the service of inventing anything new in terms of what art "is" or "represents," but inventing new questions, juxtapositions, modes of provocation (which is, of course, what conceptual and performance art has *become*: a series of discourses and practices as much as it is a series of discreet objects). Likewise, the early C20 conundrums that forced painting into the abstract expressionist and then pop art realms (which is to say, the economic and technological truism that photography had by that point completely taken over figuration) have for a long time now hung over literature as well, even moreso poetry: if advertising and the

greeting card industry have completely territorialized short, pithy expressions of "authentic" sentiment, showing us how to re-enchant even
the most mundane corners of everyday life (everything's an opportunity for self-actualization, even doing the laundry, succeeding at your
job, or driving your car), then what's left for poetry to do in the contemporary world?

For the avant-garde of mid- to late-C20 American poetry (from the
Black Mountain poets and Beats of the 1950s through the Language
Poets in the '80s and '90s), the job of poetics in a world of commodified subjective experience was to attack or avoid the whole banal world
of easily assured "meaning" in language usage, and in the process to
reinvent or reemphasize alternative uses for poetry—for intense language usage—that had long since been forgotten as the lyric became
the safe repository for our belief in authentic, "true feelings" or affects.
Take, as an example of that kind of deconstructive work, the poetry of
Bruce Andrews, whose composition method consists of writing down
phrases and sentences on small rectangles of paper, and editing them
together into discontinuous onslaughts of phrasing.[16] The result looks
something like this, a more or less randomly chosen chunk from the
opening section of his 1992 *I Don't Have Any Paper So Shut Up:*

> Brandish something clean—there is no more reason to limit
> ourselves to the customary rhetorical confinement. White
> commission, piss shall triumph.
>
> Get busy looking at immaculate doves; I *couldn't* stab
> myself . . . you want subgum?—fuck your kitchen. Gandhi
> becomes handsome cholo. I hate scenes.
>
> And palpitating! Candle suckers, don't react to the given.
> Dignity for resale ankle be sister farm fear swallows the
> unwary unison feeble heard such me mug
> sauce plenitude preservatives; spores,
> variable halvah. Thinking about genocide all the time make
> me hopeful. Catholics fly to the lips & smoke out the sting,

you can poop my duck, mastery of craft; turquoise makes the I
dumb stick. Buckets of chicken urine in the blue gauzy non-urban
    sounds
apocryphal. Brood of drum majors to cause their trouble.
Once bread got that staff of life crap attached to it, it became
Inedible. Wasn't it Solzhenitsyn that pardoned Patty Hearst?[17]

In Andrews's machine-gun style of poetry, it's as if the entirety of
poetic meter wants to be reduced to nothing but stressed syllables.
And literature is thereby reduced by Andrews, like a watery sauce is
reduced, to its strongest version: not the job of meaning or edification
("Get busy looking at immaculate doves") or even the job of pleasure
("there is no more reason to limit ourselves to customary rhetorical
confinement") but the austere task of relentless provocation: "fuck
your kitchen."

Literature gets repurposed in Andrews's work precisely because of
its too-easy links to the sacred trace of lost or future meaning: "Once
bread got that staff of life crap attached to it, it became / Inedible."
Of course, there's certainly a certain kind of "interruption" of meaning
here, parataxis in its perhaps strongest form, but the focus is not so
much on deforming wholeness (where would totalization rest in the
force-field that is this page?) but obsessively on production of all kinds,
all the myriad productive powers of language: reflexive or "critical" statements, nonsense, insults, porn lingo, slightly changed "adbuster" style
slogans, hate speech, bureaucratic discourse, religious mantras, news
headlines, therapy tropes, and so forth. Andrews speeds up language
as series of practices, rather than primarily slowing it down and territo-
rializing it on one function, language's meaning (or lack thereof). It's
the confrontation of performative or inventive force that you see on
every line; in every "gap" there's not meaning waiting to burst forth
(or not), but a kind of hinge, linkage, movement, intensification—
what Andrews calls "torque." And this torque returns to poetry a series
of other jobs, the functions it had years, even centuries, before poetics
became linked inexorably to the question of meaning and its discontents: here, we see poetry function as discourse that's ceremonial,

aggressive, passive, communal, seductive, repulsive, humorous, meditative, persuasive, insulting, praising, performative, and lots more. But one thing it doesn't do—or even really attempt—is to "mean" something on the sentence or stanza level. What you get in Andrews's texts is a kind of massive overcoding operation or a schizoid dialectic: language from myriad cultural places, forms, and practices, mishmashed all at once. Reading then becomes less a hermeneutic operation than the kind of performance that Andrews sometimes does with dancers and musician improvisers—they respond to his words with their own riffs, do their own "readings" of these provocations as bodily and sound gestures, movements, translations.

For all its radicality, though (and Andrews is the kind of guy who can clear a room of "poetry" lovers pretty quick), Andrews's work does continue to participate obliquely in Morris's "banality/fatality" dialectic. Andrews takes the banality of everyday speech and overcodes it, torques it, with a certain kind of fatal attraction. Though the poetry itself may not be interested in "meaning," the overcoding practice of the poetry itself is highly charged with meaning—attempting to show the violent fatality buried not too far below the surface of everyday, banal speech. Or more simply, think of the distinction between Andrews and Goldsmith this way: love it or hate it, Andrews's work is designed to be nearly impossible to ignore, and is thereby a far cry from Goldsmith's endgame of deliberately being boring or banal.

Goldsmith's project is certainly related to the avant-gardist project of something like Language poetry—but goes in a slightly different direction: As Goldsmith writes about work like Andrews's, "Language Poetry has fulfilled the trajectory of modernist writing and as such, has succeeding in pulverizing syntax and meaning into a handful of dust. At this point in time, to grind the sand any finer would be futile."[18] For Goldsmith, the critique (if there is to be one) is not to be found so much within the work but in what might come after it—the discourses, acts, and further appropriations that surround, circumscribe, and respond to the work. As Goldsmith continues, "The simple act of moving information from one place to another today constitutes a significant cultural act in and of itself."[19] This post-postmodern (what else could you call it?) project constitutes a decisive turn away from the linguistic turn of resistant, infinite "meaning," and returns a different kind of density (a new set of everyday concerns concerning how one manages language overload) to the complexities of contemporary language use. If everyone's a poet in this sense, it's not because everyone has to find meaning in her life, or to look outside into the world to create or free that meaning, but because everyone must sculpt his linguistic identity out of a vast sea of available, iterable texts and practices.

This anti-originalist performativity was the project or home terrain of postmodernism and deconstruction as well, although it's hard to imagine either of those discourses working without some sense of linguistic "meaning," if only negatively. In that sense, the practice of Goldsmith's conceptual writing is less "other than postmodern" (wholly foreign to it or simply beyond it) than it is post-postmodern: intensifying certain strains within postmodernism in order to render it not so much a "new" postmodernism, but a kind of intense, hyper-postmodernism of positive usage. The performance of poetry sparks other types of performance, provokes other practices of response, rather than primarily calling for contemplation or understanding of the poem's content, or the truisms contained therein. This sentiment is, of course, as old as the hills—or, in New American poetic terms, at least as old as Jack Spicer's 1959 pronouncement, "No / One listens to poetry":[20] which is to say, *no one* listens to poetry—harkens after or obeys its hidden truths. No, one *listens* to poetry—responds to it in some way.

Of course, an antihermeneutic strain runs directly through the mainstream of modern and postmodern poetics, from Ezra Pound's 1914 thoughts about his own "In a Station of the Metro" ("I dare say it is meaningless unless one has drifted into a certain vein of thought") right up through Susan Sontag's "Against Interpretation," all the way to Deleuze and Guattari's indictment of "interpretosis" and the work of Hans Ulrich Gumbrecht.[21] Even thinkers within the tradition of hermeneutics will quibble with interpretation: for example, Martin Heidegger's "The Origin of the Work of Art" insists that a certain kind of interpretation "does not lay hold of the thing as it is in its own being, but makes an assault upon" the artwork.[22] In general, this critique of interpretation is of a piece with the pervasive modernist questioning of instrumental rationality, wherein a crude "this-means-that" style of criticism reduces an individual artwork's complexity (its "being") by too hastily translating the messy, overflowing encounter with an artwork into a neat, general, or universal example of some "higher" meaning or content—a philosophical idea, a social issue, an identity position, and so on. As Sontag puts it, "Interpretation, based on the highly dubious theory that a work of art is composed in terms of content, violates art. It makes art into an article for use."[23] Though we could of course note that this kind of "interpretation 2.0" was already under construction in Heidegger, and his sense that any technological or "ontic" use of language is already based on (forgetting) a poetic or "ontological" one. "Poetry proper," Heidegger insists, "is never merely a higher mode of everyday language. It is rather the reverse: everyday language is a forgotten or used-up poem."[24]

Now exactly what characterizes that ontological, nebulous, "forgotten" pre-interpretive moment, and how one preserves it in responding to or interpreting artworks differently, remains a question about which there's substantially less agreement. For Heidegger, that moment is characterized by the opening of Being, for Derrida the structure of *différance,* for Deleuze and Guattari the plane of immanence, for Sontag the "luminousness of the thing itself."[25] All of these disparate theories, however, perhaps converge under the banner of an originary event or encounter—which is to say, they focus on that privileged moment of affective undecidability that precedes any given interpretation of an artwork. For example, in "Music—Drastic or Gnostic," Carolyn Abbate insists not on a "Gnostic" or hermeneutic treatment of music as text (emphasizing the written musical score or the recorded performance), but a "drastic" attention to "music-as-performed," an encounter "that engenders physical and spiritual conditions wherein sound might suggest multiple concrete meanings and associations, conflicting and interchangeable ones, or also none at all, doing something else entirely. Real music, the event itself, in encouraging or demanding the drastic, is what damps down the Gnostic."[26]

If interpretation has become a name for artistic disenchantment (for the violent betrayal and reduction of the artistic work's power), then this kind of antihermeneutic project is undertaken in the name of a deconstructive re-enchantment of art: something like Abbate's "drastic" response would honor the affective eventhood of the artwork, the ontological multiplicity that is inevitably betrayed in the ontic discourse of interpretation. If, as Sontag puts it, "interpretation is the revenge of the intellect upon art,"[27] then the antihermeneutic gesture tries to get the body, the senses, and the encounter back into the processes of making meaning. In short, meaning itself (understood as multiple, rich, conflicting, open-ended, maybe even impossible) is not the thing to be avoided in most modern and postmodern critiques of artistic interpretation; rather, it's an instrumental, totalizing, or univocal notion of meaning that's the bad guy.

In any case, such an antihermeneutic re-enchantment of the artwork—gesturing always toward the multiplicity of its meanings, against any single interpretation—seems quite foreign to Goldsmith's practice, and even moreso to the somatic encounter of reading his work. There is little that is overflowing, drastic, or fatally significant in his work; indeed, a transcript of the nightly weather report seems less the province of authentic *Dasein*, listening for the mysterious call of Being, and more like a staging of the meaningless, banal chatter of *das Man*. In other words, Goldsmith's antihermeneutic gesture seems radically different from the mainstream modernist or postmodernist critique of meaning: rather than trying to re-enchant, enliven, or reinvent what I've called a "bodacious" artistic hermeneutics, Goldsmith's work seems to want to abandon it altogether—which is of course easier said than done, and thereby remains a certain kind of utopian project nonetheless.

It's the literal banality of language usage that Goldsmith is looking to foreground in his texts and readings: what he wants you to hear is the ubiquitous functioning of language as a set of practices, not the fatality of redemptive meaning or innovative epiphany that poetry is famous for adding to the banal experience of the everyday. As Goldsmith puts it in an interview, "The moment we shake our addiction to

narrative and give up our strong-headed intent that language must say
something 'meaningful,' we open ourselves up to different types of
linguistic experience, which . . . could include sorting and structuring
words in unconventional ways: by constraint, by sound, by the way
words look, and so forth, rather than always feeling the need to coerce
them toward meaning."[28] To experience a "real feel" chunk of that banality without fatality, one need only look on YouTube for a video record
of Goldsmith reading from *The Weather* at the Whitney Museum in New
York in April 2009, at a high-profile summit for avant-garde American
poetry's next big things, conceptual writing and Flarf.[29] Hipsters of
all sorts look on as Goldsmith reads verbatim weather reports from
the spring of 2003. They wait, and wait some more, for an injection of
fatality (commentary, mockery, something), but just get the weather—
complete with umms, ahhs, and the most banal clichés of the trade:
"it's 44 in Central Park, going up to 46." A few minutes into the reading, you can see that people who had expected the product launch of
a hot new poetry movement find themselves fidgeting, sorely disap-
pointed. You see heads lean into others, presumably remarking, "He's
just reading weather reports." "Where's the poetry?" "This is dull."

Of course, for that Whitney reading, Goldsmith had cleverly chosen
to read the most "exciting" set of passages from his documentation of
The Weather for the year 2003: the passages that take us through the
first days of the US-led invasion of Iraq in March. At this point in *The
Weather,* local weather reports in New York unexpectedly begin to talk
about battlefield weather around Baghdad as well—quite literally inject-
ing overtones of fatality into the banality of the nightly weather report.
After more than fifty sections taking us through the excruciating banality of January and February weather in the tri-state area, Section 2,
"Spring," begins like this:

> Oh, we are looking at, uh, weather, uh, across, uh, Iraq obviously here
> for the next several days, uh, we have, uh, actually some good, good
> weather is expected. They did have a sandstorm here earlier, uh, over the
> last twelve to twenty-four hours those winds have subsided and will actu-
> ally continue to subside. Uh, there will be enough of a wind across the

southern portion of the country that still may cause some blowing sand tomorrow. Otherwise we're looking at clear to partly cloudy skies tonight and tomorrow, uh, the weekend, uh, it is good weather, and then we could have a storm, uh, generating some strong winds, uh, for Sunday night and Monday, uh, even the possibility of a little rain in Baghdad. Uh, currently we have, uh, uh, increasing cloudiness, uh, forecast locally tonight, uh, it's gonna be brisk and chilly, temperatures getting down into the middle-thirties, and then some, uh, intermittent rain is expected tomorrow and tomorrow night. It'll become steadier and heavier late in the day and, uh, actually a pretty good soaking tomorrow night. Uh, temperatures getting into the mid-forties tomorrow, and then staying in the forties tomorrow night. Friday it's a breezy and warmer day but, uh, still a few more showers maybe even a thunderstorm, the high of sixty degrees. Currently we have sunshine and forty-four with an east wind of ten. Repeating the current temperature forty-four, going up to forty-six in midtown.

We still have clouds, we still have some fog outside of the city this morning but, uh, during the afternoon the sky can brighten, the sun can peek on through, temperatures get on up into the sixties. A couple of showers and maybe a thunderstorm this evening, and then the weekend to follow looks pretty good, at least partly sunny. It'll be breezy tomorrow, the high about sixty and in the, uh, fifties for a high on Sunday. As for Middle East weather, it continues to be favorable for military operations, and that'll remain the case through Sunday, but Monday and Tuesday, there may be another episode of strong winds, poor visibilities, and, uh, even some sandstorms. Right now fifty-seven and cloudy in Central Park, temperature today going up to sixty-two. . . .

A nice evening, clear to partly cloudy skies overnight. We'll be in the mid-forties come daybreak, uh, tomorrow another mild day but, uh, clouds and, uh, limited sun, a couple of showers around associated with a cold front which will be moving through, especially in the afternoon and evening. Clears out later tomorrow night, and Thursday and Friday lots of sunshine and only, uh, a bit cooler, fifty-four Thursday, fifty-eight Friday. The battlefield forecast, uh, the weather is nasty over there right now. Strong winds accompanying a powerful cold front, uh, really kicking up the sand and making for poor visibility. Uh, that wind speed will gradually come down over the next twenty-four hours, but it'll still be causing some problems. Rain, in mountains, snow in northern Iraq on Wednesday, a couple of showers still down in Baghdad, uh, then better weather Thursday, right on through the weekend. Back home we have fifty-seven in Caldwell, fifty-three and sunshine in Central Park, the southeast wind at eleven. Repeating the current temperature fifty-three going down to forty-seven in midtown.

Rather than comment on this excerpt myself, I'll follow Goldsmith's practice and cede the floor to our finest critic of contemporary experimental poetry, Marjorie Perloff:

> This passage nicely exemplifies the powers of 'mere' transcription, mere copying, to produce new meanings. From the perspective of the weather forecaster, Iraq is experiencing some 'good good weather'—good visibility, no doubt, for bombing those targeted sites, and not too much wind. The risk of 'blowing sand' is slight. After the reference to 'a little rain in Baghdad,' the 'we' shifts back to the New York area, as if the Baghdad rain or wind were merely a brief diversion from everyday life in the Tri-State area where it's a nice average day with temperature in the forties and a chance of rain.[30]

While Perloff's strikes me as a very instructive and insightful interpretation of the passages, I can't help but highlight this reading's complete reliance on the "banality/fatality" dialectic of "meaning" that Morris diagnosed for us earlier in this chapter.

As Perloff interprets it, Goldsmith's work is not really about the surface banality of the weather as a series of global practices that connect (or don't) with other practices: the emphasis that Perloff reads in Goldsmith is not so much on what the weather *does* but what the weather *means*. Perloff argues, quite persuasively, that Goldsmith's reinscription of the New York weather report's banality allows us to see something deeply, fatally meaningful about the forces behind something as ordinary as the weekend weather forecast: this passage shows how our everyday desires for leisure and ease in the late capitalist first world are made possible by imperialist bloodshed happening far away. In other words, Goldsmith's text offers the close reader a kind of ideology critique, which looks through the banality of the surface discourse to its deeper, more disturbing meaning: the March 2003 weather reports function as the mystical shell that hides the rational kernel of American imperialism.

Ironically though, however expertly done, such an exposing of hidden meaning behind or below the surface tends to rebuild the very ideological "mystical shell" that Marx long ago located for us as the target of ideology critique (for example, the bourgeois faith that war and imperialism are primarily enabled and sustained by airy abstractions like "meaning"). In language that's particularly instructive for its trying (a bit too hard, I might suggest) to produce meaning from the most mundane of topics, Perloff concludes her commentary on this passage: "The Baghdad thread is thus the clinamen that gives the 'classical narrative' of *The Weather* its piquancy."[31] For Perloff, these passages are not bland or banal at all, but are in fact brimming with the spice of multiple, hidden meaning; they are in fact nothing less than the Lucretian "clinamen" that gives the entire project "piquancy," the seeming swerve that is also the text's hidden skeleton key. And thereby on Perloff's reading, Goldsmith's work follows a recognizable recipe for preparing contemporary poetry: begin with the flavorless, everyday banal; find the meaningful detail or swerve, and make it palatably piquant by adding the spice of multiple meanings; in addition, suggest strongly that poetry's exposure of a such new meaning comprises its primary political or critical upshot. As Perloff sums up *The Weather,* these "'mere' retypings of the daily reports have their own poetic force—a force that relates them to science fiction rather than to the boredom of everyday fact."[32]

Of course, whatever one might say about it, Perloff's emphasis on the flavorful piquancy of multiple meaning puts her reading at some odds with Goldsmith's self-described practice, a project which he calls "Uncreative Writing": "I'm interested in quantifying and concretizing the vast amount of 'nutritionless' language; I'm also interested in the process itself being equally nutritionless."[33] Perloff is here trying to

weave into Goldsmith's project some recognizable threads within contemporary avant-gardist American poetry (threads that Perloff herself
has expertly explored for many years).[34] But I think that attempted
annexing of hermeneutic depth (the sense that this is all done "to produce new meanings"—which is to say, Goldsmith's work is read as an
oblique continuation of Pound's "make it new" modernism) downplays the singularity of Goldsmith's work, and tends in fact to obscure
the factors of his work that do positively connect him to strands of
American avant-gardism of the C20. And Perloff is by no means alone
in thematizing Goldsmith's project as a continuation of the postmodernist liberation of multiple meanings. Molly Schwartzberg reads
"Goldsmith's tomes" as continuations of the "encyclopedic" tradition
of the long novel (from *Tristram Shandy* to *Gravity's Rainbow*), with all
that genre's attendant Bakhtinian excess: on Schwartzberg's reading,
Goldsmith's work "pushes us to look beyond the solid physical boundaries of the conventional object of our attention, the heavy book sitting
in front of us, and out into the endless possibilities of intertextuality."[35]

As compellingly "right" as such interpretations of Goldsmith's project undoubtedly are (read a certain way, his works can suggest some
multiplicity buried in or hidden behind the mundane everyday), I'm
here trying to suggest another, more intensely antihermeneutic map
for *The Weather*, wherein the banality of Goldsmith's work is not primarily in the service of producing "endless possibilities" or "new
meanings." I'm not sure if Goldsmith's work is "in the service" of anything in particular (other than rethinking the practices and status of
poetry itself), but *The Weather*'s primary effect is to invoke a kind of
phenomenology of banality: an attention to the emergence and transformation of discourse itself, outside the "fatal" circuits of meaning. I
take at least part of Goldsmith's trickster gambit to be asking readers a
deceptively simple question: Does the weather primarily "mean" something? Do thunderstorms or cold snaps harbor hidden meaning? Or
does one have to find some other vocabularies for talking about the
weather—or, for that matter, for talking about *The Weather*?

Perhaps this brand of antihermeneutic poetic project is akin to what
Foucault tries to do in his *Archaeology of Knowledge:* to treat discourse

as a practice, rather than a representation; to treat linguistic events as "statements" rather than individual creative "expressions" of this or that possible, hidden, or future meaning. As Foucault writes, "archaeology tries to define not the thoughts, representations, themes, preoccupations that are concealed or revealed in discourses; but those discourses themselves, those discourses as practices obeying certain rules. It does not treat the discourse as a document, as a sign of something else, as an element that ought to be transparent . . . ; it is concerned with discourse in its own volume, as a monument. It is not an interpretive discipline: it does not seek another, better-hidden discourse. It refuses to be 'allegorical.'"[36] In the early pages of *Archaeology of Knowledge,* Foucault sets up his sense of archaeology by juxtaposing it to the dominant mode of the "new" modality of historical research birthed with the Annales School, and its attempts to make *monuments* into *documents*— to have mute monuments speak to us, express themselves. Which is to say, the project of the newer historicisms is to narrativize history by imbricating the silences of monuments within the conversations and documents that surround them, so forgotten monuments and moments can "speak" and "mean" again, in dialog with the concerns of the present.

As productive as this "narrative history" is and was in its time, Foucault suggests his archaeological project is precisely the inverse: not to make monuments into documents but to make documents into monuments—to transform discourses into inert markers of a certain time and place, material practices without the additional metaphysical burden of hidden significance or lost narrative complexity. The methodological imperative here is to treat documents as what they are— monuments to their place and time, combination machines or primitive linking functions—rather than as opportunities to produce ever more documents through endless restagings and updatings of commentary. Language practices, in short, do a lot more than reveal meaning. It may be worth noting, if only in passing, that this endlessly reassuring ability to produce meaning or commentary (as the upshot of a certain kind of narrative undecidability) also constitutes Foucault's most thoroughgoing critique of Derrida, and his wholesale "'textualization' of discursive practices." Recall the specific reason why Foucault infamously tags deconstruction as a "historically determined little pedagogy": such a generous ventriloquism dedicated to reanimating "undecidable" objects and texts "inversely gives to the master's voice that unlimited sovereignty that allows it indefinitely to re-say the text."[37] Or perhaps Nietzsche put it most succinctly, commenting on Wagner's Hegelianism: "The two words 'infinite' and 'meaning' were really sufficient: they induced a state of incomparable well-being in young men."[38]

And to paraphrase an old *Saturday Night Live* routine, just as undecidabilty was very, very good to deconstruction, the narrativizing of "silent" objects—this dream to make monuments into documents—has been very good not only to history but to poetics over the past century. Just think of the ways that mundane events like fishing or finding old, forgotten paintings reveal hidden truths in Elizabeth Bishop's poetry. Or how William Carlos Williams's "Red Wheelbarrow," upon which "so much depends," is in the end not just a Red Wheelbarrow, but a marker for a series of ideas that, famously, can be located only through the detour of mute objects ("no ideas but in things"). Such a poetic transforming of the banal, everyday monument into a kind of readable or interpretable document is, I take it, something like the "new meaning" that Perloff sees on display in Goldsmith's *The Weather*: when contextualized in a certain way by savvy readers, these otherwise uninteresting, utterly banal monuments (just an archive of weather reports) become documents, which is to say that they reveal traces of depth or value-added hidden meaning.

There is, however, yet another vein or strand in C20 American poetry, one more akin to the Foucauldian project of making documents into monuments: the extensive use of unchanged source material on display in modernists like Muriel Rukeyser or Louis Zukovsky, and intensified in various found, concrete, and sound poetries in the later C20.[39] In this vein, consider again Jack Spicer, this time rewriting the obscure work done by William Carlos Williams's infamous "Red Wheelbarrow":

Rest and look at this goddamned wheelbarrow. Whatever
It is. Dogs and crocodiles, sunlamps. Not

For their significance.
For their significant. For being human
The signs escape you. You, who aren't very bright
Are a signal for them. Not,
I mean, the dogs and crocodiles, sunlamps. Not
Their significance.[40]

Subtly bending Williams's sentiment that "so much depends" on reve-
latory singular objects like a red wheel barrow and the ideas that we
can access through them, Spicer here intensifies our attention not so
much to the ideas or multiple meanings that might surround the thing
but to "this goddamned wheelbarrow" itself, and also a series of other
random things ("dogs, crocodiles, sunlamps") that seem not to conjure
much in the way of ideas upon which anything at all might depend. In
short, Spicer here challenges us readers ("You, who aren't very bright")
to concentrate on the objects themselves, "Not / Their significance."

If there's the continuation of an American poetics project, utopian or
otherwise, in Goldsmith's work, it's the project of displacing the entire
apparatus of poetics from any vestige of the category of "meaning,"
either as a rare and valuable commodity, or a kind of value-added quality of interestingness. (Warhol's project in the realm of visual art, as
Goldsmith has suggested many times, is more an inspiration for his
project than any strictly speaking poetics of the C20.)[41] And that reassuring sense of hidden meaning in the everyday may constitute a dead
end for cultural poetics today precisely because of the ideological quality of life's reassured meaningfulness that we see played out in the contemporary culture and lifestyle industries—which of course no longer
sell things, but brand "experiences" (of everything from education and
tourism to toilet paper).

For example, something as banal as the temperature, that staple
of the nightly weather report, is no longer merely a number ("it's 62 in
midtown"), nor even an experience ruled over by the outmoded "wind
chill index" (which hopes to represent not so much what the temperature *is,* but how cold it *feels* if you factor in the wind). Since November
2002 (only two months before Goldsmith started his documentation

of *The Weather*), all of that has been replaced by a "RealFeel"[42] temperature, invented by meteorological giant AccuWeather (headquartered
in my home town of State College, Pennsylvania). On the company's
website, the RealFeel temperature system is touted by the company's
president, Joel Myers, in breathlessly innovative terms:

> Dr. Myers is so confident of his new measure that AccuWeather.com, his
> firm's industry-leading weather Web site, now offers it with every fore-
> cast, and AccuWeather TV and radio weathercasters across the country
> are adopting this new, more accurate measure as a way of expressing
> how cold and warmth actually feel. . . . "Our goal is to set the record
> straight and provide average Americans more accurate information
> which can help them live better lives," says Dr. Myers. "If in five years,
> no one remembers the Wind Chill, all the better. It's time to retire this
> antiquated index, and the RealFeel Temperature is the best indicator yet
> for measuring how warm or cold it really feels."[43]

RealFeel has succeeded in making something as mundane as the temperature into a sibling of modernist poetics: the Fahrenheit scale has
been made new; or, it could even be that AccuWeather has succeeded
in making the temperature the kind of news that stays news.[44]

In the end, virtually any emphasis on cultural meaning has a kind of
"RealFeel" effect to it: nothing seems "real" until it's made-interesting,
made-personal, made-new, and thereby made-significant in some way.
But insofar as the real of everyday life in late, later, or just-in-time capitalism is inexorably bound up with "feeling" or a subject's investment
in "meaning" (the recent flood of scholarly work on affect and biopower can only confirm this), that's precisely why adding more "feeling" or "meaning" to the deluge of discourse that surrounds us seems
like it may be something of a dead end in the present climate—why
Goldsmith's practice might invite us to evacuate and flee from that
entire discourse. The breathless fatality of multiple meaning has, one
might say, finally become-banal in our post-postmodern world.[45]

But what, the skeptical reader might ask, is left for poetry if you sub-
tract the thematics of "meaning"? Isn't poetry finally all about meaning

(which of course also includes demonstrating the multiplicity, or even impossibility of meaning)? Well, yes and no. Certainly, since the triumph of the New Criticism in the mid-C20, the question of meaning has become the central question of poetics: "poems are there to be interpreted" is a truism as clear for New Critics like Brooks and Warren as it is for deconstructionists like J. Hillis Miller (who has written, quite straightforwardly, that "Deconstruction is neither nihilism nor metaphysics but simply interpretation as such").[46] However, before the academic apparatus of literary interpretation and commentary (which Evan Kindley has called "Big Criticism")[47] got up and running in the mid-C20, it's not at all clear that poetry was primarily meant for close reading–style interpretation and commentary. Certainly what Foucault might call the "monumental" functions of poetry (archiving a time or place, enshrining a memory, passing along an event or legend, rousing collective ire, functioning within various spiritual or religious practices, simply passing the time) obtained for centuries before the founding of academic journals dedicated to interpreting literary works.

Given such a genealogy of poetics and its relations to myriad practices outside the search for meaning, one might look at Goldsmith's antihermeneutic project not as a spring-green avant-gardism but as an attempt to reconnect poetry to what Jane Tompkins has called the "long history of critical thought in which the specification of meaning is not a central concern":[48] a poetics based not so narrowly on the subject-centered or formal relations among texts and meanings but focused instead on what one might call the banal everyday, what Tompkins calls "the relations of discourse and power."[49] Indeed, the question "what does it mean?" which seems so central to poetics, looks hopelessly confining and inadequate in the context of many other art forms (music, dance, sculpture, architecture); and Goldsmith's work, among many other provocations, asks us to rethink what poetry "is" primarily by focusing our attention on what poetry "does," or what it can do, if you remove the regulative idea that poetry primarily contains, expresses, or releases meanings. Why literary critics want (or even need) to interpret poetry is clear enough; however, whether poetry exists primarily to be interpreted is another question altogether.

Or, to put the point slightly differently: I would certainly agree with Perloff when she writes that "*The Weather* is a work of radical defamiliarization. It forces the reader to think about the weather in new ways."[50] However, a thornier question remains concerning whether a discourse that would dedicate itself to unleashing multiple "new" meanings from within the banal everyday remains an effective or defamiliarizing bulwark against the affective capitalism that dominates our present.[51] Is Goldsmith's primary defamiliarization located in unleashing the excessive meanings buried under the everyday banality of our lives (a re-enchanting project that seems awfully familiar—certainly within postmodern poetics, but just as certainly within contemporary advertising)? Or does his work gesture toward evacuating the thematics of poetic meaning altogether? (Now *that's* defamiliarizing.) It's nearly axiomatic to point out that linguistic meaning is irreducibly slippery, and that identity in the social-media era is largely a cut-and-paste operation rather than an authentic flowering of the one true you. Those realizations, in other words, don't offer much in the way of a critical wedge to defamiliarize the present, but in fact tend to intensify the biopolitical mandate of endlessly producing this thing called our lives within an information- and commodity-saturated world. One might venture that the multiplicity of meaning is today no longer the lead story on the C21 Headline News, but functions more like the weather—the wider ambient context within which everything else happens.

In the end, while there may or may not be a creative modernist, make-it-new brand of "uncreative genius" lurking behind Goldsmith's work, there certainly remains something like "innovation" on display there, and in conceptual poetry on the whole. However such innovation can, it seems to me, no longer be measured solely by Perloff's gold standard: "the production of new meanings."[52] Rather, the force of Goldsmith's phenomenology of banality finds itself in honing our ability to respond to performative practices as practices: it provokes what Goldsmith calls a diffuse "thinkership" rather than a hermeneutic "readership" around the poem, and this ongoing building and maintenance of a "thinkership" is maybe what "making literature now" is all about. The challenge is perhaps to hear the weather report and its everyday, banal force as a series of discursive events, without the mediating (and, finally, too-reassuring) discourses of added, hidden meaning. Or at least this is the primary provocation of Goldsmith's *The Weather*: it asks us to learn how to take the banality of statements seriously, as a series of productive biopolitical performances, without translating the banal everyday into the breathless fatality of meaning's "RealFeel."

Conclusion

On the Returns of Realism and the (Supposed) Exhaustion of Critique

> I believe one's point of reference should not be to the great
> model of language and signs, but that of war and battle.
> The history which bears and determines us has the form
> of a war rather than that of a language: relations of power,
> not relations of meaning.
>
> —MICHEL FOUCAULT, "Truth and Power"

For me, the New Realism definitively arrived on Wednesday, February 18, 2015, at or around 7:30pm EST. That evening I was guest-lecturing in a graduate theory seminar on Posthumanism, filling in for my colleague Claire Colebrook, who was out of town. The topic was Foucault's *The Order of Things* (*Les mots et les choses*; that is, "words and things" in the original French, I dutifully begin by pointing out), and about an hour into talking about the dramatic epistemic changes at the beginning of the C19 in Europe (with special emphasis on the discursive formations of life, labor, and language, and the distributions of objects they make available), seemingly out of nowhere comes the question: "So, Foucault's work is hostile to realism, then? He doesn't believe that 'things' are independent of their discursive articulation? Isn't that blatant, correlationist anthropomorphism?" There it was, the arrival of "realism" on the inland theory shores of State College, Pennsylvania. Just as someone of my generation had probably asked a similar

Foucauldian "gotcha" question in the Marxism seminar several decades earlier ("So Marx believes that power is scarce and held by certain people or social groups? It doesn't circulate through the socius? There's a central conflict—the class struggle—that organizes all the others?"), here was a potential "passing of the torch" moment.

In response, I try to suggest that for Foucault, if you're asking after the "truth" or "essence" of things (or if you're asking for clarification of philosophical positions), you're already asking anthropomorphic, largely political questions—what does the chipmunk, the folding chair, or the delphinium care for finding the truth? As I noted earlier in this book, truth is our problem, not theirs. Similarly, I tried to suggest in class that evening that Foucault seems somewhat ill-chosen as the fall guy (or cheerleader) for humanist anthropomorphism, what with his insistence that "man is an invention of recent date. And one perhaps nearing its end."[1] In fact, *The Order of Things* is largely given over to looking at the historical preconditions for the (very recent and precarious) emergence of something like "correlationism," the word coined by Quentin Meillassoux in *After Finitude* in his attempt to get back behind Kant's Copernican revolution of subjectivity. Meillassoux defines the term quite simply: "Correlationism consists in disqualifying the claim that it is possible to consider the realms of subjectivity and objectivity independently of one another."[2] For Meillassoux, and a series of other recent thinkers from speculative realism through the new materialism, it's the great "outside" of the real that was lost with Kant, then further mystified by Hegel, bracketed by Husserl, and ignored as "essentialist" or "metaphysical" by virtually all continental existentialism and phenomenology, and denounced as a dangerous totalizing fiction by the linguistic turn of social constructionism. These modern and postmodern discourses remain (on Meillassoux's account) hopelessly filtered through (and thereby openly centered on) the mediations of human subjectivity, precisely insofar as these philosophies all follow Kant in resolutely refusing to say anything at all about the real, or at least not without saying something at the same time about the perceiving subject. To put it another way, at a certain point in Western thinking, the mediation between subject and object becomes the only way to think subject or object, and thereby the anthropomorphic question of signs or language becomes the necessary and irreducible detour in any theoretical work.

In *The Order of Things,* Foucault is in fact following out a version of this itinerary—trying to show how "things" became inexorably entangled with human "words." (Foucault's earliest work was on Kant's anthropology, after all, and in fact he suggests that philosophy becomes anthropology with Kant). However, Foucault is certainly no fan of this linguistic turn, nor of phenomenology or subject-centered thought in general, and his analysis of "life, labor, language" and their emergence at the beginning of the C19 concerns nothing less than the birth of biopower within the episteme of the human sciences, a knowledge-power regime primarily characterized by a misplaced confidence that nothing is "real" until and unless it passes through the mediation of the human and the discourses of its sciences (biology, economics, linguistics).[3] Finally, Foucault shows that, like the representational regimes of the early modern period and the fabulation and magic practices dominant in the Renaissance, this myopic C19 centrality of "man" is doomed to historical eclipse and anachronism, and was in fact already on the way out in 1966, when Foucault published *Les mots et les choses.* But all that didn't seem very convincing to the New Realists on the block.

So I give it one more try on Foucault and realism, by suggesting that for Foucault, the contemporary question surrounding realism has little to do with the veracity of various philosophical or scientific positions. If you're a Foucauldian, you can forget tracking the seemingly endless blog posts that attempt to mark out the nuanced differences in philosophical realism among Object-Oriented Thinkers, New Materialists, Post-Critical Critics, Digital Humanists, or Actor-Network Theorists—all of them arguing, quite vehemently and apparently in all sincerity, that we should stop focusing on what (individual) humans think, because The Truth Is Out There. In *Onto-Cartography,* Levi Bryant perhaps speaks for the Object-Oriented Ontology group when he dismisses Foucauldian critique because "discussions of the role played by technology and non-humans in the formation of social ecologies is severely underdetermined."[4] (As one reviewer wryly notes, "To anyone who has read *Discipline and Punish* or any of the *History of Sexuality* series, this statement will come as a great surprise.")[5] In the end, though, the point perhaps is this: for Foucault the archaeologist or genealogist, the primary question about philosophical realism is not, "Is it true that things possess an essence, to which we do have scientific, speculative, or diffracted access?" (the "dogmatic" position that was bracketed by Kantian critique, but had a prior life as either medieval "equivocity" or Duns Scotus's "univocity").[6] Far rather, the Foucauldian question would be, "Why at a certain historical juncture (for example, this one) does realism become an attractive position to adopt or espouse? What comprises the historical a priori that allows realism to reemerge now— positioned as the latest thing, something new, against the hegemony of the present?" As Rita Felski blurbs on the back cover of *Vibrant Matter,* for example, "This manifesto for a new materialism is an invigorating breath of fresh air. Jane Bennett's eloquent tribute to the vitality and volatility of things is just what we need to revive the humanities and to redraw the boundaries of political thought." Looking back over cratering student enrollments and moribund tenure-line job prospects in the decade since that book's publication, it seems in retrospect that we needed a lot more than new materialism "to revive the humanities." And going forward, I'm not convinced that any shiny new paradigm shift in critical theory, any more than a god, will save us now.

In any case, realism is back in critical theory largely because its archnemesis social constructionism has run aground; there are just no new articles, books, or dissertations to be written about the social construction of x or y. And to many jaundiced new materialist eyes, it looks like those social-construction years were tragically hubristic as well, with the tenets of the linguistic turn harboring a secret investment in what turns out to be an earth-destroying humanism. As Jane Bennett writes in "Systems and Things: On Vital Materialism and Object-Oriented Philosophy," almost all of these recent postcritical models "share a critique of linguistic and social constructivism" and thereby "see the nonhuman turn as a response to an overconfidence about human power that was embedded in the postmodernism of the 1980s and 1990s."[7] As an aside here, one might note that critique in the modern, Kantian sense is grounded in a severely austere humility concerning the power of human logos, not a celebration of its unbounded powers to know everything—the one point of agreement that made postmodernism and Kant such unlikely bedfellows. As Adorno insists, "The crucial feature of the Kantian work . . . is that it is guided by the conviction that reason is denied the right to stray into the realm of the Absolute. . . . The power of the *Critique of Pure Reason* resides not so much in responses to the so-called metaphysical questions as in its highly heroic and stoical refusal to respond to these questions in the first place."[8] In short, it completely escapes me how turning back toward realist metaphysical questions constitutes anything other than massively hubristic "overconfidence about human power": the new realism suggests humans can know the absolute truth, and indeed must.

In fact, the only way something as hopelessly old-fashioned as metaphysical, scientific realism can return as the hopeful "new" in the C21 is precisely as a symmetrical and inverse reaction to the prior (post) structuralist triumph of the linguistic turn and its narrow sense of C20 performativity, the axiom that any "truth" about the world is produced and transformed solely by humans and their sign systems. As a certain reading of Austin showed us, saying can and does make it so, and this performative truism about linguistic social constructionism is clearly Latour's issue with climate change deniers and other flat-earth types in his early C21 salvo in favor of realism, "Why Has Critique Run Out of Steam?" In short, the new realists follow Latour when he argues that critique isn't progressive anymore because bad guys like the Koch brothers have caught onto social constructionism: with their fake news and alternative facts, the C21 finds people in power undermining anything that injures them or their interests by labeling it an unreal, merely constructed, untrue "hoax." Realism has newfound luster at least in part because linguistic-turn strategies of endless recontextualization have tarnished the critical, progressive powers previously associated with unmasking the truth as a social construction; likewise, these postmodern strategies have shown themselves to be in league—or at least oftentimes in sync—with the sinister neoliberal imperatives of spin doctors and regressive Mad Men everywhere.

Perhaps the most thoroughgoing rehearsal of the argument for the abandonment of critique is offered by Mitchum Huehls, whose *After Critique* is dedicated to "demonstrating . . . that it's actually the politics of oppositional critique that remains perpetually complicit with neoliberalism [!], while it's actually those post-normative ontological forms and modes, which might at first glance look like mere capitulations to neoliberalism, that offer the most possibility for undoing neoliberalism as we know it. Critique capitulates, but apparent capitulation opens potentially new modes of being, and politics."[9] The recent triumph of neoliberalism, Huehls argues, entails accepting "the impossibility of generating any critical representation of the world that doesn't in some way reinforce neoliberalism" (12): "to echo Latour once more, the left's capacity for political and social critique has run out of steam. Those argumentative descriptions of the world that aim to defamiliarize, disillusion, and debunk our commonly held beliefs, values and norms, exposing their ideological or discursive construction, their aporias and contradictions, their constitutive blind spots, their racism or economic self-interest—those representational acts are not as effective as they used to be" (14). That cooptation being the case (a claim that is vigorously asserted but never actually demonstrated), Huehls argues that critique as we knew it must be abandoned and reinvented on an "ontological" rather than "representational" basis. As he writes in "Risking Complicity," today literary authors and critics are "thinking about meaning ontologically, as a matter of location, relation, and presence, not epistemologically, as a matter of representation, signification, and reference."[10]

One might pause to pose several questions about this postcritical project: for example, how is a different way of "thinking about meaning" anything other than an anthropomorphic (or even epistemological) problem? Isn't a primary, linguistic-turn dependence on "meaning" the fatal problem with social-constructionist demystification—insofar as all such a discourse can do is endlessly undermine "true" meaning by unmasking it as a social power play? Or one might wonder how antiracist critique like Black pessimism or hardcore Marxist critique is just as "neoliberal" as the dogma of Chicago School economics or the white supremacy of *The Daily Stormer*, or what evidence exists that recent progenitors of capitalism without democracy—Trump, Putin, Xi—have nothing to fear from demystification-as-critique (their common hit lists of enemies have made it seem pretty clearly the opposite), not to mention the question of how critique itself gets associated wholly with the paranoid unmasking move characteristic of axiomatic social constructionism? Likewise, I've already suggested substantial skepticism concerning the idea that the force of critique can be reinvigorated as easily as performing a discursive shift from social-constructionist epistemology to scientific ontological realism—if that were the case, analytic philosophers like Rudolf Carnap would be the unacknowledged legislators of the C20 world; or if you prefer a more abstract notion of ontology, Carnap's nemesis Heidegger would have turned out to be the great continental political thinker of our time, dedicated as he is to thinking about ontological Being rather than ontic beings. Finally, as I've noted throughout this book, one of the oddest things about proponents of the new realism is the way they fiercely hang onto the "fact-value" relation (and the concomitant prestige-value of the truth)—as when Huehls argues that a relatively simple change in philosophical vocabulary, from that epistemological worldview to an ontological one, will somehow leave anthropomorphism in the dust and open up possibilities of positive social change that C20 modes of critique sought (but failed) to bring about. Throughout various instantiations of the new materialism, one maneuver remains nearly constant: it's as if appealing to realist ontology, rather than relativist epistemology, to ground political claims would redeem a legitimate (dare I say "critical"?) role for philosophy in political and social discourse.

As Barad writes, for example, hanging desperately onto Butler's performative thesis concerning Lacanian (social-constructionist) exclusion, "Objectivity and agency are bound up with issues of responsibility and accountability. Accountability must [!] be thought in terms of what matters and what is excluded from mattering."[11] As much as I like this sentiment, and want to affirm it, I can't see how this isn't a completely anthropomorphic formulation, or at least a reinvention of the very fact-value ("objectivity and agency") relations that are wholly constitutive of the social-construction thesis and its human exceptionalism (insofar as plants and animals don't decide to accept or reject performing any given action based on their understandings of nature and culture). Here I'd have to side with Carnap and suggest that if you really are a hardline scientific realist, then virtually all truth claims related to or dictated by (human) values are dubious at best, nonsense at worst.[12] Indeed, consider the ersatz humanism of Barad's assertions here: we humans are accountable for our actions, ethically required to respect the universe's becoming by adapting our agency to its objectivity; but in what sense is the black hole "responsible" or "accountable" to the matter it scoops up, the parasite responsible to its host, or the river accountable to the farmer's flooded field? If everything is part of the same mesh of intra-active becoming, whence comes this additional, exceptional form of human sociopolitical "accountability" that we "must" heed?

On Barad's new materialist grid of intelligibility, nature is no longer understood as a place of timeless and stern directives, but is far rather a lively mesh where everything constantly (re)configures itself in an intra-active realm of performativity, just like us. For better or worse, once we accept this insight into the entangled performativity of everything, we can no longer so simply be consoled, or enlivened, or chastened, or limited by these ontological inquiries into the nature of things: in terms of post–linguistic turn political thought, these strong realist claims about "the way things are" no longer translate into a series of prescriptions for the way things "should be" politically. After the linguistic turn of social constructionism (as freedom from a determinative or prescriptive understanding of nature), ontological realism then ceases politically to "matter," to deploy for one last time that ubiquitous term from the performativity literature.

Given the fact that the realist insights of new materialism don't necessarily entail any values socially, it's not odd that almost all the emphasis in those new materialist discourses falls on the whiz-bang novelty of such realist claims. Indeed, I sometimes wonder whether the new materialism is such a hot property these days precisely because people really, really don't want to talk anymore about the old materialism—otherwise known as dialectical materialism, which is to say Marxism, plain and simple. On another reading, however, I suppose the "new" in new materialism or new realism can be read or understood as a series of attempts to update Marxism's commitment to materialism (to separate the rational kernel of practices from the mystical shell of ideological meanings), to continue transforming materialism in such a way as to extend Marx's original project: the attempt to describe or diagnose the workings of capitalism as a disastrously unequal system that nonetheless offers myriad potentials for its own transformation. As Antonio Negri has argued, if you take Marxism to be a prophetic or predictive discourse (tied to a moralistic vocabulary of denunciation), then of course it's been an outright failure (having failed to bring about heightened proletariat consciousness leading to international communism). Or, as Foucault more snarkily puts it in *The Order of Things*, as a revolutionary discourse Marxism seems historically anachronistic, a "minor Ricardian" fish that can't swim outside its home waters of mid-C19 Europe.

However, if you take Marxism not as an anticapitalist moralism but as a *diagnostic* discourse that will inevitably require rewriting to remain as nimble as the object of its analysis (capitalism), then some aspects of the project of new materialism become a potential extension or intensification of dialectical materialism, rather than an outright scrapping of it. Or at least a kind of diagnostic Marxism lives on decisively in new materialism's updating of the tools of materialist analysis: from analog to digital economic processing; from the labor theory of value to the attention theory of value; from a disciplinary, factory society of mass production to biopolitical, synoptic society of niche-market consumption; from alienated labor to overloaded symbolic analysis; from workers being enslaved by the machines of capital to the machinic enslavement of each and every one of us to the everyday machines of biopolitical capitalism, where in addition to whatever it is we do for a living, we are all tied to the performative project of sculpting our own subjectivity, making meaning out of our lives 24/7. Which, again, is only to say that the ongoing analysis of capitalism, the ways that we're imbricated with it or may be able to resist it, should be front and center in work on the new materialism. However, at the end of the day, a thoroughgoing insistence on ontological realism leaves you with nothing much to say about the human-value system that is capitalism. In the end, the workings of quantum physics or the essences of objects simply don't imply, much less dictate, the workings of this or that economic system.

Going forward, such a diagnostic project, aimed at the neoliberal present rather than the eternal verities of realism, would strongly suggest, at least to me, that it's the wrong time to give up on the force of critique, trading it out for the lively, overfull modes of making meaning that are waiting for us in our new materialist ontological future. It may in fact be that demystifying social constructionism has run aground, lost its effectiveness, for a whole series of social, scientific, and academic reasons. For example, we may simply have witnessed the historical becoming-dominant of what used to be an emergent, social-constructionist cynical reason: as Leonard Cohen puts it, today "everybody knows that the dice are loaded," so that maybe puts demystification out of a critical job. Or maybe there's a simpler market (neoliberal) explanation: as an academic commodity, paranoid social constructionism is perhaps just like a leisure suit, very popular in the 1970s and '80s, but since fallen out of fashion (though without the leisure suit's possibility of substantial retro appeal). Or it may be that decades of endless cable news shouting matches between flacks hired by various think tanks to defend industry interests has worn the sharpness of critical argumentation and demystification down to a cliché.

Whatever the explanation for the fall of the linguistic turn, my concluding point here is this: the procedure of exposing the social construction of this or that seemingly natural formation does not constitute the whole of "critique"—especially neo-Marxist, feminist, queer, postcolonial, ethnic and Afrocentric modes of critique, which are deeply invested in diagnosing and responding to the developments of capitalism (social mutations that nobody besides Lou Dobbs thinks are "natural"). In his calls to move beyond critique, Huehls for example has conflated the whole of critique with linguistic-turn's social-constructionist demystification of meaning, which I think is a serious underestimation of critical discourse's toolkit. And similarly, the primary thing that's simply "wrong" in Huehls's provocative diagnosis of the present, a diagnosis he shares with many of the postcritical new realists, is its continued investment in the new social modes of value and meaning making that will inevitably be born from accepting and promoting a lively new ontology. As Huehls writes, we need to become postcritical specifically because "Neoliberalism owns critique, but it has not achieved an exhaustively totalizing grasp on all possible forms of post-normative value production" (28). To put it bluntly, this formulation diagnoses the current neoliberal situation exactly backwards: I would say that neoliberalism definitively owns the project of postnormative value production, but it has not achieved an exhaustively totalizing grasp on all possible forms of critique. From Jonathan Beller's *Attention Theory of Value* to Mariana Mazzucato's *The Value of Everything*, any glancing look at the recent economics of "value" will show you what neoliberalism definitively "owns"—lock, stock, and barrel: the proliferation of meaning making, biopolitical modes of value-production.

Advanced capitalism can endlessly reincorporate new or innovative forms of value (which has been capitalism's primary job for the past two hundred years: from the labor theories of value in the C19, through the mass production of value in the disciplinary factory Fordism of the C20, through the financialization of human experience itself in the C21). But neoliberalism has certainly not achieved an exhaustive grasp on all possible forms and forces of critique. In short, critique still matters, but it's the myriad forces of critique that still make a difference, not critique's tragic fate in forever demonstrating the inevitability of meaning's failures. Which is why Heuhls has the oppositional potentials of the present 180 degrees wrong when he writes that recent social and economic history "has replaced older modes of meaning making that rely on representation and critique with new modes of meaning-making that rely on connection, adjacency, being, transmission, and presence. It's not surprising, then, that today's authors and readers have changing notions of what it means to mean."[13] Contra that (oddly Habermasian) attempt to rehabilitate the communicative values of meaning in order to outflank instrumental neoliberalism, I've been arguing throughout this book that the project of restoring or producing new "meaning" is in fact one of the primary instrumentalist neoliberal ene-mies at present: producing meaning in our lives, constantly reinvent-ing our subjectivity, is the project we're all forced to perform all the time by biopolitical neoliberalism. Given that fact, the endless produc-tion of such enchanting new meaning is a privileged object of critique at present, not a golden path forward. In the end, it's not critique that's run out of steam or shown itself to be endlessly recuperable by capital, but what's run out of steam is the production of new meaning(s) as an oppositional or anticapitalist mode of value production in the biopo-litical era of neoliberalism. It's not the force of critique but the modes of value production, of making meaning, that are always already recu-perated by advanced capitalism.

On the other side of understanding performativity as inexorably tied to the linguistic question of social construction, I've tried to show throughout that the performative is a discourse that is at its core aller-gic to "meaning" in almost all of its forms. Performativity constitutes a set of practices that look axiomatically at force before meaning, and that's I think the primary reason why performativity remains impor-tant in the present: not because it can ceaselessly undercut or debunk meaning, or even produce new meanings, but because it demonstrates that meaning is always and everywhere secondary, the outcome of a series of (much larger than linguistic) processes rather than the realist ground of those processes. To say that meaning is the outcome of a process—for example, that the reality of climate change has a long his-tory and is firmly grounded in scientific discourse—is not to say that climate change doesn't exist, that the climate is a mere fiction invented by humans, or that humans are not responsible for initiating and accel-erating climate change; it is simply to say that the "meaning" of climate change is not the primary hinge for either understanding or combatting it. Not that it's false or fictional, a socially constructed story, but that climate change (as much as anything else) is best grasped as a series of practices and forces—political, scientific, geological, and so on. Maybe in the end this critique-in-motion, this critique beyond language and its meanings (or lack thereof), is finally something that the old critique and the new materialism can agree upon.

In conclusion, to make good on my opening promise to limn out what's living and what's dead in and around the performative, I'd say simply this: the social constructionist critique of meaning (demonstrating that any constative truth is undermined by its performative linguistic construction) is dead. In its wake, long live the myriad other forces of performative critique—a posthumanist world where critique focuses on relations of force, not the epiphanies of failed totalization and/or the production of new meaning. In the end, it's been a long, strange trip for the performative, as it migrated from a tiny corner of British ordinary language philosophy to become synonymous with the real itself.

Notes

Preface

1. Karen Barad, *Meeting the Universe Halfway: Quantum Physics and the Entanglement of Matter and Meaning* (Durham, N.C.: Duke University Press, 2007), 151–52; emphasis in original.

2. Ferdinand de Saussure, *Course in General Linguistics,* trans. Wade Baskin (New York: McGraw Hill, 1966), 120.

1. The Truth Is a Joke?

The original version of this essay was first delivered at the "Comedy and Philosophy" conference at DePaul University. Special thanks to Russell Ford for inviting me, and to Michael Naas and Pascale-Anne Brault for their hospitality. Thanks also to Arne De Boever and Peggy Kamuf for their comments when I gave a version of it in Los Angeles. A much shorter version was published in *Cultural Critique.*

1. See, most centrally, the collection of Derrida's epicedial pieces, *The Work of Mourning,* ed. and trans. Pascale-Anne Brault and Michael Naas (Chicago: University of Chicago Press, 2001). This English "original" was later expanded considerably and later published in French under Derrida's chosen title, *Chaque fois unique, la fin du monde* (Each time unique, the end of the world) (Paris: Galilée, 2003).

2. Here I'm using the phrasing of John Caputo's *The Prayers and Tears of Jacques Derrida: Religion without Religion* (Bloomington: Indiana University Press, 1997).

3. In fact, what one might argue that the last word in *Glas* (trans. John Leavey [Lincoln: University of Nebraska Press, 1986])—such as it has a final word—is "comedy." The penultimate paragraph in the Hegel column is the

"final" one insofar as the very last section is in fact the beginning. Page 1 is a continuation from the final page, and the column begins in mid-sentence, "what, after all, of the remains, today, for us, here, now, of a Hegel?" (1a). The penultimate (though secretly final) paragraph concludes: "The syllogism of spiritual art (epic, tragedy, comedy) leads esthetic religion to revealed religion. Through comedy then" (262a).

4. *Glas,* 2–3a.

5. See Derrida's *Spurs: Nietzsche's Styles,* trans. Barbara Harlow (Chicago: University of Chicago Press, 1981), especially pages 123ff.

6. Jacques Derrida, "Some Statements and Truisms," trans. Anne Tomiche, in *The States of 'Theory,* ed. David Carroll (New York: Columbia University Press, 1990), 80.

7. See Michael Naas's first-person summary of Bill Martin's rendition of the joke in *Derrida from Now On* (New York: Fordham University Press, 2008), 228–29. Though a controversy has sprung up around this joke and its reception. See E. A. Hartigan's very different account in "L'Oz," available online at http://mylaw2.usc.edu/why/students/orgs/ilj/assets/docs/20-1%20Hartigan .pdf.

8. See J. Hillis Miller's *Speech Acts in Literature* (Stanford, Calif.: Stanford University Press, 2002), 89.

9. J. L. Austin, *How to Do Things with Words* (Cambridge, Mass.: Harvard University Press, 1975), 124. Hereafter cited in the body of the text.

10. J. L Austin, "Performative Utterances," in *Philosophical Papers,* 3rd ed. 233–52 (Oxford: Oxford University Press, 1979), 252. Note also that Austin often used this joke in his live show; see its deployment in *How to Do Things with Words* (38).

11. Austin, "Performative Utterances," 251.

12. Austin, "Performative Utterances," 236.

13. Austin, *How to Do Things with Words,* 10; my emphasis.

14. This of course is one of the central upshots of Derrida's work on the performative, and is developed (in very different directions) in Miller's *Speech Acts in Literature,* Shoshana Felman's *The Literary Speech Act: Don Juan with JL Austin* (Ithaca, N.Y.: Cornell University Press, 1983), Eve Kosofsky Sedgwick's *Touching Feeling: Affect, Pedagogy, Performativity* (Durham, N.C.: Duke University Press, 2003), and Judith Butler's *Gender Trouble* (New York: Routledge, 1989). Much more on Butler and Sedgwick in chapter 2.

15. Austin, "Performative Utterances," 241

16. Jacques Derrida, *Dissemination,* trans. Barbara Johnson (Chicago: University of Chicago Press, 1983), 223.

17. Gilles Deleuze and Félix Guattari, *A Thousand Plateaus,* trans. Brian Massumi (Minneapolis: University of Minnesota Press, 1987), 75–110.

18. Here I think of the "apologies of the week," a regular bit on Harry Shearer's comedy radio program *Le Show*. Almost all of the apologies (offered by politicians, performers, public figures who drunk-tweeted something they shouldn't have) begin, "I apologize if anyone was offended, that's not what I intended." Apologizing, ironically, means never having to say you're sorry—it's almost always a matter of refashioning the original intention, and offloading any "offense" onto the receiver. *Le Show* can be downloaded at http://www .kcrw.com/etc/programs/ls.

19. Austin, "Performative Utterances," 251.

20. Austin, "Performative Utterances," 236.

21. On this issue, and for a more sympathetic reading of Searle's critique, see Raoul Moati's *Derrida/Searle: Deconstruction and Ordinary Language*, trans. Timothy Attanucci and Maureen Chun (New York: Columbia University Press, 2014). Moati in fact argues that Derrida's real target, even in his original critique of intentionality in "Signature Event Context," is not Austin's performative, but rather the deconstruction is directed at Searle all along. Moati writes, "in believing he is deconstructing Austin's theory, Derrida, in an increasingly involuntary way, is already aiming at Searle's theory, whose characteristics include the attempt to rethink the performative through intentionality" (67).

22. John Searle, "Reiterating the Differences: A Reply to Derrida." *Glyph* 1 (1977): 172–208, 202.

23. Searle, "Reiterating the Differences," 208.

24. The word *quite* amuses Derrida quite a bit throughout "Limited Inc abc . . . ," a pleasure taken primarily from Searle's conjecture that the "confrontation" between Austin and Derrida "never quite took place." Derrida is of course interested in the critique of presence implied here (*différance* as deferral and delay), but he also deploys throughout the idiom of bemused British dismissal that accrues to the English word *quite*.

25. Jacques Derrida, *Limited Inc.*, trans Samuel Weber (Evanston, Ill.: Northwestern University Press, 1988), 105. Hereafter cited in the text.

26. The phrase that encapsulates this critique is "post-truth politics." See Alterman's *When Presidents Lie: A History of Official Deception and Its Consequences* (New York: Viking, 2004).

27. Giorgio Agamben, *Homo Sacer: Sovereign Power and Bare Life*, trans. Daniel Heller-Roazen (Stanford, Calif.: Stanford University Press, 1998), 120, 123.

28. Slavoj Žižek, *Žižek's Jokes* (Cambridge, Mass.: MIT Press, 2014), 35. Either in passing or on topic, note that Žižek alerts us to "an old Jewish joke, loved by Derrida" (52).

29. See Paolo Virno's *Multitude: Between Innovation and Negation*, trans. Isabella Bertoletti, James Cascaito, and Andrea Casson (New York: Semiotext(e),

2008). On the tragic in Butler, see especially her *Antigone's Claim: The Kinship between Life and Death* (New York: Columbia University Press, 2002).

30. Searle, "Reiterating the Differences," 199.

31. Searle, "Reiterating the Differences," 207.

32. Rita Felski, *The Limits of Critique* (Chicago: University of Chicago Press, 2015), 151–85.

33. Jacques Derrida, "Living On / Border Lines," trans. James Hulbert, in *Deconstruction and Criticism*, ed. Harold Bloom et al. 75–176 (New York: Seabury Press, 1979), 81.

34. Terry Eagleton, *Literary Theory: An Introduction* (Minneapolis: University of Minnesota Press, 1983), 125.

35. For recent related attempts to further this line of reasoning concerning Derrida, see Michael Marder's *The Event of the Thing: Derrida's Post-Deconstructive Realism* (Toronto: University of Toronto Press, 2011) and Clayton Crockett's *Derrida After the End of Writing: Political Theology and New Materialism* (New York: Fordham University Press, 2017).

36. Theodor Adorno, *Kant's "Critique of Pure Reason,"* ed. Rolf Tiedmann, trans. Rodney Livingstone (Stanford, Calif.: Stanford University Press, 2001), 4.

37. Samantha Frost, *Biocultural Creatures: Toward a New Theory of the Human* (Durham, N.C.: Duke University Press, 2016), 34. Hereafter cited in the text.

2. Two Paths You Can Go By

1. John McGowan, *Democracy's Children: Intellectuals and the Rise of Cultural Politics* (Ithaca, N.Y.: Cornell University Press, 2002), 112.

2. Bruno Latour, "Bruno Latour Tracks Down Gaia," https://lareviewofbooks.org/article/bruno-latour-tracks-down-gaia.

3. Judith Butler, *Subjects of Desire: Hegelian Reflections in Twentieth-Century France* (New York: Columbia University Press, 1987), 214 (emphasis added).

4. Eve Kosofsky Sedgwick, *Epistemology of the Closet* (Berkeley: University of California Press, 1990), 41. Hereafter cited in the text.

5. Ferdinand de Saussure, *Course in General Linguistics*, trans. Wade Baskin (New York: McGraw, 1966), 73.

6. Graham Harman, *Immaterialism: Objects and Social Theory* (London: Polity, 2016), 14.

7. Sedgwick, *Epistemology of the Closet*, 23.

8. Susan Bordo, *Unbearable Weight: Feminism, Western Culture, and the Body* (Berkeley: University of California Press, 1995), 291–92.

9. Judith Butler, *Bodies That Matter: On the Discursive Limits of "Sex"* (New York: Routledge, 1993), 32. Hereafter cited in the text.

10. Given the centrality of inevitable failure in her work, one might venture that the entirety of Butler's later itinerary is guided by her abiding early interest in Hegel, whose dialectic is fueled from beginning to end by the work of the failing negative.

11. Judith Butler, *Gender Trouble: Feminism and the Subversion of Identity* (New York: Routledge, 1989), 143.

12. See, for example, Elizabeth Grosz's *Becoming Undone: Darwinian Reflections on Life, Politics, and Art* (Durham, N.C.: Duke University Press, 2011).

13. Barad, *Meeting the Universe Halfway*, 88.

14. Barad, *Meeting the Universe Halfway*, 89.

15. Vicki Kirby, "Natural Convers(at)ions: Or, What If Culture Was Really Nature All Along?" in *Material Feminisms*, ed. Stacy Alaimo and Susan Hekman, 214–35 (Bloomington: Indiana University Press, 2008), 221.

16. Barad, *Meeting the Universe Halfway*, 135.

17. Gilles Deleuze and Félix Guattari, *A Thousand Plateaus: Capitalism and Schizophrenia, Volume 2*, trans. Brian Massumi (Minneapolis: University of Minnesota Press, 1987), 84.

18. Eve Kosofsky Sedgwick, "Paranoid Reading and Reparative Reading; Or, You're So Paranoid, You Probably Think This Essay Is About You," in *Touching Feeling: Affect, Pedagogy, Performativity* (Durham, N.C.: Duke University Press, 2003), 128. Hereafter cited in the text.

19. Barad, *Meeting the Universe Halfway*, 170.

3. The Bodacious Era

1. Henry David Thoreau, *Walden*, in *The Portable Thoreau*, ed. Carl Bode (New York, Viking Press, 1964), 351. Quotations from *The Portable Thoreau* are hereafter cited in the text.

2. Henry David Thoreau, "Civil Disobedience," in *The Portable Thoreau*, ed. Bode, 109.

3. Henry David Thoreau, "Life without Principle," in *The Portable Thoreau*, ed. Bode, 636.

4. Thoreau continues: "Commerce is unexpectedly confident and serene, alert, adventurous, and unwearied. It is very natural in its methods withal, far more so than many fantastic enterprises and sentimental experiments, and hence its singular success" (371).

5. Jane Bennett, *Thoreau's Nature: Ethics, Politics, and the Wild* (Thousand Oaks, Calif.: Sage, 1994), 42.

6. For some sense of the spread on the question of Thoreau's politics—whether they're leftist activism, apolitical individualism, right-leaning libertarianism, or something else altogether—see the essays in *A Political Companion to Henry David Thoreau*, ed. Jack Turner (Lexington: University of Kentucky

Press, 2009). Most of these articles laud Thoreau as an engaged thinker of the leftist variety, especially on questions of the environment, the abolition of slavery, and ethical self-fashioning in a democracy. For a quite different Thoreau, see the numerous essays on his work at the Cato Institute website. Thoreau is in fact a linchpin in their history of libertarian thought and figures prominently in their home-study course for conservative activists: https://www.cato .org/cato-university/home-study-course/module9.

7. Bennett, *Thoreau's Nature*, 3.

8. Jane Bennett, *Vibrant Matter: A Political Ecology of Things* (Durham: Duke University Press, 2010), 5. Hereafter cited in the text.

9. Bennett, *Thoreau's Nature*, 42–43 and 27

10. Bennett, *Thoreau's Nature*, 114.

11. See for example section 27, "Everyday Being a Self and the They," in Martin Heidegger, *Being and Time*, trans. Joan Stambaugh and Dennis Schmidt (Albany: State University of New York Press, 2010).

12. John Dewey, "The Need for a Recovery of Philosophy," in *Creative Intelligence: Essays in the Pragmatic Attitude*, ed. John Dewey et al. (New York: Henry Holt, 1917), 63.

13. Virginia Woolf, *The Essays of Virginia Woolf, Volume 4: 1925 to 1928*, ed. Andrew McNeille (London: The Hogarth Press, 1984), 160.

14. Friedrich Nietzsche, *Thus Spoke Zarathustra*, trans. Clancy Martin (New York: Barnes and Noble Classics, 2005), 114.

15. "Bill and Ted on the Word Bodacious," https://www.youtube.com/watch ?v=HCehmc_YrEI.

16. If you don't like "Bodacious era" as a handle for the present, I'd offer as an alternative Sam Lipsyte's sense that we live in the era "of aggressively marketed nachos," in his novel *The Ask* (New York: Farrar, Straus, and Giroux, 2010), 31.

17. Georg Simmel, *The View of Life: Four Metaphysical Essays with Journal Aphorisms*, trans. John A. Y. Andrews and Donald N. Levine (Chicago: University of Chicago Press, 2010), 13.

18. G. W. F. Hegel, *Phenomenology of Spirit*, trans. A. V. Miller (Oxford: Oxford University Press, 1976), 100 and 107.

19. Simmel, *The View of Life*, 17. Compare Bennett on Thoreau's "Wild": "Wildness is the remainder that always [!] escapes taxonomies of flora and fauna or inventories of one's character or conscience; it is the difference of the woods that remains no matter how many times one walks them; it is the distance never bridged between two humans, no matter how well acquainted" (*Thoreau's Nature*, 36).

20. Diana Coole and Samantha Frost, "Introducing the New Materialisms," in *New Materialisms: Ontology, Agency and Politics* (Durham, N.C.: Duke University Press, 2010), 9.

21. Jeffrey T. Nealon, *Plant Theory: Biopower and Vegetable Life* (Stanford, Calif.: Stanford University Press, 2016). See especially chapter 1, from which the following few paragraphs borrow and condense.

22. Michel Foucault, *The Order of Things: An Archaeology of the Human Sciences*, trans. Alan Sheridan (New York: Pantheon, 1970), 137; cited hereafter in text.

23. Simmel, *The View of Life*, 29.

24. Simmel, *The View of Life*, 104.

25. Simmel, *The View of Life*, 101.

26. Giorgio Agamben, *Homo Sacer: Sovereign Power and Bare Life*, trans. Daniel Heller-Roazen (Stanford, Calif.: Stanford University Press, 1998), 9.

27. Jacques Derrida, *The Beast and the Sovereign, Volume 1*, trans. Geoff Bennington (Chicago: University of Chicago Press, 2011), 330.

28. Foucault, *The Order of Things*, 127–28 and 160.

29. See for example the essays collected in *Anthropocene or Capitalocene? Nature, History and the Crisis of Capitalism*, ed. Jason W. Moore (New York: PM Press, 2016).

30. William Wordsworth, "The World Is Too Much With Us" (1807), https://www.poetryfoundation.org/poems/45564/the-world-is-too-much-with-us.

31. Neil deGrasse Tyson, *Astrophysics for People in a Hurry* (New York: W.W. Norton, 2017), 197. Compare Karen Barad's similar sentiment in *Meeting the Universe Halfway* (Durham: Duke University Press, 2007): "If we hold on to the belief that the world is made of individual entities, it is hard to see how even our best, most well-intentioned calculations for right action can avoid tearing holes in the delicate tissue structure of entanglements that the lifeblood of the world runs through. Intra-acting responsibly as part of the world means taking account of the entangled phenomena that are intrinsic to the world's vitality and being responsive to the possibilities that might help us flourish. Meeting each moment, being alive to the possibilities of becoming, is an ethical call, an invitation that is written into the very matter of all being and becoming" (396).

32. Fredric Jameson, *Postmodernism; or, The Cultural Logic of Late Capitalism* (Durham, N.C.: Duke University Press, 1991), 5.

33. Shoshana Zuboff, *The Age of Surveillance Capitalism* (New York: Public Affairs, 2019).

34. For more on this, see Andrew Epstein, *Attention Equals Life: The Pursuit of the Everyday in Contemporary Poetry and Culture* (Oxford: Oxford University Press, 2016).

35. See Barad, *Meeting the Universe Halfway*: "The fundamental discontinuity of quantum physics disrupts the nature of difference: the relationship between continuity and discontinuity is not one of radical exteriority but rather agential

separability, each being threaded through the other. 'Otherness' is an entangled relation of difference. Questions of space, time, and matter are intimately connected, indeed entangled, with questions of justice" (236).

36. See Zuboff for some chilling examples of attention-based surveillance capitalism—the revelation for example that the (outdoor treasure hunting with your cellphone) game *Pokémon Go* was largely birthed by Google engineers as a way to push foot traffic toward sponsoring businesses. On the birth of the attention economy, see Jonathan Beller, *The Cinematic Mode of Production: Attention Economy and the Society of the Spectacle* (Hanover, N.H.: Dartmouth University Press, 2006).

4. Biopolitics, Marxism, and Piketty's *Capital in the Twenty-First Century*

1. Thomas Piketty, *Capital in the Twenty-First Century*, trans. Arthur Goldhammer (Cambridge, Mass.: Harvard University Press, 2014), 10–11. Page references hereafter cited in the text.

2. This, though, is a faith in social science that I fear is misplaced—for all the pseudo-scientific, ideological mystification that Piketty outlines concerning his home discipline of economics, and more. For example, in social science fields like psychology, a recent replication study has shown that more than 60 percent of the published research in the field's most highly respected journals is, to put it bluntly if unkindly, just plain bullshit [https://www.nature.com/news/over-half-of-psychology-studies-fail-reproducibility-test-1.18248]. If 61 percent seems a high rate of shenanigans, note the comment in that article by a Stanford epidemiologist who suggests that if one took into account all work published in psychology journals, not just the top-tier ones used in this study, "the true replication-failure rate could exceed 80%." Though I'm pretty sure you could easily replicate published social-science research that shows that studying economics as a college major makes you a worse person: self-interested, callous, deceitful, uncaring about the needs of others—the core principles of mainstream economic thinking. See http://www.businessinsider.com/psychology-of-studying-economics-2013-10.

3. Marco Revelli, *The New Populism: Democracy Stares into the Abyss*, trans. David Broder (London: Verso, 2019), 200–201.

4. Antonio Negri, "At the Origins of Biopolitics," trans. Diana Garvin, in *Biopower: Foucault and Beyond*, ed. Vernon W. Cisney and Nicolae Morar, 48–64 (Chicago: University of Chicago Press, 2016), 50.

5. Though they mention Foucault and Negri each only once, this shift within capitalism is also something like the extended thesis of Luc Boltanski and Eve Chiapello in their *The New Spirit of Capitalism* (trans. Gregory Eliot [London: Verso, 2018]).

6. Read about it here: www.nytimes.com/2013/06/16/world/asia/chinas-great-uprooting-moving-250-million-into-cities.html.

7. Michel Foucault, *"Society Must Be Defended": Lectures at the College de France, 1975–76*, trans. David Macey (New York: Picador, 2003), 242.

8. Michel Foucault, *Discipline and Punish*, trans. Alan Sheridan (New York: Vintage, 1979), 138.

9. Michel Foucault, *The Birth of Biopolitics: Lectures at the College de France 1978–79*, trans. Graham Burchell (New York: Picador, 2010), 259–60.

10. Negri, "At the Origins of Biopolitics," 51. Page references hereinafter cited in the text.

11. Carolyn Dicey Jennings, "I Attend, Therefore I Am: You Are Only as Strong as Your Powers of Attention," *Aeon: A World of Ideas*, July 10, 2017, https://aeon.co/essays/what-is-the-self-if-not-that-which-pays-attention.

12. Jonathan Beller, "Paying Attention," *Cabinet* 24 (2006–7), http://www.cabinetmagazine.org/issues/24/beller.php.

13. Jonathan Beller, *The Cinematic Mode of Production: Attention Economy and the Society of the Spectacle* (Hanover, N.H.: Dartmouth College Press, 2006), 4.

14. Beller, *The Cinematic Mode of Production*, 27.

15. Beller, *The Cinematic Mode of Production*, 3.

16. Theodor Adorno and Max Horkheimer, "The Culture Industry: Enlightenment as Mass Deception," in *Dialectic of Enlightenment*, trans. Edmund Jephcott (Stanford, Calif.: Stanford University Press, 2002), 94–136.

17. Pierre Bourdieu, *Distinction: A Social Critique of the Judgment of Taste*, trans. Richard Nice (Cambridge, Mass.: Harvard University Press, 1987), 30–31.

18. See on this topic Judith Butler's "Merely Cultural," *New Left Review* 227 (January–February 1998): 33–44.

19. Michel Foucault, *Foucault Live: Interviews 1961–84*, ed. Sylvere Lotringer, trans. Lysa Hochroth and John Johnston (New York: Semiotext(e), 1996), 73.

20. "Vladimir Putin Says That Liberalism Has 'become obsolete,'" *Financial Times* (UK), June 27, 2019: https://www.ft.com/content/670039ec-98f3-11e9-9573-ee5cbb98ed36.

21. Revelli, *The New Populism*, 198–99.

22. Revelli, *The New Populism*, 199.

5. What Is a Lecturer?

1. I have regularized the transliterated spelling of this Greek word, and will refer to it as "parrhesia" even in texts where it's transliterated differently (in the 1982–83 lectures, for example, it's rendered as "parresia").

2. Michel Foucault, *The Government of Self and Others: Lectures at the Collège de France, 1982–83*, trans. Graham Burchell (New York: Palgrave, 2010). Hereafter referred to in the text.

3. Michel Foucault, *The Archaeology of Knowledge and The Discourse on Language*, trans. A. M. Sheridan Smith (New York: Pantheon, 1972), 83. Hereafter cited in the text.

4. Compare the lectures on "The Problematization of Parrhesia" that Foucault gave later that year (in English) at Berkeley, where he turns to the question of the performative in the opening section of the first lecture, to distinguish it from the parrhesiastic utterance: "I use the phrase 'speech activity' rather than John Searle's 'speech act' (or Austin's 'performative utterance') to distinguish the parrhesiastic utterance and its commitments from the usual sorts of commitment which obtain between someone and what he or she says" (2–3). In short, the performative (for Austin) binds subjects to their words and the conventional actions that should follow (as in the promise or the marriage ceremony, for example), whereas parrhesiastic utterances rebound immediately on the speaking subjects themselves, putting them in some danger. Find these "Problematization of Parrhesia" lectures online at https://foucault.info/parrhesia/.

5. See, for example, Timothy O'Leary's *Foucault and the Art of Ethics* (London: Bloomsbury, 2003) and Edward McGushin's *Foucault's Aekesis: An Introduction to the Philosophical Life* (Evanston, Ill.: Northwestern University Press, 2007).

6. Thomas Flynn, "Foucault as Parrhesiast: His Last Lecture Course at the Collège de France," *Philosophy and Social Criticism* 12, no. 2–3 (1987): 213–29.

7. Michael Hardt, "The Militancy of Theory," *South Atlantic Quarterly* 110, no. 1 (2011): 19–35; https://read.dukeupress.edu/south-atlantic-quarterly/article-abstract/110/1/19/3490/The-Militancy-of-Theory?redirectedFrom=fulltext.

8. Michel Foucault, *Security, Territory, Population: Lectures at the Collège de France, 1977–78*, trans. Graham Burchell (London: Picador, 2009), 3.

9. For a different rendering of the relation between parrhesia and performative in Foucault, one that tries overtly to reconcile Foucault and Stanley Cavell on truth-telling by emphasizing perlocutionary outcome over illocutionary force, see Daniele Lorenzini, "Performative, Passionate, and Parrhesiastic Utterance: On Cavell, Foucault, and Truth as Ethical Force," *Critical Inquiry* 41 (Winter 2015): 254–68.

10. Michel Foucault, *The Courage of Truth: Lectures at the Collège de France, 1983–1984*, ed. Frédéric Gros, trans. Graham Burchell (New York: Palgrave, 2011). Hereafter cited in the text.

11. Flynn, "Foucault as Parrhesiast," 227.

12. For what is to my mind the definitive retort to the "parrhesia is a weapon for today" line of reasoning, see Gordon Hull, "The Banality of Cynicism: Foucault and the Limits of Authentic Parrhesia," *Foucault Studies* 25 (2018): 251–73.

13. Ed Pluth, review of Alain Badiou, *Malebranche: Theoretical Figure, Being 2*, trans. Jason E. Smith and Susan Spitzer (New York: Columbia University Press, 2019). Pluth continues wondering: "since this seminar was delivered

when Badiou was actively working on *Being and Event* (1988), maybe it played a hidden role in that book's formation? Is there an underground Malebranche influence there? In his preface to this edition of his seminar, Badiou answers this question rather bluntly: not at all. 'This seminar is without a doubt the only one in my entire career that, in terms of the construction of my own system, has been of no use to me' (xxxvii). The clever thing to do here would be to disagree with him, but I can't bring myself to do it, because he's entirely right." Online at *Notre Dame Philosophy Reviews*, https://ndpr.nd.edu/news/malebranche-theological-figure-being-2/.

14. Michel Foucault, "What Is an Author?" in *The Norton Anthology of Theory and Criticism*, ed. Vincent Leitch et al., 1475–89 (New York: Norton, 2010). Hereafter cited in the text. I cite this version as a performative salute to teaching and lecturing, because it's the version of the essay that I most often teach.

15. See Stephen Best and Sharon Marcus, "Surface Reading: An Introduction," *Representations* 108, no. 1 (2009): 1–21; on postcritical reading, see Rita Felski's *The Limits of Critique* (Chicago: University of Chicago Press, 2015); for various neuroscientific accounts of reading, see Lisa Zunshine's *Oxford Handbook of Cognitive Literary Studies* (Oxford: Oxford University Press, 2015); on descriptive reading, see Heather Love, "Close But Not Deep: Ethics and the Descriptive Turn," *New Literary History* 41 (2010): 371–91.

16. As Frédéric Gros notes in discussing the "distinctiveness" of Foucault's 1981–82 course *The Hermeneutics of the Subject* (ed. Gros, trans. Graham Burchell [London: Palgrave, 2010]), it's not until 1982, when Foucault is finally forced to abandon the practice of offering a research seminar in tandem with his public lecture, that Foucault pays regular, substantial, and sustained attention to textual analysis in his lectures. As Gros notes, "The 1982 course at the Collège de France has, if only formally, some specific features. Having abandoned his research seminar parallel to the main course, Foucault extends the length of his lectures, which, for the first time, extend over two hours divided by a break. The old difference between a lecture course and a more empirical and precise research is thereby erased. *A new style of teaching is born*; Foucault does not expound the results of his work so much as put forward, step by step, and almost hesitantly, the development of a work of research. *A major part of the course now consists in patient reading of selected texts and word-by-word commentary on them*" (518, my emphasis).

17. Michel Foucault, *"Society Must Be Defended": Lectures at the Collège de France, 1975–1976*, trans. David Macey, ed. Mauro Bertani and Alessandro Fortana (New York: Picador, 2003), 2. Hereafter cited in the text.

18. Find the archive here: http://www.law.columbia.edu/foucault1313.

19. Michel Foucault, *Lectures on the Will to Know: Lectures at the Collège de France, 1970–1971*, ed. Daniel Defert, trans. Graham Burchell (New York: Palgrave, 2013), 198.

20. Compare Timothy O'Leary's worries in his review essay "New Books 'By' Foucault," where he argues that all these recent publications ultimately "raise a question about where one should draw the line in publishing Foucault's minor works. It is well known that Foucault's will contained the injunction 'no posthumous publications.' One wonders how he would view the fact that more than thirty years after his death new books 'by' Foucault continue to be published. Not that his feelings about the matter should necessarily concern us; after all, the author is dead in more senses than one. And yet, by adding more and more of such books to Foucault's oeuvre, we risk changing that oeuvre in ways that don't necessarily add to its value." In *Foucault Studies* 21 (2016): 231–37; https://rauli.cbs.dk/index.php/foucault-studies/article/view File/5017/5448.

21. See https://www.theguardian.com/books/2018/feb/12/key-fourth-book -of-foucaults-history-of-sexuality-published-in-france.

22. The Melville poem is "The House-top": https://www.poetryfoundation .org/poems/55905/the-house-top.

23. See the essays collected in *Heidegger's Black Notebooks: Responses to Anti-Semitism*, ed. Andrew J. Mitchell and Peter Trawny (New York: Columbia University Press, 2017); see also Jean-Luc Nancy's thoughts on this question in *The Banality of Heidegger*, trans. Jeff Fort (New York: Fordham University Press, 2017).

24. Consult, for example, Shelley Tremain's "Educating Jouy," in *Hypatia* 28, no. 4 (2013): 801–17, an analysis that's expanded in her *Foucault and Feminist Philosophy of Disability* (Ann Arbor: University of Michigan Press, 2017). Foucault discusses the Jouy case at some length in the final (March 19, 1975) lecture of *Abnormal: Lectures at the Collège de France, 1974–75*, ed Valerio Marchetti and Antonella Salomoni, trans. Graham Burchell (New York: Picador, 2003), 291–322.

25. For a sense of that discourse, peruse the essays collected in *Foucault and Neoliberalism*, ed. Daniel Zamora and Michael C. Behrent (New York: Polity, 2015).

26. In "On the Limits and Promise of New Materialist Philosophy," for example, Kyla Wazana Tompkins writes, "It is of deep concern to me how much New Materialism . . . cannot deal with race; how it ignores or misreads the work of feminist and queer theory; and how the move to a kind of ontology-centered hermeneutic suppresses the question and problem of difference. Here I am particularly worried by the ongoing citation of 'the power of language' or 'representationalism' as a problem that is corrected by new materialism, as well as worried by loose and vague references to 'identitarian thinking' or 'identity politics' as a failure to ground and create productive political thought." In *Lateral: Journal of the Cultural Studies Association* 5, no. 1 (2016): http://csalateral .org/issue/5-1/forum-alt-humanities-new-materialist-philosophy-tompkins/.

27. See Felski's *The Limits of Critique.*

28. Christopher Nealon, "Reading on the Left," *Representations* 108, no. 1 (2009): 22–50. "Hermeneutics of suspicion" is of course Paul Ricoeur's phrase for critical discourse inspired by demystifying masters of suspicion like Marx, Freud, and Nietzsche.

29. Franco Moretti, *Distant Reading* (London: Verso, 2013), 48.

30. Andrew Piper, "Reading's Refrain," *ELH* 80 (2013): 373–99 at 380.

31. See https://media2.proquest.com/documents/bowker-selfpublishing-re port2019.pdf.

32. Foucault, *The Archaeology of Knowledge and The Discourse on Language,* 231.

33. Foucault, *Hermeneutics of the Subject,* 17.

34. Kathleen Stock, "Changing the Concept of 'Woman' Will Cause Unintended Harms," *The Economist,* July 6, 2018: https://www.economist.com/open-future/2018/07/06/changing-the-concept-of-woman-will-cause-unin tended-harms.

35. See for example retired Yale Law School dean Anthony Kronman's book *The Assault on American Excellence*: "In endless pronouncements of tiresome sweetness, the faculty and administrators of America's colleges and universities today insist on the overriding importance of creating a culture of inclusion on campus," Kronman writes. "They stress the need to respect and honor the feelings of others, especially those belonging to traditionally disadvantaged groups, as an essential means to this end. In this way they give credence to the idea that feelings are trumps with a decisive authority of their own. That in turn emboldens their students to argue that their feelings are reason enough to keep certain speakers away. But this dissolves the community of conversation that the grown-ups on campus are charged to protect." Quoted from the *New York Times,* August 2, 2019: https://www.nytimes.com/2019/08/02/opinion/university-campus-diveristy-inclusion-free-speech.html.

6. Literary RealFeel

1. See Steven Shaviro, *Post-Cinematic Affect* (Winchester, UK: Zero Books, 2010).

2. This is the final line of Archibald MacLeish's 1926 poem, "Ars Poetica." https://www.poetryfoundation.org/poetrymagazine/poems/17168/ars-poet ica.

3. Amy Hungerford, *Making Literature Now* (Stanford, Calif.: Stanford University Press, 2016), 430.

4. Hungerford, *Making Literature Now,* 47.

5. David Antin, *Tuning* (New York: New Directions, 1984), 109, 147, 151.

6. I'm staking my claims here for poetry; for some thoughts on how drama as a genre cuts across the biopolitics story, see Hedwig Fraunhofer, *Biopolitics,*

Materiality, and Meaning in Modern European Drama (forthcoming from Edinburgh University Press).

7. Meaghan Morris, "Banality in Cultural Studies," in *The Cultural Studies Reader*, 3rd ed., ed. Simon During, 119–46 (1990; London: Routledge, 2009), 122; hereafter cited in the text.

8. This antihermeneutic strain runs deep in Australian cultural studies; see also Tony Bennett's foundational *Outside Literature* (London: Routledge, 1990).

9. Goldsmith, "Being Boring," Electronic Poetry Center, online at http://epc.buffalo.edu/authors/goldsmith/goldsmith_boring.html.

10. For the unfamiliar reader, the best general introductions to conceptual writing are probably Craig Dworkin's *The Ubuweb Anthology of Conceptual Writing* (http://www.ubu.com/concept/), Dworkin and Kenneth Goldsmith's *Against Expression: An Anthology of Conceptual Writing* (Evanston, Ill.: Northwestern University Press, 2011), and Rob Fitterman and Vanessa Place's *Notes on Conceptualisms* (Brooklyn, N.Y.: Ugly Duckling Presse, 2009). On Goldsmith specifically, see the essays in *Open Letter* 12, no. 7 (2005), edited by Lori Emerson and Barbara Cole, as well as Goldsmith's *Uncreative Writing* (New York: Columbia University Press, 2011), which collects many of his writings that I cite in their more readily available web versions. See also *American Book Review* 32, no. 4 (2011), which contains a focus on Goldsmith and Uncreative Writing.

11. Goldsmith, "Being Boring," n.p.

12. Buried under the pseudo-controversy that rapper Common was on the bill (as were Rita Dove and Billy Collins, among others), note that Goldsmith read sections of *Traffic* (along with poetry by Walt Whitman and Hart Crane) at Michelle Obama's White House Poetry Celebration on May 11, 2011. http://www.whitehouse.gov/blog/2011/05/11/celebration-american-poetry-white-house.

13. For all this and more (including Goldsmith reading the entirety of *The Weather*—clocking in at more than four and a half hours), see Goldsmith's author page at PennSound: http://writing.upenn.edu/pennsound/x/Goldsmith.html.

14. Goldsmith, "Being Boring," n.p.

15. Kenneth Goldsmith, "Flarf Is Dionysus. Conceptual Writing Is Apollo. An Introduction to the 21st Century's Most Controversial Poetry Movements," *Poetry*, July/August 2009, http://www.poetryfoundation.org/journal/article.html?id=237176.

16. Here I follow in the footsteps of Sianne Ngai's *Ugly Feelings* (Cambridge, Mass.: Harvard University Press, 2007). In the closing pages of her book, she calls Andrews's *Shut Up* "insistently ugly. Indeed, most readers would agree that no contemporary American poet has continued the modernist avant-garde's

project of decoupling art from beauty . . . as consistently or aggressively as Andrews" (348). I'm less interested in the work's aesthetic beauty or ugliness than I am in its diagnostic power, the kind of force it deploys and/or asks—maybe even forces—its reader to redeploy. In fact, I tend to think of Andrews's work in the terms that Gilles Deleuze uses to talk about Proust's (which is far from "ugly"): "the poet learns what is essential is outside of thought, in what forces us to think. The leitmotif of *Time Regained* is the word *force:* impressions that force us to look, encounters that force us to interpret, expressions that force us to think" (*Proust and Signs,* trans. Richard Howard [Minneapolis: University of Minnesota Press, 2004], 95). These next few paragraphs are adapted from chapter 7 of my *Post-Postmodernism* (Stanford, Calif.: Stanford University Press, 2012).

17. Bruce Andrews, *I Don't Have Any Paper So Shut Up; or, Social Romanticism* (Los Angeles: Sun and Moon, 1992), 10.

18. Goldsmith, "After Language Poetry." Online at http://www.ubu.com/papers/oei/goldsmith.html.

19. Goldsmith, "Being Boring," n.p.

20. From Spicer's poem, "Thing Language," in *My Vocabulary Did This to Me: The Collected Poetry of Jack Spicer,* ed. Peter Gizzi and Kevin Killian (Middletown, Conn.: Wesleyan University Press, 2008), 373. For an insightful discussion of this poem, and its importance for experimental American writing after Spicer, see Christopher Nealon's *The Matter of Capital* (Cambridge, Mass.: Harvard University Press, 2011), 126–39.

21. See Pound's "Vorticism," in *The Fortnightly Review* 96 (September 1914): 461–71; online at https://fortnightlyreview.co.uk/vorticism/; Sontag's 1964 "Against Interpretation," in *Against Interpretation and Other Essays,* 3–14 (New York: Farrar, Straus and Giroux, 1966); and Deleuze and Guattari's *Anti-Oedipus* (Minneapolis: University of Minnesota Press, 1983), where they write, "Interpretation is our modern way of believing and being pious" (171). Deleuze and Guattari coin the word "interpretosis" in *A Thousand Plateaus* (Minneapolis: University of Minnesota Press, 1987), 127–29. Re: Gumbrecht, see his *Production of Presence: What Meaning Cannot Convey* (Stanford, Calif.: Stanford University Press, 2004).

22. Martin Heidegger, *Poetry, Language, Thought,* trans. Albert Hofstadter (New York, Harper and Row, 1971), 25.

23. Sontag, "Against Interpretation," 10.

24. Heidegger, *Poetry, Language, Thought,* 208.

25. Sontag, "Against Interpretation," 13.

26. Abbate, "Music—Drastic or Gnostic," in *Critical Inquiry* 30, no. 3 (2004): 532.

27. Sontag, "Against Interpretation," 7.

28. From *The Believer*, "Interview with Kenneth Goldsmith," (n.p.): https://
believermag.com/an-interview-with-kenneth-goldsmith/.

29. See http://www.youtube.com/watch?v=3Uc7pvdVWEE&feature=related—
Kenneth Goldsmith reading at Whitney Museum.

30. Marjorie Perloff, "'Moving Information': On Kenneth Goldsmith's *The Weather*," *Open Letter* 12, no. 7 (2005): 84–95, 87.

31. Perloff, "Moving Information," 88.

32. Perloff, "Moving Information," 88.

33. Goldsmith, "Uncreativity as a Creative Practice," http://writing.upenn
.edu/epc/authors/goldsmith/uncreativity.html, n.p.

34. See Perloff's *Unoriginal Genius: Poetry by Other Means in the New Century* (Chicago: University of Chicago Press, 2010), an exploration of modern and postmodern collage and antisubjectivist poetics that begins with considerations of "The Waste Land" and Benjamin's *Arcades* Project, and ends with a final chapter on Goldsmith's *Traffic*.

35. Molly Schwartzberg, "Encyclopedic Novelties: On Kenneth Goldsmith's Tomes," *Open Letter* 12, no. 7 (2005): 21–36 at 34.

36. Foucault, *Archaeology of Knowledge*, 155. I should also note that, contra this Foucauldian refusal of allegory that I'm trying to harness in the service of conceptual writing, Fitterman and Place begin their *Notes on Conceptualisms* with the premise that "1. Conceptual writing is allegorical writing" (6) that maintains a great "potential for excess" (8). And their final lines are, "This brings us back to meaning, and the / possibility of possibility. // This is allegorical" (67). While I can see and affirm the compelling quality of this "excessive meaning" reading of conceptual poetry (as I do Perloff's similar take on Goldsmith), I'm here trying to take things in a different, maybe even opposite, direction.

37. Michel Foucault, "My Body, This Paper, This Fire," in *History of Madness*, trans. Jonathan Murphy and Jean Khalfa, 550–74 (London: Routledge, 2006), 573.

38. Friedrich Nietzsche, *The Birth of Tragedy* and *The Case of Wagner*, trans. Walter Kaufmann (New York: Vintage, 1967), 178.

39. For a vast archive of those sound and concrete poetries, see UbuWeb [ubu.com], which was founded by Goldsmith, as well as PennSound, where he's a senior editor [http://writing.upenn.edu/pennsound/].

40. Jack Spicer, *My Vocabulary Did This to Me: The Collected Poetry of Jack Spicer*, ed. Peter Gizzi and Kevin Killian (Middletown, Conn.: Wesleyan University Press, 2008), 325.

41. Goldsmith has edited the *Selected Interviews of Andy Warhol*, and writes the following in "Being Boring": "Andy Warhol, for instance, said of his films that the real action wasn't on the screen. He's right. Nothing happened in the

early Warhol films: a static image of the Empire State Building for eight hours, a man sleeping for six. It is nearly impossible to watch them straight through. Warhol often claimed that his films were better thought about than seen. He also said that the films were catalysts for other types of actions: conversation that took place in the theatre during the screening, the audience walking in and out, and thoughts that happened in the heads of the moviegoers. Warhol conceived of his films as a staging for a performance, in which the audience were the Superstars, not the actors or objects on the screen" (n.p.).

42. Perloff, it should be noted, also discusses RealFeel temperature in her essay on Goldsmith's *The Weather,* but she threads her consideration through a strong, meaning-based hermeneutics of suspicion: "Whose RealFeel is this? Does everyone *realfeel* 19° when the temperature is 31°, the humidity 41%, and winds gusting thirty-one miles per hour? Who decides, and doesn't specific predisposition, location, or clothing have anything to do with it? More important, how do we process all this accurate information, given the continuous references to chance, to the *possibility* of this or that happening? Indeed, the further we read into *The Weather,* the more we note that the only certainty has to do with *present* time and place (but whose present?), whereas the forecast is always, so to speak, under a cloud" ("Moving Information," 90). Perloff of course has her own critique concerning a discourse of "meaning," but her polemical force is directed at the sense of univocal, top-down, or totalized meaning ("who decides"?), thereby restaging a familiar "postmodern" battle between the open-ended multiplicity of avant-garde poetics (good meaning—deconstructive, antisubjectivist, and dependent on the "new") versus the supposedly closed totalized systems of some other kind of poetics (desiring closure, subjectivist, expressive, etc.).

Given the rollout of RealFeel only two months before, one could map its recurrence in *The Weather* (the phrase appears approximately forty times, almost always on extreme days of cold or hot) as a kind of documentation of RealFeel's product launch and slow triumph—the further corporatization and privatization of the weather, that discourse that was once the epitome of collective interest and folk practice. The canonical cultural studies text here would be Andrew Ross's *Strange Weather: Culture, Science, and Technology in the Age of Limits* (London: Verso, 1991); see especially 214–49.

43. "Wind Chill Replaced by More Accurate RealFeel Temperature™," AccuWeather.com.

44. These of course mimic the two famous slogans of Poundean modernism: "Literature is news that STAYS news" (*ABC of Reading* [New York: New Directions, 1960], 29), and "Make It New," the Poundean battle cry and title of his essay collection (New York: Faber and Faber, 1934).

45. For poetry's part, one need only recall Target's 2011 "Haikupon" (Haiku coupon) marketing strategy: see http://www.flickr.com/photos/vacuumboy9/5692655218/.

46. J. Hillis Miller, "The Critic as Host," in *Deconstruction and Criticism* (New York: Seabury Press, 1979), 230; revised and expanded from the essay first published in *Critical Inquiry* 3, no. 3 (1977): 439–47.

47. Evan Kindley, "Big Criticism" in *Critical Inquiry* 38, no. 1 (2011): 71–95.

48. Jane Tompkins, ed., *Reader-Response Criticism: From Formalism to Post-Structuralism* (Baltimore: Johns Hopkins University Press, 1980), 221.

49. Tompkins, *Reader-Response Criticism*, 226.

50. Perloff, "Moving Information," 92.

51. I remain sympathetic to this aesthetic project; I just don't see it as Goldsmith's. For a text that does defamiliarize the weather in this direction (toward language with a high "overflow" quotient), see Lisa Robertson's brilliant 2001 book, also called *The Weather* (Vancouver, B.C.: New Star Books, 2001). In her Introduction, a separate page insert that comes with the text, she writes: "The weather is a sketchy, elaborate, delicate trapeze, an abstract and intact conveyance to the genuine future which is also now. Mount its silky rope in ancient makeup and polished muscle to know the idea of tempo as real" (n.p.). Unlike Goldsmith's *The Weather,* Robertson's text heightens and transforms various languages of the weather, in order to give birth to the unexpected: "To language, rain. To rain, building. Think of this stric- / ture so that the vernaculars of causation quicken" (66).

52. Perloff's *Unoriginal Genius* advances a similar argument about Goldsmith, and conceptual poetry on the whole. There she seems less interested in recuperating the category of poetic "originality" than the status of "genius"— with Benjamin's *Arcades Project* and Eliot's "The Waste Land" functioning as the paradigms for the genius of working with found materials: "Once we grant that current art practices have their own momentum and *inventio,* we can dissociate the word *original* from its partner *genius.* If the new 'conceptual' poetry makes no claim to originality—at least not originality in the usual sense—that is not to say that genius isn't in play. It just takes different forms" (21). And those forms continue to create meaning, through what we might call object-centered or curatorial means (juxtaposing or repackaging preexisting objects in an interesting way) rather than through the subject-centered force of personal style. About Goldsmith's "unoriginal genius" in *Traffic,* Perloff writes: "Submitting his JamCam reports to the Aristotlean unities of time, place and action, Goldsmith has produced a vivid representation of urban life in all its ritual, boredom, nervousness, frustration, fear, apathy—and also its pleasure. . . . One must be flexible and *inventive* so as to find another road—an alternative. Driving, in this scheme of things, becomes a mental challenge—how to get there—

rather than a preplanned move toward one's destination. Getting there, ironically, really does become half the fun!" (156–57). Again, Perloff's approach lauds the postmodern thematics of multiple meaning released in Goldsmith's work (which reveals many "alternative" ways "to get there") over against the univocity of meaning that is presumably insisted upon by other types of poetry, wherein reading becomes merely "a preplanned move to one's destination."

Conclusion

1. Michel Foucault, *The Order of Things: An Archaeology of the Human Sciences* (New York: Vintage, 1994), 386.

2. Quentin Meillassoux, *After Finitude,* trans. Ray Brassier (London: Bloomsbury, 2010), 5.

3. For an extended rehearsal of this argument, see the Foucault chapter in my *Plant Theory: Biopower and Vegetable Life* (Stanford, Calif.: Stanford University Press, 2015).

4. Levi Bryant, *Onto-cartography: An Ontology of Machines and Media* (Edinburgh: Edinburgh University Press, 2014), 285.

5. See Bryan E. Bannon's review at *Notre Dame Philosophical Reviews*: http://ndpr.nd.edu/news/55820-onto-cartography-an-ontology-of-machines -and-media/.

6. As Eugene Thacker puts it in *After Life* (Chicago: University of Chicago Press, 2010), medieval "equivocity posits no common terms between Creator and creature, Life and the living. Equivocity is blank thought, the thought of the neutral. Being is said in several senses, each in its own way, indifferent to each other instance" (154). Compare this sense of equivocity to Graham Harman's argument [in *The Quadruple Object* (Winchester, UK: Zero Books, 2011)] that things consistently withdraw into their own (largely unknowable) essence, or Ian Bogost's seemingly endless lists of random things—turns out everything's different from everything else!—in *Alien Phenomenology; or, What It's Like to Be a Thing* (Minneapolis: University of Minnesota Press, 2012).

7. Jane Bennett, "Systems and Things: On Vital Materialism and Object-Oriented Philosophy," In *The Nonhuman Turn,* ed. Richard Grusin (Minneapolis: University of Minnesota Press, 223–41), 227.

8. Theodor Adorno, *Kant's "Critique of Pure Reason,"* trans. Rodney Livingstone (Stanford, Calif.: Stanford University Press, 2001), 6–7.

9. Mitchum Huehls, *After Critique: Twenty-First Century Fiction in a Neoliberal Age* (Oxford: Oxford University Press, 2016), 6. Hereafter cited in the text.

10. Mitchum Heuhls, "Risking Complicity,." in *Arcade: Literature, Humanities, and the World,* https://arcade.stanford.edu/content/risking-complicity.

11. Barad, *Meeting the Universe Halfway,* 184.

12. In addition to Austin's performative assault on logical positivism, which we discussed in chapter 1, see also Hillary Putnam's famous critique of Carnap's position regarding the fact-value dichotomy (wherein facts are said to be constative, true or false, and any talk of values is hopelessly relativist): in retort, Putnam writes, "if we do not see that facts and values are deeply 'entangled' we shall misunderstand the nature of fact as badly as logical positivists misunderstood the nature of value" (*The Collapse of the Fact-Value Dichotomy and Other Essays* [Cambridge, Mass.: Harvard University Press, 2004], 46). "Entangled" is also a word the Barad uses to talk about quantum performativity, but here Putnam simply means that you need social-value criteria that are not given in experience (for example, the sense of everlasting truth's absolute worth as opposed to the nonsense of social values) to be able to locate any such constative "facts" in the first place. In short, for Putnam, facts always already imply values, and vice versa.

13. Huehls, "Risking Complicity.," n.p.

Index

JEFFREY T. NEALON is Edwin Erle Sparks Professor of English and Philosophy at Penn State University. His most recent books are *I'm Not Like Everybody Else: Biopolitics, Neoliberalism, and American Popular Music; Plant Theory: Biopower and Vegetable Life*; and *Post-Postmodernism; or, The Cultural Logic of Just-in-Time Capitalism.*